Patenting Medical and Genetic Diagnostic Methods

Patenting Medical and Genetic Diagnostic Methods

Eddy D. Ventose

Professor of Law and Head, Intellectual Property Unit,
Faculty of Law, University of the West Indies, Cave Hill
Campus, Barbados

Edward Elgar
Cheltenham, UK • Northampton, MA, USA

Published by
Edward Elgar Publishing Limited
The Lypiatts
15 Lansdown Road
Cheltenham
Glos GL50 2JA
UK

Edward Elgar Publishing, Inc.
William Pratt House
9 Dewey Court
Northampton
Massachusetts 01060
USA

A catalogue record for this book
is available from the British Library

Library of Congress Control Number: 2012948845

This book is available electronically in the ElgarOnline.com
Law Subject Collection, E-ISBN 978 1 78100 178 3

ISBN 978 1 78100 177 6

Typeset by Servis Filmsetting Ltd, Stockport, Cheshire
Printed and bound by MPG Books Group, UK

Contents

Preface

The issue of patenting medical procedures (whether therapeutic, surgical or diagnostic) in the United States has been in a state of flux for over a hundred years. The uncertainty of an early district court decision was laid bare by the Board of Patent Appeals (BOPA), which decided in the 1950s that methods of medical treatments were patentable. This BOPA decision was also tenuous because it could easily be overruled by a district or higher court. Nonetheless, this decision was the foundation for the legal position in the United States for the next four decades. The spectre of physicians reaping monopoly profits from their patents on medical procedures on life-threatening illnesses prompted Congress to enact the Medical Procedures and Affordability Act (MPAA) in 1996. The MPAA provided immunity to physicians and health care entities from patent infringement suits.

These developments did not halt the tide of patenting medical and diagnostic treatments. With the mapping of the human genome in 2000, there was increased impetus to find genetic diagnoses of illnesses and patents on these have mushroomed. Methods of treating patients, dosage regimes, methods of determining the effectiveness of particular dosages, surgical methods and genetic diagnostic methods are now being patented. It was only a matter of time before the patentability of these came before the Supreme Court. Although missing an opportunity in 2006 (*Laboratory Corporation*), the Court in 2012 (*Prometheus*) finally determined that medical treatment and diagnostic methods are patentable under section 101 of the Patents Act, reversing decisions of the Federal Circuit that held the contrary. The issue of patenting genetic diagnostic methods is now on remand for reconsideration by the Federal Circuit, so the Court may soon have another opportunity to revisit the issue of patent protection for medical treatment and diagnostic methods and, consequently, finally decide on whether genetic diagnostic methods are patentable under section 101.

Chapter 1 provides an introduction. Chapter 2 considers the early decisions relating to patentability of methods of medical treatment in the United States, while Chapter 3 investigates the legislative history and provisions of the MPAA. Chapter 4 examines in detail the leading court authorities on patent-eligibility, namely, the *Benson*, *Flook* and *Diehr* trilogy and *Bilski*. It proceeds to assess the post-*Bilski* Federal Circuit authorities to determine whether they have heeded the Court's mandate in *Bilski*. Chapter 5 analyses early and recent Federal Circuit authorities on medical treatment and diagnostic methods. Chapter 6 builds on this by exploring the dissenting judgment in *Laboratory Corporation* and the decision of the Court in *Prometheus*. It also examines a decision of the District Court applying *Prometheus* to similar medical diagnostic claims, and a decision of the Federal Circuit which seemingly eschewed many of the mandates of the Court in *Prometheus*. Chapter 7 concludes by providing some suggestions concerning how the issue of patent-eligibility of medical treatment and diagnostic methods under section 101 might be resolved.

This book is a completely revised and expanded version of Chapter 10 of my book, *Medical Patent Law: The Challenges of Medical Patents*, published by Edward Elgar in 2011. It follows themes I first addressed in my doctoral thesis at the University of Oxford between 2001 and 2004.

Abbreviations

COURTS AND TRIBUNALS

BOPA	Board of Appeal of the Patent Office (US)
CCPA	Court of Customs and Patent Appeals
EBA	Enlarged Board of Appeal of the European Patent Office
TBA	Technical Board of Appeal

LEGISLATION AND CONVENTIONS

EPC 1973	European Patent Convention 1973
GRDA	Genomic Research and Diagnostic Accessibility Act
MPAA	Medical Procedures and Affordability Act 1996

ORGANISATIONS AND BODIES

AMA	American Medical Association
EPO	European Patent Office
USPTO	US Patent and Trademark Office

Table of cases

EUROPEAN PATENT OFFICE

Table of national and international legislation

1. Introduction

While European countries carved out an exception for methods of treatment of the human or animal body by therapy, surgery and diagnostic methods practised on the human or animal body (Article 52(4) European Patent Convention (EPC) 1973 (later confirmed in Article 53(c) EPC 2000)), no legislative change dealing with medical methods/procedures occurred in the United States until 1996. However, the Board of Patent Appeals of the United States Patent Office (USPTO) (BOPA) and the courts, namely, the Federal Circuit and the Supreme Court of the United States (Court), did have occasion to consider the issue of patent protection for methods of medical treatment.

This book examines the scope of patent protection for methods of medical treatment and genetic diagnostic methods in the United States. Since the question of patent protection has not been finally decided legislatively, the issue is still a live one for the courts in the United States. The jurisprudence considered will mainly examine the central issue of whether medical and genetic diagnostic methods are patent-eligible under section 101 of the Patents Act. An in-depth consideration of the issue is important in light of the continued uncertainty medical patents might have on public health, investment by pharmaceutical companies in research and development, and the impact that uncertainty might have on medical and veterinary practitioners.

The book first considers how the Board of Patent Appeals (BOPA) and the courts in the United States had to deal with the issue as it arose previously. One of the seminal cases, *Morton v New York Eye Infirmary*,[1] will be considered in detail to determine whether it is in fact authority for the unpatentability of medical treatment methods, as is widely assumed. In addition, much needed guidance on this issue will be provided by the decisions of the various courts which applied or referred to *Morton*. Of equal significance too in this historical exegesis is an examination of the decisions of the BOPA, which have addressed this issue. Two important decisions will be explored fully, namely, *ex parte Brinkerhoff*[2] (which seemingly held

---

[1] (1862) 17 F Cas 879.
[2] (1883) reprinted in 27 JPOS 797 (BOPA (1945)).

that methods of medical treatment were not patentable subject matter) and *ex parte Scherer*[3] (which overruled *ex parte Brinkerhoff* to the extent to which it held that medical treatment methods were not patent-eligible). While *ex parte Brinkerhoff* might have settled the question, other decisions had applied *ex parte Brinkerhoff* and *Morton*, holding that medical and diagnostic methods were unpatentable. These early decisions are explored to determine what was the status of the patentability of medical and diagnostic methods before the Federal Circuit, at least initially, joined in the debate on patent-eligibility.

Before that is considered, the book takes an important but necessary diversion from an examination of the case law in this area to consider the legislative intervention, which was precipitated by potential infringement liability of medical and veterinary practitioners who treat their patients. As will be seen, the courts and the USPTO oscillated on the issue of patent protection for methods of medical treatment. Medical procedures were initially excluded from patent protection, but, in 1954, the BOPA in *ex parte Scherer* decided affirmatively that such procedures were not outside the scope of patent protection. The patenting of medical treatments continued unhindered, without posing any serious threat to the medical profession and health care, after the decision in *ex parte Scherer*. The issues only climaxed in the aftermath of the *Pallin v Singer*[4] litigation, where one physician sought to enforce a patent for a method of medical treatment against another physician. The publicity given to this case in the media alerted the public to the possibility of patents negatively impacting health care. The legislators were quick to respond to what was perceived to be an upsurge in patents for methods of medical treatment. The Medical Procedures and Affordability Act (MPAA) was the resulting compromise that provided immunity to physicians and related health care entities against suits for patent infringement. The legislation, the drafters thought, achieved a proper balance between, on the one hand, the public health considerations and, on the other hand, the economic incentive of the patent system. This book examines comprehensively the numerous drafts and the debates surrounding the passage of the MPAA, including the various versions of House Bills and Senate Bills that dealt with similar subject matter. This provides cogent evidence for the rationale for the enactment of the MPAA. A detailed examination of the provisions of the MPAA is also undertaken in order to properly determine its scope and the manner in which it was expected that the immunity provision would work.

---

[3]   103 USPQ 107 (BOPA (1954)).
[4]   36 USPQ 2d 1050 (US DCDY 1995).

Even before considering the decisions of the Federal Circuit dealing directly with medical treatment and diagnostic methods, it is important to consider the controlling precedents of the Court on the question of patent-eligibility under section 101 of the Patents Act. This is important because many of the earlier Federal Circuit decisions applied the Court's precedent to decide those issues relating to medical patents. Since the Court precedent is not static, this book considers the main Court precedents, which articulate the first principles by which section 101 is to be construed, namely, *Gottschalk v Benson*,[5] *Parker v Flook*[6] and *Diamond v Diehr*.[7] These seminal decisions provide the backdrop against which the issue of patent protection for medical treatment and diagnostic methods are considered. As such, it is necessary to consider them in some detail. Additionally, the recent Court decision in *Bilski v Kappos*,[8] which has also reconsidered that trilogy, is also examined to the extent that it sheds any light on the way section 101 is to be construed, in particular, with advancements in technology and the information age – a point which was repeated by the Court in *Bilski*. Since the Federal Circuit is burdened with interpreting the Court's decisions to provide answers to the myriad of section 101 issues that usually confront it, decisions of the Federal Circuit that have applied *Bilski* are considered, especially since, in *Bilski*, the Court stated categorically that, '[i]n searching for a limiting principle, this Court's precedents on the unpatentability of abstract ideas provide useful tools' and that if the Federal Circuit 'were to succeed in defining a narrower category or class of patent applications that claim to instruct how business should be conducted, and then rule that the category is unpatentable because, for instance, it represents an attempt to patent abstract ideas, this conclusion might well be in accord with controlling precedent'.[9]

The Federal Circuit lost no time in heeding the words of the Court and, in approximately seven decisions, since the Court's decision in *Bilski* in June 2010, unrelated to medical treatment or diagnostic methods, it has attempted to interpret the Court's precedents, including *Bilski*, to provide a workable test or method by which to determine which claims fall within the Court's exceptions for the laws of nature, natural phenomena and abstract ideas. An examination of the post-*Bilski* Federal Circuit's jurisprudence in this area, particularly, *Research Corp Technologies Inc. v*

---

[5]   409 U.S. 63 (1972).
[6]   437 U.S. 584 (1978).
[7]   450 U.S. 175 (1981).
[8]   130 S. Ct. 3218; 177 L. Ed. 2d 792 (2010).
[9]   Ibid. at 805.

Microsoft Corp.,[10] is important. In these decisions, the Federal Circuit is trying to carve out a consistent theme in its section 101 jurisprudence and this has implications for its consideration of patents for medical treatment and genetic diagnostic methods. The manner in which the Court and the Federal Circuit interpret section 101 determines, to a considerable extent, the scope of protection for medical and diagnostic method patents.

The Federal Circuit, therefore, is a filtering mechanism for decisions on section 101 of the Patents Act. By having a unified court dealing with patents it was hoped that, to a large extent, its jurisprudence would be mainly uniform. However, since the Federal Circuit sits in panels, there are sometimes diverging views on some issues, which is usually resolved by using an *en banc* panel, as happened in the *Bilski* litigation. More importantly, though, is that many of the decisions on section 101 are resolved at the Federal Circuit. The Supreme Court seldom forays into section 101 jurisprudence. Since the trilogy of decisions of *Benson* (1972), *Flook* (1978) and *Diehr* (1981), it took the Court approximately 30 years before it next considered a section 101 case: *Bilski* (2010). The Federal Circuit, therefore, provides the bulk of such cases, so it was not surprising that even as early as 1982, in *In re Meyer*,[11] and in 1989, in *In re Grams*,[12] the Federal Circuit was already dealing with related medical patents. These early decisions provide some insight into the way in which the Federal Circuit considered the issue of medical treatment and diagnostic method patents. The book considers what the Federal Circuit had to say about the Court's decision in *Laboratory Corporation v Metabolite Labs*,[13] which dealt with a medical diagnostic method. It also examines the District Court and Federal Circuit decisions in the recent trilogy of decisions dealing with treatment regimes, diagnostic methods and genetic diagnostic methods in *Classen Immunotherapies Inc. v Biogen Idec*,[14] *Prometheus Laboratories Inc. v Mayo Collaborative Services*[15] and *Association for Molecular Pathology v U.S. Patent & Trademark Office (AMP v USPTO)*.[16] These decisions provide the basis for recent Federal Circuit opinion on the issues considered in this book.

This upsurge in decisions relating to methods of medical treatment and

---

[10]   627 F.3d 859 (Fed. Cir. 2010).
[11]   688 F.2d 789 (CCPA 1982).
[12]   888 F.2d 835 (Fed. Cir. 1989).
[13]   548 U.S. 124, 126 S. Ct. 2921, 165 L. Ed. 2d 399 (2006).
[14]   659 F.3d 1057 (Fed. Cir. 2011).
[15]   628 F.3d 1347 (Fed. Cir. 2010), cert. granted (June 20 2011). See the Federal Circuit's first decision in this case: 581 F.3d 1336 (Fed. Cir. 2009).
[16]   653 F.3d 1329 (Fed. Cir. 2011).

diagnostic methods reaching the Federal Circuit did not go unnoticed by the Court. After delivering its judgment in *Bilski*, the Court remanded both *Prometheus* and *Classen* for reconsideration by the Federal Circuit. The two decisions had applied the 'machine or transformation test' and had provided different conclusions on broadly similar claims. On further reconsideration, the *Prometheus* case was first to get back onto the Court's docket, with a unanimous decision by the Court handed down in March 2012. The Court missed its first opportunity to consider patent-eligibility of medical and diagnostic patents in 2006 in *Laboratory Corporation* when it dismissed the writ as improvidently granted, causing Breyer J to pen a vigorous dissent. However, his dissent, which did not find favour with most of the decisions of the Federal Circuit in *Prometheus*, *Classen* or *AMP*, anticipated the unanimous decision of the Court in *Prometheus*.[17] Not surprisingly, Breyer J wrote the decision of the Court. *Prometheus*, although not deciding that methods of medical treatment, including diagnostic methods, are not patent-eligible, provides much needed guidance on the scope of section 101 of the Patent Act in relation to medical and diagnostic methods in the United States. This book: first, explores the rationale for the dissent in *Laboratory Corporation*; second, examines the decision of the Court in *Prometheus* to determine how it sheds light on the issue of patent protection for medical treatment and diagnostic methods in the United States; and third, examines a recent District Court decision in *SmartGene Inc v Advanced Biological Laboratories SA*[18] that has already applied the Court's decision in *Prometheus* to medical patent claims.

---

[17] Supreme Court decision dated 20 March 2012.
[18] 212 U.S. Dist. LEXIS 44138 (March 30 2012).

2. Initial determination

A INTRODUCTION

The question of patent protection for medical patents has long engaged the attention of the courts in the United States. There was no question that substances and compositions of matter for treating the human body were patentable.[1] The question, then, was whether methods of medical treatment were patent-eligible; although, in some cases, the issue did not directly arise for consideration by the court.[2] The Board of Patent Appeals (BOPA) initially held that methods of medical treatments were not protected under United States patent laws[3] but their decisions were not well reasoned. *Ex parte Brinkerhoff*[4] was based on a dubious legal analysis and the subsequent decisions did not strictly adhere to the supposed rule enunciated therein. The retreat from the *ex parte Brinkerhoff* decision was crystallised in *ex parte Scherer*,[5] where the BOPA expressly overruled *Brinkerhoff* to the extent that it held methods of medical treatment were unpatentable subject matter. There was no consideration of the nature of the exclusion, or whether it only applied to methods of *medical* treatment or covered all methods of treatment. Similarly, there was no discussion as to whether the exclusion covered humans only, or whether it extended to animals. It seemed that only methods for the medical treatment of humans were excluded from patent protection before the decision in *ex parte Scherer*. Diagnostic methods of treatment were, however, considered to be patentable subject matter.[6]

---

[1] *Bayer Co. v United Drug Co.*, 272 F. 505 (1921); and *Ruskin v Coe*, 58 F. Supp. 424 (1945).

[2] In *Baxter Travenol Laboratories, Inc. v Smith Laboratories, Inc.* 227 U.S.P.Q. (BNA) 67 (1985).

[3] See, generally, I.J. Fellner, 'Patentability of Therapeutic Methods' (1946) 28 JPOS 90.

[4] (1883) reprinted in 27 JPOS 797 (BOPA (1945)).

[5] 103 USPQ 107 (BOPA (1954)).

[6] *Ex parte Kettering* 35 USPQ (BOPA (1936)).

B DECISIONS OF THE COURTS

The first case that dealt with the issue of patenting methods of medical treatments was decided just over 140 years ago. In *Morton v New York Eye Infirmary*,[7] the plaintiff sought to recover damages for infringement of a patent for an 'improvement in surgical operations' which used sulphuric ether in producing nervous quiet and insensitivity to pain, especially during operations. The court, which had doubts as to the validity of the patent, directed that it be decided first whether it was a patentable invention.[8] Section 6 of the Patents Act 1836 provided, in relevant part, 'that any person or persons having discovered or invented any new and useful art, machine, manufacture, or composition of matter, or any new and useful improvement on any art, machine, manufacture, or composition of matter not known or used by others before his or their discovery or invention thereof, and not, at the time of his application for a patent, in public use, or on sale with his consent or allowance as the inventor or discoverer . . .' shall be entitled to receive a patent. The question for the court was whether the invention fell within the words of section 6.[9] It explained that '[a] discovery of a new principle, force, or law operating, or which can be made to operate, on matter, will not entitle the discoverer to a patent'.[10] However, where the person 'has gone beyond the mere domain of discovery, and has laid hold of the new principle, force, or law, and connected it with some particular medium or mechanical contrivance by which, or through which, it acts on the material world, that he can secure the exclusive control of it under the patent laws'.[11] In other words, although a mere discovery is not patentable, where a person connects it with some medium by which it makes a contribution to the material world and acts upon it, then he can have a patent for that discovery as applied through this medium but not otherwise. Without the application of the discovery to make it a patentable invention, the court ruled that it would be 'a naked discovery, and not an invention'.[12] What mattered then was that there should be an application of that discovery to make the invention a patentable invention. It was not sufficient for the patentee merely to lay claim to the discovery alone. The court continued that, although a discovery 'may be the soul of an invention, . . . it cannot be the subject of the exclusive

---

[7] (1862) 17 F Cas 879.
[8] Ibid. at 881.
[9] Ibid.
[10] Ibid.
[11] Ibid.
[12] Ibid.

control of the patentee, or the patent law, until it inhabits a body, no more than can a disembodied spirit be subjected to the control of human laws'.[13]

The court was in no doubt that the invention in question was a discovery and that it was new at the date of the invention.[14] It then sought to determine the precise nature of the discovery before it began its assessment of whether the claimed invention was patentable. The court noted that the invention was described, in general terms, for 'a new and useful improvement in surgical operations on animals'.[15] It held that the 'real discovery' made was 'that this well-known inhalation of well-known agents (in increased quantities) would produce a state of the animal analogous to complete intoxication accompanied with total insensibility to pain'.[16] For the purposes of determining whether this was a patentable invention, the court reasoned that '[t]he effect discovered was produced by old agents, operating by old means upon old subjects'.[17] Importantly, it was of the opinion that the 'effect alone was new' and this can only be termed a 'discovery', which 'however novel and important, [was] not patentable, need[ed] neither argument nor authority to prove'.[18] Although the court was there dealing with patent-eligibility under section 101, it was also making it clear that the invention was not a new one but merely comprised using old products in an old way.

The court claimed that this was apparent to the applicant who, noting that it had a 'mere discovery' attempted to 'struggle . . . to grapple it to something in active existence' in the form of 'combining it with, or applying it to, any surgical operation'.[19] It was of the opinion that the utility of the application was not in question and the object of applying it to surgical operations was apparent. This was to 'shelter the discovery under those terms of the patent act which protect "any new and useful improvement on any art"'.[20] The court was of the opinion that the application was 'clearly not the discovery or invention of an "art", or "machine", or "manufacture", or "composition of matter"' and it was not 'an "improvement" on any one of the last three'.[21] It was for this reason, the court claimed, that the application was 'called, in substance, an improvement in the art

---

13   Ibid. at 882.
14   Ibid.
15   Ibid.
16   Ibid.
17   Ibid.
18   Ibid.
19   Ibid.
20   Ibid.
21   Ibid.

of surgery'.[22] However, it continued that one could not change a thing by calling it something else. The court held that the patent was 'nothing more, in the eye of the law, than the application of a well-known agent, by well-known means, to a new or more perfect use, which is not sufficient to support a patent'.[23] In other words, the process was a well-known one and the discovery of the effect of increased quantities of the substance was not new.

Because the patent was clearly for the 'discovery', the court noted that it was for that reason why there was the 'perpetual struggle in the specification to draw from the surgical operation some support to the patent beyond that of its utility'.[24] It was for that main reason why the court was of the opinion that a reading of the specification 'demonstrate[d] the impossibility of sustaining this patent on any grounds known to the law'.[25] The court explained that, '[b]y increasing their quantity, [the applicant] discovered that a new or more complete effect was produced, by which the subject was rendered wholly insensible'.[26] In the court's view, '[t]his can be no more patentable than the discovery that the increased quantity of liquors, taken into the stomach, would produce a like result', claiming that in 'both cases there is only a naked discovery of a new effect, resulting from a well-known agent, working by a well-known process'.[27] This effect, the court explained, was 'a temporary suspension of sensibility and motion in the animal body', adding that it was there that 'what is new in the alleged invention begins and ends'.[28] It continued that the 'fact that the surgeon can operate upon the body in the condition to which it is thus reduced, forms no part of the invention or discovery' and that it 'simply furnishes evidence that it can be applied to at least one useful purpose; a fact quite independent of the other elements necessary to make a discovery patentable'.[29]

Although the discovery was ranked 'among the great discoveries of modern times; and one of them remarked that its value was too great to be estimated in dollars and cents', the court was nonetheless of the opinion that this could not 'change the legal principles upon which the law of patents is founded, nor abrogate the rules by which judicial construction

---

22 Ibid.
23 Ibid. at 883.
24 Ibid.
25 Ibid.
26 Ibid.
27 Ibid.
28 Ibid.
29 Ibid.

must be governed'.[30] These principles and rules, the court explained, 'are fixed, and uninfluenced by shades and degrees of comparative merit'.[31] It continued that '[t]hey secure to the inventor a monopoly in the manufacture, use, and sale of very humble contrivances, of limited usefulness, the fruits of indifferent skill, and trifling ingenuity, as well as those grander products of his genius which confer renown on himself, and extensive and lasting benefits on society'.[32] However, it explained that they 'are inadequate to the protection of every discovery, by securing its exclusive control to the explorer to whose eye it may be first disclosed. A discovery may be brilliant and useful, and not patentable'.[33] A discovery alone was not patentable. The patentee has to invent a useful application of that discovery for it to fall within the realm of patentability.

The court explained that the 'new force or principle brought to light must be embodied and set to work, and can be patented only in connection or combination with the means by which, or the medium through which, it operates'.[34] In other words, as mentioned above, the new principle must be practically applied before it can be patent-eligible. It continued that '[n]either the natural functions of an animal upon which or through which it may be designed to operate, nor any of the useful purposes to which it may be applied, can form any essential parts of the combination, however they may illustrate and establish its usefulness'.[35] The discovery that increased quantities of the inhaled ethers could result in a complete insensitivity to pain was not sufficient to confer novelty on the claim. The invention was, therefore, for the use of an old substance (the ethers) in an old way (by inhalation) for inducing insensitivity in mammals (old purpose). The usefulness or otherwise of the invention could not be a substitute for satisfying the statutory requirement of patentability. The District Court did not determine that, as a matter of law, patents could not be granted for methods of medical treatment. The patent, as the court held, was 'nothing more, in the eye of the law, than the application of a well-known agent, by a well-known [method], to a new or more perfect use, which is [not] sufficient to support a patent'.[36] Indeed, the court proceeded on the basis that patent protection was available for methods of medical treatment. There was no discussion about the patentability of methods of medical treatment

---

[30] Ibid.
[31] Ibid. at 883–4.
[32] Ibid. at 884.
[33] Ibid.
[34] Ibid.
[35] Ibid.
[36] Ibid.

per se – the issue was whether the alleged invention satisfied the requirements for patent protection. The court was of the view that a discovery was
not patentable per se, but where the inventor had 'connected [the discov-
ery] with some particular medium or mechanical contrivance' where it 'acts
on the material world' she can secure its exclusive control with a patent
monopoly.[37] The patentee would control the method by which she brought
the discovery to some practical application. If the discovery is severed from
its practical application the claim becomes 'a naked discovery and not an
invention'[38] and would not be patentable. The applicant in the instant case
had not found a useful way to embody the discovery in a useful object, so
it was therefore not patentable.

There is no question the method of treatment of the human body in
Morton was a 'discovery' and this is how it was treated in subsequent
decisions.[39] Interesting, too, was that it was also cited for the principle that
'laws of nature may not be patented'.[40] It also stood for the principle that
'a new idea, to become patentable, must be embodied in working machinery, and adapted to practical use; and that a new force or principle can be
patented only in connection with the means by which it operates'.[41] In
addition, it was pointed out, citing *Morton*, that 'the question whether the
discoverers have wholly covered their discovery by a patent, and if not,
then how far have they appropriated it to their exclusive use, within the
principle that in its naked sense a discovery is not patentable and can be
embraced in and controlled by a patent only when and to the extent that
its principle is developed into invention by the disclosure of a medium or
means which brings it into practical action'.[42] Similarly, it was pointed out
that the applicant in *United Verde Cooper v Peirce-Smith Converter Co*[43]
'grasped the principle of his discovery and sought to develop it into invention by finding and disclosing a medium or means which would bring it
into practical action'.[44]

So while *Morton* was the authority for the principle that a naked discovery of a medical treatment, without any practical application, is not

---

[37] Ibid.
[38] Ibid. at 883.
[39] *Cunningham Piano Co. v Aeolian Co.*, 255 F. 897 (1919) at 900.
[40] *American Patents Development Corp. v Carbice Corp.*, 38 F.2d 62 (1930) at
64.
[41] *Burke v Partridge*, 58 N.H. 349 (1878) at 352.
[42] *Miami Copper Co. v Minerals Separation*, 244 F. 752 (1917) at 756.
[43] 7 F.2d 13 (1925).
[44] Ibid. at 15.

patentable, it was left to the court in *Dick v Lederle Antitoxin Laboratories*[45] to show how an applicant could successfully overcome that difficulty and get a patent for his invention. The claim in *Dick* was for a method of securing scarlet fever toxin and injecting that toxin into the skin of a human being. The toxin was useful for the development of a skin test for susceptibility to scarlet fever, preventative immunisation and the production of an antitoxin.[46] The District Court claimed that 'no patent can be granted for a discovery, no patent can be granted for finding out what is a law of nature' and that it was important to 'draw the line as to when the processes with which we are concerned passed beyond the point of being merely a conception or passed beyond the point of being merely in the experimental stage and became entitled to be called an invention as distinguished from a discovery'.[47] It explained that 'when the experimental form of the processes had been employed to the point when it had been proved what was the cause of the disease, thereupon they became an invention'.[48] In other words, 'whatever the processes that might be employed, until it had been determined and proved what was the cause of scarlet fever, none of such processes had been carried out to the point where it was an invention'.[49] As a result, the District Court reasoned that the proof of the date of discovery of the cause of scarlet fever is in effect substantially the same as the determination itself of the date of the invention.[50] After examining the evidence, the court concluded that, in fact, the processes described in the patent constituted the invention.[51]

The District Court noted that the claims in question were the proper subject matter of patent laws, an art, based on the *Morton* precedent.[52] It was of the opinion that it was not necessary to engage in any discussion of whether methods of medical treatment were patentable, because the processes claimed by the plaintiff embraced 'method' claims, which were the proper subject of a patent.[53] In his dissenting opinion in *ex parte Scherer*, the Chief Examiner asserted that cases such as *Dick* 'were concerned with a method of testing for susceptibility and not a claim to a medical

---

45   D.C., 43 F.2d 628 (1930).
46   Ibid. at 630.
47   Ibid. at 631.
48   Ibid.
49   Ibid.
50   Ibid. at 631–2.
51   Ibid. at 633.
52   Ibid. at 630.
53   Ibid.

treatment'.[54] Despite the decision of the BOPA in *ex parte Brinkerhoff*, the District Court implicitly accepted that methods of medical treatment could, nonetheless, be patented.

The courts did not embrace or consider the ethical considerations in determining the patentability of methods of medical treatment until the decision of the District Court in *Martin v Wyeth*,[55] where the patent was for a special form or kind of treatment for the disease, mastitis, of milk cows.[56] The court claimed that the 'dominant question in the case, however, is whether the plaintiff's idea is legally patentable under the federal statute and judicial decisions'.[57] In other words, 'the particular question of patent law that is here applicable is whether this new use for medicated bougies meets the required standard of invention for a valid patent'.[58] The plaintiff, in support of its claim that the patent was valid, argued that its method of treatment of mastitis was new and useful and had achieved commercial success.[59] The court noted that, in final analysis, really all the defendant had done was to apply the long and well-known bougie to the new use of treatment of mastitis in milk cows.[60] It then questioned whether this met the standard of invention required for a valid patent. The defendant argued that 'under the well-established judicial decisions the application of merely an old device to a new and analogous use is not patentable, and that the use of the bougie for the treatment of mastitis is clearly a use which is analogous to many former uses of medicated bougies'.[61]

The court then proceeded to examine whether the patent, as claimed, met the requirement of a patentable invention. After quoting the constitutional power and the relevant section in the Patents Act, the court claimed that 'the thing patentable must be either (1) art; (2) machine; (3) manufacture; or (4) composition of matter. The statute does not expressly mention as patentable a process or method of medical or surgical treatment; and unless the latter can be classed as an art, it is not patentable.'[62] Importantly, the court pointed out the patent in question claimed neither 'a particular medicament as a composition of matter' nor 'an exclusive

---

[54] *Ex parte Scherer* at 111.
[55] 96 F Supp 689 (DC DM (1951)).
[56] Ibid. at 691.
[57] Ibid. at 692.
[58] Ibid.
[59] Ibid.
[60] Ibid.
[61] Ibid.
[62] Ibid. at 694.

right in the *administration* of penicillin or other drug'.[63] It claimed, '[t]o be patentable the subject matter must also be new and useful, not in public use or a matter of public information for more than a year prior to the patent application, and it must have been invented or discovered by the patentee'.[64] The court claimed, although the Patents Act does not define the words 'invention or discovery', the 'proper application of this phrase is therefore necessarily left for judicial construction'.[65]

The District Court pointed out that '[i]nstances of valid patents for a method of medical or surgical treatment have been rare indeed, although a few cases may be found in which therapeutic agents, such as aspirin, have been held patentable'.[66] It continued that there were previous cases which dealt with methods of medical treatment, namely, a method of applying an inoculation against scarlet fever.[67] The District Court emphasised that '*Doctors and surgeons have seldom thought it desirable to try to patent their new procedures for human relief.*'[68] This indicated that the policy of the medical profession was not to encourage patents for methods of medical treatment. Noting that the 'grant of a patent carries with it the right to exclude others from its use for a period of seventeen years', the court explained that '*[t]he professional ethics of doctors and surgeons are more consistent with the widespread use of their medical and surgical discoveries for the benefit of mankind than in obtaining a monopoly to control their discoveries for personal commercial advantage.* In this respect it would seem also that public interest is here involved.'[69] The District Court recognised, for the first time, that patenting of methods of medical treatment raised ethical and public policy considerations. This rationale was not expanded upon or adopted in the cases that followed.

The District Court in *Martin* pointed out that 'a medical or surgical method may, if otherwise patentable, be placed in the category of an art and therefore within reach of the statute'.[70] This statement was inconsistent with the traditional understanding of *ex parte Brinkerhoff*, which was not cited in the judgment. It suggests that medical and surgical procedures

---

63   Ibid. (emphasis added).
64   Ibid.
65   Ibid.
66   Ibid. at 694–5, citing *Bayer Co., Inc. v United Drug Co.*, D.C., 272 F. 505, 507; *Ruskin v Coe*, D.C., 58 F.Supp. 424; *Dick v Lederle Antitoxin Laboratories*, D.C., 43 F.2d 628 (1930).
67   *Martin* at 695.
68   Ibid. at 695 (emphasis added).
69   Ibid. (emphasis added).
70   Ibid.

are patentable under section 101 of the Patents Act. Nonetheless, the patent was invalidated because it involved the use of an old device for a new purpose. This conclusion was also surprising in light of the District Court's previous observation that the plaintiff's discovery of the new use met many of the objective tests for patent protection. *Morton* was referred by the District Court too, but the invention in the *Morton* case was directed at the use of an old substance in an old way to achieve the same purpose. The court in *Martin* stated that, in *Morton*, the court held, in a fully considered opinion, the administration of ether (a well-known subject) to induce anaesthesia in animals was not patentable.[71] It continued that in *Morton*, as in the instant case, 'the instrument used in the surgical process was old, while the use to which it was put was new'.[72] The court then concluded by stating that *Morton* 'has frequently been cited with approval' and, as far as it was aware 'has never been overruled'.[73] The patent in *Martin* was found invalid for want of *required standard of invention.*[74] The *Morton* case was applied to invalidate the patent although it, arguably, stood for a different principle.

In *Ellis v Coe*,[75] the applicant sought a patent covering a method and apparatus for determining a characteristic of living animal tissue. The actual claims, in full, were as follows:

16. The method of determining the electrolytic condition of a living animal organism which comprises applying a pair of dissimilar electrodes at spaced points to the tissue surfaces of the organism in order to create a non-pulsating direct current potential difference between said electrodes due to the electrolytic nature of the organism, and measuring the non-pulsating direct current potential or current generated between said dissimilar electrodes; and 18. An apparatus for determining the pathological condition of a living animal body comprising a pair of electrodes of dissimilar materials, each of said electrodes being shaped to facilitate its application to the tissue surface of the body at spaced points, and electric circuit connections including means for measuring the non-pulsating current generated between the electrodes by the contact thereof with the tissue of the body.[76]

The court did not engage in a detailed examination of the applicable legal principles but concluded that, *inter alia*: first, the invention covered by the claims of the plaintiff's application for patent possesses usefulness

---

[71]   Ibid.
[72]   Ibid.
[73]   Ibid. at 695.
[74]   Ibid. at 696.
[75]   49 U.S.P.Q. (BNA) 232 (1941).
[76]   Ibid. Editor's Note.

adequate to comply with the statutes; second, the method claim 16 defined an art within the purview of the statute and the apparatus claims 18 defined a machine or manufacture in accordance with the statute; and third, the art defined by method claim 16 consisted in controlling the forces of nature to effect a new result and to this end a characteristic of tissue was transformed to another physical form in which it might be quantitatively measured.[77] The head note of the case claimed that the '[a]pplicant utilises discovery of principles or forces of nature in such a manner as to produce new result; art defined by method claims consists in controlling forces of nature to effect new result and to this end a characteristic of living animal tissue is transformed to another physical form (electrical effect) in which it may be quantitatively measured; in utilizing forces of nature to effect such measurement, applicant has done unobvious thing that amounts to an invention; method and apparatus claims are allowed.'[78]

In addition, the court claimed: first, it was no objection to the method claims that the measurements or recordations resulting from practising the invention might be subject to the intellectual appraisal of an operator; second, the method claims involved more than a mere 'mental concept'. This was summarised in the head note as follows: '[i]t is no objection to method claims that measurements or recordations resulting from practicing invention may be, subject to the intellectual appraisal of an operator; claims involve more than mere mental concept.'[79] As a result, the court concluded that '[i]n utilizing the forces of nature to effect measurement of a characteristic of living tissue, the plaintiff has done an unobvious thing that amounts to invention'.[80]

C   DECISIONS OF THE BOPA

One of the first BOPA decisions that dealt with the issue directly was the 1883 decision of *ex parte Brinkerhoff*,[81] where it held methods of medical treatment were not patentable subject matter. The claimed invention was for the use of surgical instruments for the treatment of the human body. The BOPA emphasised that the applicant had already obtained a patent for the surgical instruments and that their sale should allow the purchaser

---

[77]   Ibid.
[78]   Ibid.
[79]   Ibid.
[80]   Ibid.
[81]   (1883) reprinted in 27 JPOS 797 (BOPA (1945).

the right to use them in any way that they desire.[82] It was weary of the patentee gaining secondary protection for his invention by patenting specific uses of the already patented surgical instruments. In particular, the BOPA explained that 'methods or modes of treatment of physicians are not patentable'.[83] It continued that they were 'discoveries which may in a majority of cases under certain conditions accomplish certain results, but no particular method or mode of treatment under all circumstances, and in all cases will produce upon all persons the same result'.[84] In other words, methods of medical treatment of certain diseases by physicians were not patentable because they could not provide 100 per cent certainty of curing any particular patient because of the vagaries of medical treatment.[85] The patentability of an invention should not be determined by a mathematical calculation of the success rate of the invention. This is especially so since it cannot ever be determined with any accuracy whether a particular result of any method of medical treatment would be the same in all cases.

There was no discussion about the propriety, or otherwise, of granting patents for methods of medical treatment in *ex parte Brinkerhoff*. The references to the human body were to simply illustrate the nature of the invention and to reiterate that no method of treatment could ever guarantee the same result for each patient. According to the BOPA, patents for methods of medical treatment 'would have a tendency to deceive the public by leading it to believe that the method therein described and claimed would produce the desired result in all cases'.[86] The public would therefore presume that the invention could guarantee 100 per cent certainty of results when, conceivably, this could not be the case. In addition, it claimed it did 'not think that the statute providing for the issuance of patents was intended to cover applications of this kind'.[87] The BOPA claimed that '[i]t should be reasonably certain in every case that the invention . . . sought to be patented will produce a certain result', which, it held, 'cannot be said of any mode of treatment used by physicians in curing diseases'.[88]

The BOPA held, on the 'authority' of *Morton*, that the invention in *ex parte Brinkerhoff* could not be patented.[89] The invention was for a mode of treatment 'which must be treated as a discovery, and falls clearly . . . under

[82] Ibid.
[83] Ibid. at 798.
[84] Ibid.
[85] Ibid.
[86] Ibid.
[87] Ibid.
[88] Ibid.
[89] Ibid.

the class of discoveries, held not to be patentable in the *Morton* case'.[90] The *Morton* case, it must be emphasised, simply reiterated that a discovery must have *some* practical application before it could be patented, and was *not* based on the unpatentability of any particular class of inventions. Therefore, it should not be taken as the authority for the unpatentability of methods of medical treatment.

In *ex parte Appeal*,[91] the claim at issue was for a method of treating animal tissues by subjecting them to the action of light rays lying within a certain region of the spectrum, the tissues being shielded from the wave length lying within other regions of the spectrum.[92] The method was effective for the treatment of skin infections and assisted in the proper function of enzymes associated with healing. The Examiner rejected the patent on the basis that it was for a method of medical treatment of the human body and that type of claim was condemned in *ex parte Brinkerhoff*.[93] On appeal, the BOPA held that the ground on which the Examiner rejected the claimed method was 'warranted' and it affirmed the decision of the Examiner.[94]

The later decisions merely paid lip service to the *ex parte Brinkerhoff* decision. In *ex parte Wappler*,[95] the claims were for a method of shrinking living tissue. The exact claims were for:

> 1. The herein-described method of shrinking living tissue, which consists in heating the same to a degree sufficient to devitalize the tissue cells but insufficient to impair the liquid state of the blood and lymph, whereby the blood and lymph flow are stimulated and the devitalized cells may be promptly absorbed.
> 4. The herein-described method of shrinking living tissue, which consists in passing therethrough a high-frequency electric current whose concentration is approximately four milliamperes per square millimetre.[96]

Relying on the 'fact that completion of the process is not immediate and is dependent upon the operation of natural forces and laws', the Examiner rejected the claimed method as not patentable. In arriving at his decision, the Examiner relied on *Morton* and *ex parte Brinkerhoff* and was of the opinion that 'in so far as the claims define a procedure different from that of the recognized prior art, it is one of degree rather than of kind'.[97]

---

90 Ibid.
91 27 JPOS 797 (BOPA (1945).
92 Ibid.
93 Ibid.
94 Ibid.
95 26 U.S.P.Q. (BNA) 191.
96 Ibid.
97 Ibid.

On appeal, the BOPA held that 'the present claims are not of a type, the granting of which is precluded by' *Morton* and *ex parte Brinkerhoff*.[98] It continued that '[c]laims are frequently allowed for methods in which dependence is placed upon the operation of some natural law. In fact, practically all methods are more or less dependent on nature's laws.'[99] The BOPA claimed that *Dick* also involved 'the operation of nature's laws and also a procedure ultimately intended to combat disease'.[100] It explained that the claims 'are not directed to the treatment of any specific disease, but they do define an act or a series of acts performed upon a definite subject matter for the purpose of *reducing it to a different state*'.[101] In addition, it was made clear by the BOPA that the process satisfied the conditions found in the classic definition of a process given in *Cochrane v Deener*[102] and that the procedure outlined was sufficiently certain in its results to avoid the criticism made in *ex parte Brinkerhoff*.[103] Although not disapproving the dictum in *ex parte Brinkerhoff*, the BOPA ensured its decision could withstand an *ex parte Brinkerhoff* challenge.

The *ex parte Brinkerhoff* case was discussed in *ex parte Kettering*,[104] where the claims were for a process which involved subjecting the human body to the effect of a high-frequency field to create a fever in the human body while keeping it dry at the same time.[105] The Examiner rejected the claimed methods on the basis that they were drawn to subject matter not within the protection of the patent statutes, citing *ex parte Brinkerhoff*, 'which in general holds that modes of treatment of certain diseases are not patentable'.[106] The BOPA expressly stated that the *ex parte Brinkerhoff* case did not preclude the granting of a patent in the instant case because the claims considered by the court covered a procedure that did not have the object of, or had any direct relation to, the curing of any particular disease.[107] This was particularly startling since the court had already correctly pointed out that the ultimate purpose of the invention was the creation of fever in the human body *to cure* a disease.[108] The BOPA accepted that the question of whether the disease could be cured depended, to a considerable

---

98 Ibid. (emphasis added).
99 Ibid.
100 Ibid. at 192.
101 Ibid. (emphasis added).
102 94 U.S. 780 (1954).
103 26 U.S.P.Q. (BNA) 191, 192.
104 35 U.S.P.Q. (BNA).
105 Ibid.
106 Ibid. at 343.
107 Ibid.
108 Ibid.

extent, on the skill with which the treatment is applied and the response of the patient.[109] However, the BOPA, ever fearful of the dictum in *ex parte Brinkerhoff*, stated that in so far as the production of fever is concerned, the results at which the process was aimed were sufficiently certain to avoid the limitation of *ex parte Brinkerhoff*.[110]

The decision in *In re Saunders*,[111] although not that of the BOPA, but that of the Federal Circuit on appeal from a decision of the BOPA, deserves to be mentioned here. The patent was for a method for administering gonadotropic pituitary hormones. Specifically, the claims were for:

> 7. A method of administering the gonadotropic fraction of the hormones of the anterior pituitary gland, which consists in the subcutaneous implantation of said hormone in a desiccated condition as a dispersion of said desiccated hormone in a solid waxy medium. 11. A method of administering the gonado-tropic fraction of the hormones of the anterior pituitary gland which consists in the subcutaneous implantation of said hormone in a desiccated condition in a synthetic hydro-carbon wax having substantially the composition of 85 1/2 percent by weight of carbon and 14 1/2 percent by weight of hydrogen.[112]

The Federal Circuit noted that the 'claims, which relate to the method of administering the hormones, were rejected [by the BOPA] not only as lacking invention over the prior art but also "as being for an unpatentable method in view of the *Brinkerhoff* decision cited by the examiner"'.[113] Since the Federal Circuit held that 'where an old method or process is used by an applicant in the administration of a new and analogous material, and the improved result is due solely to the quality of the material used, no inventive method or patentable process is involved in what the applicant has done',[114] it rejected the appeal. It further held that, in view of its con-clusion, it was 'unnecessary to discuss in this opinion and pass upon the further question of the rejection of the appealed claims on the ground that methods of treating the human body are not patentable'.[115]

In *Ex parte Campbell*,[116] the claimed method related to a process for combating the clotting of blood in human beings. The BOPA claimed that: first, the process comprised administering to a living human being

---

[109]   Ibid.
[110]   Ibid.
[111]   154 F.2d 693; 69 U.S.P.Q. (CCPA 1946) 341.
[112]   Ibid.
[113]   Ibid.
[114]   Ibid. at 494.
[115]   Ibid. at 495.
[116]   99 U.S.P.Q. (BNA) 51.

a regulated amount of a substantially pure coumarin compound of the class consisting of 3,3'-methylene-bis (4-hydroxycoumarin) and its alkali metal, alkaline-earth metal, ammonium, and substituted ammonium salts; and, second, the coumarin compound so administered has the property of lowering the blood prothrombin level and lengthening the clotting time of the blood in the patient.[117] The BOPA rejected claim 8 'on the ground that it is drawn to a mental process', claiming that the 'the portion of the claim which the examiner considers to involve the mental step is that part which reads, "and the regulation of the quantity of the substantially pure coumarin compound administered at later intervals is based on the blood prothrombin level following administration at earlier intervals"'.[118] It also explained that the Examiner had noted that it was:

> not contended that the mere fact that a mental determination is involved renders the claim objectionable but that there is no defined way of obtaining the result once the calculation is made. In brief, after the prothrombin time of the treated patient is determined there is no prescribed method either disclosed or claimed by which the proper dosage is to be calculated.[119]

The first point to note is that the Examiner accepted that, in principle, the mere fact a mental step was involved in the claimed method meant that it was not patent-eligible; and, second, the exact dosage to be administered to the patient was not disclosed or claimed by the patent itself. In addition, the Examiner noted that:[120]

> While the specification is extensive as to the isolation of the compound, the disclosure on the question of dosage is meagre. There is no schedule of dosages and the necessary dosage is not disclosed for any particular observed prothrombin time. There is no disclosure as to the dosage to be administered after the determination is made. There are no criteria of regulation in the claims and little basis in the disclosure to support the regulation limitation.

He further noted that:[121]

> The claims do not point out how to determine the quantity of Dicumarol needed after a higher than desired prothrombin level has been determined. On the other hand, no Dicumarol administration would be required in case the prothrombin level is too low.

---

[117] Ibid.
[118] Ibid. at 53.
[119] Ibid.
[120] Ibid. at 54.
[121] Ibid.

The BOPA reiterated the point made above that the claimed method failed to disclose the actual dosage to be administered to the patient. The BOPA claimed that '[a]fter careful consideration of the examiner's remarks and the above disclosure we are constrained to hold that in our opinion the determination of the proper dosage would be within the skill of the physician'.[122] In its view, the determination of the actual dosage regime fell within those skills that the physician, by virtue of her training, would have in treating and diagnosing patients. The BOPA continued that '[c]laim 8 embodies the steps of claim 1 of administering the Dicumarol to the patient, and regulating the amount of Dicumarol so administered'.[123] The BOPA accepted that, first, these 'steps are positive, physical steps, and no contention to the contrary has been made by the examiner'; and, second, the 'advance over the art appears to us to reside in these steps of administering regulated amounts of the Dicumarol to the patient'.[124] It continued that the 'portion of claim 8 which involves the mental step appears to us to be but an incidental feature of the process which does not constitute the advance over the prior art', citing *In re Abrams*.[125] As a result, it concluded that '[u]nder these particular circumstances we are of the opinion that the rejection of claim 8 as drawn to a mental process should not be sustained'.[126] In other words, the mental step did not constitute the inventive concept in the invention and, as such, the patent should not have been rejected on the basis that it constituted the invention.

Since there was no strict adherence to the learning in *ex parte Brinkerhoff*, it was time that the courts or the BOPA either rejected or reaffirmed its reasoning and central ruling. The issue then arose directly for consideration in *ex parte Scherer*,[127] where the claim was for a method of injecting fluids into the human body in which the epidermis acts as a passive member. The main claim, claim 29, was as follows:

> 29. The method of injecting fluids into the human body comprising the steps of placing a container of an injecting instrument having a jet orifice tightly against the epidermis to provide a hydraulic seal between the edge of the orifice and the epidermis, displacing liquid from the container through the jet orifice at a pressure sufficiently high to produce a jet velocity which causes the jet to puncture the epidermis and penetrate the body tissues therebeneath, including the steps of continuing the high pressure acting on the jet until it has reached a desired

---

[122]   Ibid.
[123]   Ibid.
[124]   Ibid.
[125]   89 188 F.2d 165; USPQ 266 (CCPA 1951).
[126]   *Ex parte Campbell* at 54.
[127]   103 USPQ 107 (BOPA (1954)).

depth, and abruptly stopping the high pressure and thereafter continuing the jet at a lower pressure after the high pressure has been exerted and until the liquid has been dispersed at such desired depth.[128]

The Examiner rejected the claim because it was not 'directed to a method that falls within the statutory class of patentable methods (35 U.S.C. Section 101)'.[129] In addition, it was the 'view of the examiner that methods in which the subject matter treated is the human body are *ipso facto* unpatentable merely because the body is involved and his viewpoint is based on the premise that such methods are excluded from the field of patentable subject matter by prior decisions of the courts and the Patent Office'.[130] In other words, the claimed method was not patentable because this was established by prior decisions of the courts and the BOPA, and also because the human body was involved in the process. The appellant argued that:

> the subject matter upon which the acts are performed may be either the fluid to be injected or the tissue, and when the fluid is taken as the subject matter, then it has its state changed from a dormant quantity of liquid to a dynamic jet which produces the result recited above, whereas when the tissue is taken as the subject matter, its state is changed by the addition of the fluid thereto and he concludes from the foregoing that the method recited in the rejected claims is not included in the type of method claims condemned in such cases as *Morton* and *ex parte Brinkerhoff*.[131]

This meant that the type of claim at issue was not the same as that in either of these decisions since it was not practised directly on the human body.

In relation to claim 29, the BOPA claimed that: first, it was the 'only claim which in terms recites injecting fluid into the human body and will be considered first'; second, '[i]t recites a series of manipulative steps performed outside the body, including the step of placing the jet orifice against the epidermis to provide a hydraulic seal between the edge of the orifice and the epidermis, with the body acting as a passive member without any reference to the nature of the liquid injected or to any reaction of the body to the liquid'; and, third, '[i]t is not asserted by the examiner that the method of this claim is not an advance over the prior art and it is our view that the advance or novelty resides in the manipulative steps

---

128   Ibid. at 108.
129   Ibid.
130   Ibid.
131   Ibid. at 109.

performed outside of the body'.[132] It explained that it was 'not impressed with the examiner's contention that the only useful result flowing from the manipulative steps of the claim is dependent on the reaction of the human body to the injected fluid, as an objection to the allowance of the claim' for two main reasons.[133] The first was that in the 'instant specification the expressed result appellant seeks to achieve is the accurate placing of a fixed quantity of medicament of any kind at a predetermined position beneath the epidermis'.[134] Second, that 'result is attained by the appellant's method is not denied by the examiner, and the utility of the injection of medicaments as a mode of administering medicaments cannot be denied'.[135] As a result, it held that 'the method specified in claim 29 must be considered as useful within the provisions of' section 101.[136] Therefore the BOPA was of the opinion that the claimed method satisfied the requirements of section 101 because, first, the invention had some utility and, second, the beneficial aspect of the invention did not rely on the reaction of the human body to the medicament, but related only to the correct placement of that medicament on the patient.

The BOPA stated that 'the method claimed is of a character which would *normally be regarded as within the field of patentable subject matter*, except for the fact that the human body is the subject acted upon'.[137] As a result, it thought it 'necessary to consider the status of method claims involving treatment of the human body both under the patent statutes and the two decisions', namely, *Morton* and *ex parte Brinkerhoff*.[138] This was all the more necessary since the two decisions were 'frequently cited in this connection' with the unpatentability of methods of medical treatment and were cited by the Examiner in the instant decision. In addition, the BOPA noted that 'a basic question involved in this case is whether methods in which the subject matter treated is the human body and the object of the method is some medical or surgical purpose are within the field of subject matter capable of being patented'.[139] It was of the 'opinion that it cannot be categorically stated that all such methods are unpatentable subject matter merely because they involve some treatment of the human body' and that claims 'involving treatment of the human body have been allowed

---

[132] Ibid.
[133] Ibid.
[134] Ibid.
[135] Ibid.
[136] Ibid.
[137] Ibid. (emphasis added).
[138] Ibid.
[139] Ibid.

on appeal', for example, in *ex parte Wappler* and in *ex parte Kettering*.[140] The BOPA continued that there was 'nothing in the patent statute which categorically excludes such methods, nor has any general rule of exclusion been developed by decisions'.[141]

It was stated correctly that the *Morton* case did not establish the principle that all methods involving the treatment of the human body were unpatentable,[142] and that the patent in the *Morton* case was invalidated for lacking novelty.[143] The BOPA continued that 'no proper inference that any and all medical or surgical methods are excluded from the field of patentable subject matter can be drawn from the opinion, and neither do the facts upon which the opinion is based warrant such a broad generalization'.[144] It held that the uncertainty of results, which was one of the grounds on which *ex parte Brinkerhoff* was decided, was 'more properly considered under the question of utility which is a separate and distinct requirement for patentability'.[145]

The BOPA then held that '[t]o the extent that *ex parte Brinkerhoff* holds or implies that all medical or surgical methods are unpatentable subject matter merely because they involve treating the human body, that decision is expressly overruled'.[146] If there was any uncertainty about whether or not *ex parte Brinkerhoff* was an authority for the unpatentability of methods of medical treatment, *ex parte Scherer* made clear that it was *never* such an authority, and if this was the *correct* interpretation of *ex parte Brinkerhoff*, then it should *no longer* be the case.

Geniesse, Examiner-in-Chief, dissenting from the decision of the BOPA, noted that Claim 29, 'which has been treated as a typical claim, is restricted to injection of the fluid through the skin into the underlying tissues of the body' and that the 'process is useful only as a part of a physician's treatment of a patient'.[147] He pointed out that the decisions in *ex parte Wappler* and *ex parte Kettering* did not represent the unanimous opinion of the BOPA and that '[u]nfortunately those decisions taking an opposite view have not been reported'.[148] He continued that the BOPA's decision, which was reviewed by the court in *In re Saunders*, 'took the view that claims

---

140 Ibid. at 109–10.
141 Ibid. at 110.
142 Ibid.
143 Ibid.
144 Ibid.
145 Ibid.
146 Ibid.
147 Ibid. at 111.
148 Ibid.

relating directly to a medical treatment of the body were nonstatutory'.[149] As a result, he explained that it, therefore, appeared to him 'that there are no controlling precedents in so far as decisions of this [BOPA] are concerned'.[150] Geniesse, Examiner-in-Chief, distinguished *Dick* on the basis that 'the claim approved by the court involved only a method for testing for susceptibility and not a claim for medical treatment',[151] and *Ellis* on the basis that the claim therein 'was likewise a claim for a testing method'.[152]

He argued that the majority were in error in suggesting that the claimed process came within the acceptable definitions of processes previously accepted by the courts.[153] In addition, he claimed that '[i]n the long history of patent litigation there does not appear to be a decision of a competent court sustaining a claim to a process which comprises steps performed by a practicing physician in treating a patient to alleviate his condition'.[154] Therefore, he concluded that '[i]n the absence of a clear precedent compelling the allowance of claims of the present character, ... the claims on appeal should be refused as not directed to a proper statutory process'.[155] In addition, Geniesse, Examiner-in-Chief, claimed that the decision in *Morton* is 'an authority for refusing claims to processes which in their practical aspects depend upon reaction with the human body for success'.[156] He continued that, although discussion of *Morton* was rather confused, he was of the view that the court, in that decision, 'suggested that the natural functions of the body could not become a part of a patentable process' and that, in his opinion, 'the success of the claimed process when read in the light of the specification and the expected usage is dependent upon the reaction of the body to the treatment given'.[157]

He explained that, although there 'should not be discrimination against inventors in the medical field', he was 'of the opinion that that objection is answered by the observations of the examiner to the effect that the claimed process is no more than the necessary functions of the apparatus used to carry out the asserted process'.[158] Also, he stated that the instant decision

---

[149]   Ibid.
[150]   Ibid.
[151]   Ibid.
[152]   Ibid.
[153]   Ibid.
[154]   Ibid.
[155]   Ibid.
[156]   Ibid.
[157]   Ibid.
[158]   Ibid.

was not unlike that of *ex parte Brinkerhoff*, noting that that decision was 'reviewed on appeal by the Supreme Court of the District of Columbia and the patent refused because *Brinkerhoff* had obtained all the protection he was entitled to in his patents to the instrumentalities used'.[159] He therefore ruled that the Examiner's decision should be affirmed.

At least at the level of the BOPA, *ex parte Scherer* finally settled the question and accepted that methods of medical treatment were patentable subject matter in the United States. It was not until 1994, some 50 years later, that the next significant decision relating to methods of medical treatment emerged. In *Pallin v Singer*,[160] the action was for patent infringement on a surgical technique for use during cataract surgery in a manner that would allow the wound to be 'substantially self-sealing'. The court denied the defendant's plea for summary judgment because there were genuine issues of fact to be considered at trial.[161] A Consent Order was later declared which invalidated the patent and stated that the plaintiff would take no action to enforce the patent against the defendants. There was much publicity about this case and it was the catalyst for the change in the law that was to follow.

D   CONCLUSION

The courts in the United States initially excluded methods of medical treatment on differing and often confusing bases. Indeed, there was even confusion on whether they were in fact excluded at all from patentability under section 101 of the Patents Act. Since there was no firm basis for the *Morton* decision, which has been universally regarded as not deciding the issue of patentability of medical procedures under section 101, and *ex parte Brinkerhoff* did not actually decide that issue, it was easy for the BOPA in *ex parte Scherer* to finally decide that methods of medical treatment were patentable subject matter in the United States. The legal basis was not articulated in a manner consistent with the reasoning of the later decisions of the Court in *Benson*, *Flook* and *Diehr*; however, *ex parte Scherer* accepted, for the time being, that methods of treatment of the human or animal body by surgery, therapy and diagnostic methods are patentable in the United States.

---

[159]   Ibid.
[160]   36 USPQ 2d 1050 (US DCDY (1995)).
[161]   Ibid.

3. Legislative intervention

A INTRODUCTION

There was an enormous outcry following the *Pallin v Singer* litigation. A coalition[1] of various interest groups led by the American Society of Cataract and Refractive Surgery quickly assembled to halt what was considered an insurgence of medical procedure patents. They lobbied Congress tirelessly to deal with the matter. The American Medical Association (AMA) criticised medical procedure patents and issued a policy document that denounced the practice amongst physicians.[2] Before the final form of the legislation was agreed, there was considerable debate and rejections of various Bills introduced in the House of Representatives[3] and Senate[4] to deal with the matter. In the end a compromise Bill[5] was agreed to, which became the Medical Procedures and Affordability Act (MPAA).[6] This legislation led to a proliferation of academic literature.[7] It has even been argued that the MPPA amounted

---

[1] American Academy of Dermatology, American Academy of Ophthalmology, American Academy of Orthopaedic Surgeons, American Academy of Otolaryngology, Head and Neck Surgery, American Association of Neurological Surgery, American College of Radiology, American College of Surgeons, American Institute of Ultrasound in Medicine, American Medical Association, American Society of Dermatologic Surgery, American Society of Plastic and Reconstructive Surgery, American Urological Association, Association of American Medical Colleges, Society of Cardiovascular and Interventional Surgery, and Society of Vascular Technology.

[2] 'Ethical Issues in the Patenting of Medical Procedures' 53 *Food & Drug LJ* 341.

[3] HR 1127, 104th Congress, 1st Session, H.R. 3814, 10th Congress, 2d Session.

[4] S. 1334, 104th Congress, 1st Session, which became the forerunner to the later HR 3610 104 Congress (1996).

[5] HR 3610, 104th Congress (1996).

[6] MPAA s.287(c).

[7] See generally B.G. Alten, 'Left to One's Own Devices: Congress Limits Patents on Medical Procedures' (1998) 8 *Fordham Intell. Prop. Media & Ent. LJ* 837; S.L. Nichols, 'Hippocrates, the Patent-Holder: The Unenforceability of Medical Procedure Patents' (1997) 7 *Geo. Mason L Rev* 227; C.J. Katopis, 'Patients

to a deprivation of property for public use without compensation contrary to the Fifth Amendment to the United States Constitution.[8]

B   LEGISLATIVE HISTORY

1   Introduction

Politicians acted hastily to enact legislation in the post *Pallin v Singer* saga. Two Bills were tabled in the United States House of Representatives (House) and two in the Senate. A compromise was finally reached when the implications of adopting various versions were argued. In the final analysis, Congress adopted a compromise Bill that exempted physicians and related health care entities from patent infringement suits. Various interest groups lobbied Congress either to reject or accept some version of the Bill. Methods of medical treatment remained patentable, while remedies against physicians that infringed patents for methods of medical treatment were removed. This solution, arguably, may have solved the ethical issues in so far as a physician could not be found liable for infringement of a medical procedure patent, and gave due consideration to the economic incentives that underpin that patent system.[9]

2   House Bill 1127

The Republican Representative Greg Ganske introduced the Medical Procedures Innovation and Affordability Act, House Bill 1127, on 3 March 1995 (HR Bill 1127).[10] HR Bill 1127 provided that:

---

v. Patents?: Policy Implications of Recent Patent Legislation' (1997) 71 *St. John's L Rev* 329; W.W. Yang, 'Patent Policy and Medical Procedure Patents' (1995) 1 *B U J Sci & Tech L* 5; R.M. Portman, 'Legislative Restriction on Medical and Surgical Procedure Patents Removes Impediments to Medical Progress' 4 (1996) *U Balt Intell Prop LJ* 91; S.D. Anderson, 'A Right Without a Remedy: The Unenforceable Medical Procedure Patent' (1999) 3 *Marq Intell Prop L Rev* 117; W.E. Havins, 'Immunising the Medical Practitioner "process" Infringer: Greasing the Squeaky Wheel, Good Public Policy or What?' (1999) 77 *Uni Det Mercy L Rev* 51; W.B. Lafferty, 'Statutory and Ethical Barriers in the Patenting of Medical and Surgical Procedures' (1996) 29 *J Marshall L Rev* 891; and B.J. Meier, 'The New Patent Infringement Liability Exception for Medical Procedures' (1997) 23 *J Leg* 265.

[8]   C.C. Brinckerhoff, 'Medical Methods Patents and the Fifth Amendment: Do the New Limits on Enforceability Effect a Taking?' (1996) 4 *U Balt Intell Prop LJ* 147. See also T.F. Cotter, 'Do Federal Uses of Intellectual Property Implicate the Fifth Amendment' (1998) 50 *Fla L Rev* 529.

[9]   See Chapter 6.

[10]   HR 1127 104th Congress (1995).

> A patent may not be granted for any discovery of a technique, method, process for performing a surgical or medical procedure, administering a surgical or medical therapy, or making a medical diagnosis, except that if the technique, method, or process is performed by or as [a] necessary component of a machine, manufacture, or composition of matter or improvement thereof which is itself patentable subject matter, the patent on such machine, manufacture, or composition of matter may claim such technique, method, or process.

The effect of this legislation was to exclude methods of medical treatment from patent protection unless the procedures are necessary components of a patentable machine or device. However, the legislation contained a provision that allowed the process to be patented if it is *a necessary part or component of a patentable machine or device*. This provision was meaningless because one would not want to carry out the particular procedure without the use of the device. Patent protection for the machine or device implicitly gave protection for the use process itself unless the procedure could be carried out in several ways. The scope of HR Bill 1127 was very wide and it would have prevented the patenting of biotechnological processes, so it came under much scrutiny from the biotechnology industry.

HR Bill 1127 received enormous criticism in the debates that followed its introduction in the House.[11] There were concerns about the patenting of new uses of unpatentable drugs.[12] Dr Noonan pointed out that there would be devastating consequences for the drug and biotechnology industries if new-use patents are eliminated[13] and that legislation is not necessary because the practical drawbacks of enforcement have limited their impact.[14] The American Society of Cataract and Refractive Surgery accepted the principles on which HR Bill 1127 was based but preferred the Senate counterpart, which achieved the same purpose while addressing the concerns of those opposing the ban.[15] Those who supported HR Bill 1127 maintained that public benefit is not enhanced with the patenting of low-cost medical procedures and that the incentive to innovate, a function of medical procedure patents, 'emanate[s] from intellectual curiosity, creativity and compassion for patients rather than the availability of capital'.[16] The

---

[11] HR Rep. No. 104-879 (1995) Medical Procedures and Affordability Act: Hearings on HR 1127 before the Subcommittee on Courts and Intellectual Property of the House Committee on the Judiciary (Hearings on HR 1127).

[12] Hearings on HR 1127 (statement of Dr Noonan).

[13] Ibid.

[14] Ibid.

[15] Hearings on HR 1127 (statement by Dr C.D. Kelman, American Society of Cataract and Refractive Surgery).

[16] Hearings on HR 1127 (statement of Dr J. Singer).

ethical obligation of physicians, it was argued, is in conflict with the patent policy.[17] The patenting of medical procedures would increase health care costs, the costs of getting a licence for the procedure and the costs of infringement actions.[18]

The Clinton Administration was cognisant of the problems associated with patents for medical procedures but was willing to conduct hearings on the actions that the USPTO could take to address those concerns.[19] One of the salient observations was that it would be unfair to single out one area of creativity and deny it the benefits of the patent system.[20] It was argued that the need for the legislation was *not* established and that the incentives of the patent system to provide new medical procedures would be lost.[21] The USPTO argued that excluding medical and surgical procedures from patentability was not the proper way to address the ethical concerns and opposed HR Bill 1127.[22]

Michael Kirk, the Executive Director of the American Intellectual Property Association, pointed out that it had not been shown that there was a demonstrated need for the legislation and that the reasons behind HR Bill 1127 were purely philosophical.[23] He emphasised that HR Bill 1127 would remove the incentive to innovate and disclosure.[24] Concerns about the United States compliance with the TRIPS Agreement were also mentioned.[25]

Supporters of HR Bill 1127 claimed that the issue went to the heart of the way in which society disseminated medical knowledge for the benefits of patients, and had serious implications for health care costs.[26] The tradition of sharing knowledge, it was argued, has been at the cornerstone of the medical profession.[27] It was noted that there is no public benefit to patenting medical procedures where there are no high costs for development

---

[17] Ibid.

[18] Ibid.

[19] Ibid.

[20] Hearings on HR 1127 (Statement by D.R. Dunner, Chair, Section of Intellectual Property of the American Bar Association).

[21] Hearings on HR 1127 (statement of M. Kirk, Executive Director, American Intellectual Property Law Association).

[22] Hearings on HR 1127 (Statement of L. Skillinton, Office of Legislative and International Affairs, US Patent and Trademark Office).

[23] Hearings on HR 1127 (statement of M. Kirk, Executive Director, American Intellectual Property Law Association).

[24] Ibid.

[25] Ibid.

[26] Hearings on HR 1127 (Statement of Dr Jack Pallin).

[27] Ibid.

testing and no manufacturing is required.[28] Medical procedure patents might also make physicians reluctant to share information as they may expose themselves to patent infringement suits.[29] Indeed, it was argued that the medical profession's culture of openness offers a goldmine of free information for opportunistic physicians to claim ownership of variations of procedures developed by others.[30] Medical patents are contrary to the American Medical Council on Ethical and Judiciary Affairs, which concluded that it is unethical for physicians to seek, secure or enforce patents on medical procedures.[31] Others opposed the HR Bill 1127 in principle but thought that it went beyond the problem that it sought to solve in so far as the effect of HR Bill 1127 was to eliminate patent protection for new uses of unpatentable drugs.[32] This, it was argued, would have serious scientific and economic consequences as these companies required patent protection to finance research into new uses of biological compounds.[33] HR Bill 1127 was claimed to be an overbroad response to the ethical problem of procedure patents in medicine.[34]

The American Society of Cataract and Refractive Surgery submitted that HR Bill 1127 would have adverse effects on the availability, cost and quality of health care.[35] It was pointed out that the *Pallin* case had caused a near firestorm in the medical community and suggested the potential for broad proliferation of medical procedure patents.[36] Such patents, it was emphasised: first, had a chilling effect on the medical profession's tradition of open exchange of information and ideas; second, impeded the quality of health care; and, third, would unnecessarily drive up the cost of health care.[37] Medical procedure patents were inherently subject to abuse and such patent protection was not needed.[38]

The American Academy of Ophthalmology pointed out that it is not against medical devices but against pure medical methods.[39] They argued

---

[28]   Ibid.
[29]   Ibid.
[30]   Ibid.
[31]   Ibid.
[32]   Hearings on HR 1127 (Statement of William N. Noonan).
[33]   Ibid.
[34]   Ibid.
[35]   Hearings on HR 1127 (Statement by Charles D. Kelman, President, American Society for Cataract and Refractive Surgery).
[36]   Ibid.
[37]   Ibid.
[38]   Ibid.
[39]   Hearings on HR 1127 (Statement by H.D. Hoskins, Executive Vice President, American Academy of Ophthalmology).

that the practice of medicine is different from a commercial enterprise and that the profession called for the treatment of patients, which, itself, called for unique judgement in every single case.[40] It is the duty of physicians, they continued, to provide the patient with the best technique available for diagnosis and treatment and, as such, the fact that patents might be held on those techniques restricts the physicians' choice.[41] The Academy of Ophthalmology concluded by positing that the policy objectives of the patent system are designed to achieve without the burdens of the patent system.[42]

3   House Bill 3814 (HR Bill 3814)

Although HR Bill 1127 had the support of the medical coalition, it was not well received. In response to criticisms of HR Bill 1127, an amendment was introduced in Congress on 18 July 1996.[43] In introducing HR Bill 3814, Senator Ganske pointed out that the amendment 'borrows from and improves'[44] HR Bill 1127 and was intended to protect patients, not physicians.[45] The Bill would allow patent protection for medical devices for use in methods of medical treatment, biological products, new uses for non-patentable drugs and biological products, and biotechnological processes.[46] The amendment reduced USPTO funding for issuing medical procedure patents except where they are a necessary component of a patentable medical device or machine.[47]

The exceptions grafted to this sweeping provision were: first, a procedure performed by, or as a necessary component to, a patentable machine, manufacture or composition of matter;[48] and, second, when the patent is for a new use or new indication for a drug or a biotechnological process.[49] New uses for old drugs would still be patentable. The amendment was

---

[40]   Ibid.
[41]   Ibid.
[42]   Ibid.
[43]   142 Cong. Rec. H8030 (1996).
[44]   142 Cong. Rec. H8030-06 (18 July 1996).
[45]   Ibid.
[46]   Ibid.
[47]   Amendment No.16 House Bill 3814 s.615(a). The amendment stated that 'none of the funds available under this Act may be used by the PTO to issue a patent for any invention or discovery of a technique, method, or process of performing a medical or surgical procedure, administering a surgical or medical therapy, or making a medical diagnosis'.
[48]   House Bill 3814 s.615(b).
[49]   House Bill 3814 s.615(c).

seen as too broad because the exceptions 'would not cover all situations where innovative science and research in the biotechnology field creates new medical therapies that have the potential of curing costly, deadly diseases'.[50] The uncertain impact on the biotechnology industry was sufficient for Senators Kennedy and Schroeder to reject the amendment.[51]

The method by which HR Bill 3814 was being passed was also challenged on procedural grounds.[52] It was pointed out that it is not appropriate to bypass the authorisation process by appending the legislation to an Appropriations Bill, especially when the matter is subject to hearings by the Committee on the Judiciary of the House.[53] The Chairman of the Appropriations Committee made it quite clear that he was opposed to the amendment because he thought that such a significant policy issue needed proper study and discussion and should *not* be rushed. The House, he proclaimed, should act on the advice of the relevant committee and should let the 'authorizers do *their* job'.[54] The Chairman of the Subcommittee of the Judiciary opposed the amendment on the ground that it was an effort to 'strip the Judiciary Committee of its jurisdiction on the issue'.[55] It was made clear that the Appropriations Committee is not the appropriate forum for discussion on matters concerning substantive patent law.[56]

Representative Ganske explained that physicians do not need incentives provided by patent law as a stimulus to innovation and that physicians should not get windfall profits at the expense of patients.[57] He continued by emphasising that new drugs, machinery and devices for treating and diagnosing disease, new uses for non-patentable drugs and biological products, would remain patentable.[58] He then urged support for the HR Bill 3814 because of the fear that: patient access would be threatened by medical procedure patents; such a patent would permit the owner to charge monopoly prices, which might increase health care costs; the obligations on physicians to share their knowledge and skills for the benefit of the

---

[50]   142 Cong. Rec H8254-03 at H8279 (17 July 1996) (statement by Senators Kennedy and Schroeder).

[51]   Ibid.

[52]   142 Cong. Rec H8254-03 at H8279 (17 July 1996) (statement by Mr Rogers).

[53]   Ibid.

[54]   Ibid. (emphasis added).

[55]   142 Cong. Rec H8254-03 at H8279 (17 July 1996) (statement by Mr Moorhead).

[56]   142 Cong. Rec H8254-03 at H8279 (17 July 1996) (statement by Mr Moorhead, Ms Eschoo and Mr Deutch).

[57]   142 Cong. Rec. H8254, 8277 (daily ed. 24 July 1996) (statement of Rep. Ganske).

[58]   Ibid.

community; medical patents are not necessary for the advancement of medical knowledge; and the United States is the only developed nation that allows patents for medical procedures.[59]

Representative Rogers pointed out that the issue of medical patents is a very complicated one and it needs to have hearings and to work its way through the authorising process of the House.[60] He noted that he had no factual basis upon which to make a judgement about whether or not the HR Bill 3814 was a good idea.[61] Representative Rogers emphasised that it would not be wise to rush forward a significant policy issue without proper study, discussion and going through the regular channels, and that this was not the appropriate forum to address such a complicated and important policy issue.[62] The Chairman of the Judiciary Committee stated that the amendment was based on HR Bill 1127, which was being considered by the Committee and the effect of the amendment was 'to strip the Judiciary Committee of its jurisdiction over the issue by attempting to legislate on this appropriations bill. For this reason alone the amendment should be rejected.'[63]

Other representatives were of the opinion that the amendment was needed because medical patents harm the patient.[64] One was of the opinion that the language was too broad regardless of the merits of what it was trying to achieve and the language of the amendment threatened to invalidate up to one-third of all biotech patents in the United States.[65] Similarly, it would serve as a disincentive for investment in medical research.[66] Another representative thought that the objective of limiting medical procedure patents could be achieved by placing a limitation on enforcement of these patents or by giving blanket immunity to physicians who might use these procedures.[67] Senator Kennedy thought that this approach was a failed one, which could be likened to cutting one's

---

[59] Ibid.

[60] 142 Cong. Rec. H8254, H8277 (daily ed. 24 July 1996) (statement by Rep. Rogers).

[61] Ibid.

[62] Ibid. (Rep. Mollohan shared similar sentiments, H8278).

[63] 142 Cong. Rec. H8254, H8277 (daily ed. 24 July 1996) (statement by Rep. Moorhead, Chairman of the House Committee on the Judiciary).

[64] 142 Cong. Rec. H8254, H8277 (daily ed. 24 July 1996) (statement by Rep. Norwood).

[65] 142 Cong. Rec. H8254, H8277 (daily ed. 24 July 1996) (statement by Rep. Dooley).

[66] Ibid.

[67] 142 Cong. Rec. H8254, H8277 (daily ed. 24 July 1996) (statement by Rep. Kennedy H8279).

fingernails with a chainsaw.[68] He was of the opinion that the two exceptions would not cover all situations where innovative science and research in the biotechnology field created new medical therapies that have the potential of curing costly, deadly diseases.[69] It was pointed out that the use of patents is crucial to the biotechnology industry, which is necessary to secure investment for research and, since the amendment might jeopardise that, it should be soundly defeated.[70]

Representative Schroeder noted that this solution was not a narrow solution for a narrow problem but would unintentionally jeopardise whole categories of biomedical research and that the House had no business legislating radical changes in patent law on an Appropriations Bill.[71] She pointed out that it was bad policy rushing the legislation and doing it in this manner was bypassing the Judiciary Committee.[72] The solution, it was emphasised, could be accomplished by leaving it to the USPTO, which was already holding public hearings on the issue at hand.[73]

4   Senate Bill 1334

Senator Frist tabled Senate Bill 1334 on 18 October 1995, seven months after the introduction of HR Bill 1127.[74] It provided that it shall not be an act of infringement for a patient, physician or other licensed health care practitioner, or a health care entity with which a physician or licensed health care practitioner is professionally affiliated, to use or induce others to use a patented technique, method or process for performing a surgical or medical procedure, administering a surgical or medical therapy, or making a medical diagnosis.[75] This exclusion of liability for infringement did not apply to the use of, or inducement to use, such a patented technique, method or process by any person engaged in the commercial manufacture, sale or offer for sale of a drug, medical device, process or other product that is subject to regulation under the Federal Food, Drug, and Cosmetic Act or the Public Health Service Act.[76]

---

[68]   Ibid.
[69]   Ibid.
[70]   Ibid.
[71]   142 Cong. Rec. H8254, H8277 (daily ed. 24 July 1996) (statement of Rep. Schroeder, H8280).
[72]   Ibid.
[73]   Ibid.
[74]   142 Cong. Rec. S15291 (daily ed. 18 October 1995).
[75]   Senate Bill 1334, 104th Cong., 1st Sess. (1995).
[76]   Ibid.

Senate Bill 1334 (Sen. Bill 1334), similarly named the Medical Procedures and Affordability Act, was also the subject of intense debate during the congressional testimony of 19 October 1995.[77] It was argued that a case for the exclusion was not made and the 'right without a remedy'[78] effect of the Ganske/Frist compromise was contrary to one of the fundamental benefits of the American patent system, namely, the right to exclusive use.[79] Such a patent 'without a meaningful remedy against infringement is *like no patent at all*.[80] The exclusion from patentability and the infringement liability section were considered discriminatory, as they would 'achieve the result by discriminatory treatment based on the identity or profession of the infringer'.[81] Sen. Bill 1334, it was argued, might ultimately increase litigation over the meaning and effort of the legislation itself.[82] Senator Kirk observed that the exception in Sen. Bill 1334 relating to the use of a composition of matter was problematic.[83] Sen. Bill 1334 provided that the exception did not apply unless the use 'directly contributes to achievement of the objective of the claimed method'.[84]

Mr Frist, who introduced Sen. Bill 1334 in the Senate, noted that there was an alarming increase in the trend of obtaining and enforcing medical procedure patents in the medical community and that a legislative solution was necessary.[85] He observed that medical procedures were not considered patentable until the Patent Office changed its policy in 1954 and that this was in conflict with broader health policy goals.[86] The publication and sharing of research findings, it was emphasised, are important elements in the advancement of health care.[87] Allowing a physician to claim ownership of years of co-operative clinical experience and research would be unfair.[88] Dr Pallin placed emphasis on the infringement lawsuit, noting that there was a growing concern that the issuance of medical procedures

---

[77] 142 Cong. Rec. S15291 (18 October 1995).
[78] 142 Cong. Rec. S11845-01 (30 September 1996) (letter by Dr O.G. Hatch).
[79] Ibid.
[80] 142 Cong. Rec. S11845-01 (30 September 1996) (letter by Senator Kirk) (emphasis added).
[81] Ibid. S11847.
[82] Ibid.
[83] Ibid.
[84] 142 Cong. Rec. S11845-01 (30 September 1996) (letter by Senator Hatch).
[85] Ibid.
[86] Ibid.
[87] Ibid.
[88] Ibid.

patents would increase the cost of health care and keep physicians from providing the best treatment available.[89]

Mr Frist emphasised that medical procedure patents were on the increase and covered all areas in health care, stating that this causes other physicians to do the same and that 'that prospect is frightening'.[90] It was noted that Sen. Bill 1334 only limited infringement lawsuits of medical procedure patents and that the legislation did not impose a ban on the issuance of medical method patents and that 'there should be no concern that the legislation would prohibit biotechnology companies from enforcing their patent rights against commercial users with respect to any patentable advancements in the areas such as gene therapy, cell therapy, or with respect to new uses for well known drugs';[91] and that there was an exception for the commercial manufacture of drugs and medical devices.[92] It was observed that more than 80 countries prohibit the issuance of medical patents and that an increase in the issuance of medical patents would 'increase health care costs, limit access to quality health care and ultimately put patient privacy at risk'.[93]

On 30 September 1996, the impact of Sen. Bill 1334 was debated and various interest groups made contributions to the debate.[94] Senator Orrin G. Hatch voiced the position of the Clinton Administration. The Clinton Administration was opposed to the passage of Sen. Bill 1334, arguing that it was impossible to state categorically that tomorrow's advances in 'pure' medical procedures would take place as expeditiously as possible in the absence of patent protection.[95] It was pointed out 'in no other field would one suggest that the incentives of the patent system be eliminated in the hope that technical progress would proceed unabated'.[96] It was argued that a case had not been made for the change in the law and that the Patent Code should not be changed on the basis of anecdotal evidence.[97] They also posited that if Sen. Bill 1334 was enacted it would violate the most fundamental benefits of the United Sates Patent system, namely, the right to exclusive use as 'a patent without a remedy against infringement is like

---

[89] Ibid.
[90] Ibid.
[91] Ibid.
[92] Ibid.
[93] Ibid.
[94] 142 Cong. Rec. S11845 (daily ed. 30 September 1996).
[95] Ibid.
[96] Ibid.
[97] Ibid.

no patent at all'.[98] Questions about the inequity in the legislation, which extended protection to the organisations that employ individual physicians, but deprived individual inventors enforcement remedies against such corporations, were also raised.[99] The Clinton Administration concluded by stating that the law should not be changed in the absence of a demonstration of a compelling need and that the omnibus appropriations should not be used as a vehicle for such a controversial change in substantive patent law.[100]

The Section on Intellectual Property Law of the American Bar Association opined that such proposals would be unfair and counter-productive.[101] Their other concerns included the negative impact on America's world leadership in scientific and technological development, the international impact of making this change to accommodate narrow domestic interests, and the unworkability and ineffectiveness of the proposals.[102] The American Intellectual Property Association pointed out that this exception should be rejected and that the proponents had failed to show a need for this amendment.[103] The Intellectual Property Owners Association observed that the amendment would harm members of their association that were investing in medical research. The American Bar Association supported these arguments and opined that they opposed the unstudied proposal.[104]

The American Bar Association, through its Chairman, John R. Kirk, noted that the Bar Association was opposed to Sen. Bill 1334 on substantive and procedural grounds.[105] It was argued that the approach would 'violate the fundamental principle of our law under which patent protection is available without discrimination as to field of invention or technology'.[106] The American Bar Association felt that the proposals, based on restrictions on remedies, were unworkable and would not achieve the intended results.[107] The Commerce Department was also opposed to Sen. Bill 1334, stating that 'we continue to oppose [Sen. Bill 1334] and any subsequent amendment that contains the substance of it. We still

---

98 Ibid.
99 Ibid.
100 Ibid.
101 Ibid. at S11846.
102 Ibid.
103 Ibid.
104 Ibid.
105 Ibid.
106 Ibid.
107 Ibid.

believe that it is premature to adopt such drastic steps when we have the opportunity to adopt administrative measures to mitigate the problem.'[108] Similarly, the USPTO Commissioner expressed the view that this would be a case of overreaction to a specific circumstance and that it was important not to kill the 'incentive for medical research'.[109]

C NATURE OF THE EXCLUSION

1 Introduction

Sen. Bill 1334 never became law but it formed the basis of House Bill 3610, which was enacted on 28 September 1996.[110] Section 287(c) of 35 USC attempted to provide a comprehensive answer to the issue of medical procedure patents by exempting physicians and medical health care entities from infringement liability. The exclusion was, therefore, a narrow one.[111] Section 287(c)(1) stipulates that the provisions dealing with infringement shall not apply against the medical practitioner or related health care entity with respect to such medical activity.[112] This exception was followed by another exception,[113] which excluded persons engaged in acts of commerce from benefiting from the immunity provided in section 287(c)(1) provided that such acts take place outside the physician's office[114] and are regulated by various Acts.[115]

A medical activity was defined as the performance of a medical or surgical procedure on the human body but did not include the use of a patented machine[116] or the practice of a patented use of a composition of matter in

---

[108]   Ibid.

[109]   Ibid.

[110]   MPAA s.287(c). This section was section 616 of House Bill 3610, which received a vote of 370 to 37 on 28 September 1996 and in the Senate passed by a vote of 84 to 15 (142 Cong. Rec. S11, 815 at S11, 816) (daily ed. 30 September 1996). This Bill was the result of a conference agreement and therefore was not subject to the usual amendment in the Senate. It could get only an up or down vote.

[111]   R.M. Portman, 'Legislative Restriction on Medical and Surgical Procedure Patents Removes Impediments to Medical Progress' (1996) 4 *U Balt Intell Prop LJ* 91, 114.

[112]   MPAA s.287(c)(1).

[113]   MPAA s.287(c)(2).

[114]   MPAA s.287(c)(2)(A).

[115]   MPAA s.287(c)(2)(B). The Food, Drug, and Cosmetic Act, the Public Health Service Act, or the Clinical Laboratories Improvement Act.

[116]   MPAA s.287(c)(3)(B)(i).

violation of the patent[117] or the practice of a patent in violation of a bio-technology patent.[118] The definition of 'medical activity' did not include diagnostic methods as practised on the human or animal body as obtained in Article 53(c) EPC. However, a Bill introduced in the United States Congress by Representative Lynn Rivers, on 14 March 2002, attempted to remedy this supposed deficiency.[119]

The medical practitioner must be a natural person licensed by the State[120] and includes someone acting under her direction in the performance of the medical activity.[121] The 'patented use of a composition of matter' does not include a claim for a method of performing a medical or surgical procedure on a body that recites the use of a composition of matter, if the use of that composition of matter does not directly contribute to achievement of the objectives of the claimed method.[122] The definition of body,[123] professional affiliation[124] and related health care entity is provided for and the subsection is not retroactive.[125]

2 Legislative Intention

The conference report on section 287(c) provided some valuable insight into the legislative intent for the new law.[126] The objective of this section was to preclude the filing of civil actions for damages, or injunctive relief for the infringement of patents for medical procedures, against a medical practitioner licensed by the state or related health care entity.[127] The approach under the MPAA is to: first, *identify* the medical practitioner or related health care entity; second, decide whether a *medical activity*

---

[117] MPAA s.287(c)(3)(B)(ii).
[118] MPAA s.287(c)(3)(B)(iii).
[119] Genomic Research and Diagnostic Accessibility Act of 2002, HR 3967, 107th Congress, 2nd Sess. (2002).
[120] MPAA s.287(c)(3)(C)(i).
[121] MPAA s.287(c)(3)(C)(ii).
[122] MPAA s.287(c)(3)(D).
[123] MPAA s.287(c)(3)(A). The term 'body' shall mean (i) a human body, organ or cadaver, or (ii) a nonhuman animal used in medical research or instruction directly relating to the treatment of humans.
[124] MPAA s.287(c)(3)(E). The term 'professional affiliation' shall mean staff privileges, medical staff membership, employment or contractual relationship, partnership or ownership interest, academic appointment or other affiliation under which a medical practitioner provides the medical activity on behalf of, or in association with, the health care entity.
[125] MPAA s.287(c)(4).
[126] HR Conf. Rep. No.104-863 (1996).
[127] Ibid.

was performed; and, third, determine whether the medical activity was *an infringement* of a patented procedure. This three-pronged approach will be used to explore the various aspects of this new legislation.

(a) Defendant

The section specifically exempts medical practitioners or related health care entities from actions for patent infringement.[128] A medical practitioner is defined as a natural person licensed by a State to provide medical activity,[129] or a natural person acting under the direction of the aforementioned in the performance of the medical activity.[130] A related health care entity includes an entity with which the medical practitioner has a professional affiliation, under which the medical practitioner performs a medical activity,[131] and includes, without limitation, an affiliation such as a nursing home, hospital, university, medical school, health maintenance organisation, group medical practice or a medical clinic.[132] Any person who is concerned with, or engaged in, the commercial exploitation and provision of pharmaceutical products and services would not be able to invoke the immunity provided in section 287(c)(1).[133] The activities excluded in section 287(c)(2) must be *directly related* to the commercial exploitation of pharmaceutical products, uses of substances or the provision of clinical or laboratory services (not being services provided in a physician's office),[134] or regulated under the various Acts.[135]

(b) Medical activity

A medical activity was defined as the performance of a medical or surgical procedure on a body,[136] but it did not cover a biotechnology patent.[137] The

---

128   MPAA s.287(c)(1).
129   MPAA s.287(c)(3)(C)(i).
130   MPAA s.287(c)(3)(C)(ii).
131   MPAA s.287(c)(3)(F)(i).
132   MPAA s.287(c)(3)(F)(ii).
133   MPAA s.287(c)(2).
134   MPAA s.287(c)(2)(A).
135   MPAA s.287(c)(2)(B), namely, the Federal Food, Drug, and Cosmetic Act, the Public Health Service Act, or the Clinical Laboratories Improvement Act.
136   MPAA s.287(c)(3)(B).
137   MPAA s.287(c)(3)(B)(iii) provides that the term medical activity shall not include the practice of a process in violation of a biotechnology patent. The report expands this definition of a biotechnology patent to include a patent on a biotechnological process as defined by 35 U.S.C. s.103(b), as well as using those materials, where those materials have been manipulated *ex vivo* at the cellular or molecular level.

section created three exceptions to this definition, namely: (a) the practice of a patented machine, manufacture or composition of matter in violation of such a patent;[138] (b) the practice of a patented use of a composition of matter in violation of such a patent;[139] and (c) the practice of a process in violation of a biotechnology patent.[140] Given the wording of these provisions, it seems clear that the intention was to prevent the activities of physicians from being hindered by medical procedure patents. It is also instructive that the exception included the major areas of research in the medical field, namely, pharmaceutical products, new uses of substances and machines. These exceptions were able to appease the lobbyists that were opposed to various versions of the Bill as it went through Congress.

The medical activity *must* be practised *on* a body, which includes the human body, organ or cadaver.[141] It is not immediately clear why the cadaver of the human body was included in this definition. If the rationale for the exclusion is to provide access to various forms of treatments for patients, then it seems unnecessary to apply this to cadavers. A patent could reasonably be granted to cover such a procedure but would be limited to human cadavers and not the live human body. Where the subject of the infringement action was non-human, it must be directed at 'research or instruction directly relating to the treatment of humans'.[142] This subsection will raise interesting questions when determining whether a particular method of treatment of an animal is one that is *directly related* to the treatment of humans. The rationale for this curious formulation was, arguably, to cover medical research on non-humans that has the treatment of humans as their specific purpose. It seems, however, that where the medical research or instruction is not *directly related* to the treatment of humans, it will be patentable. This reading of the section is in line with the objective of the statutory provision, which was to ensure that patents do not limit the actions of medical practitioners when they treat their patients. Therefore, the activities of veterinarians would not be covered by the provision as it concerns medical research or instruction relating to the treatment of animals.

(c) Patented use of a composition of matter
The most complicated aspect of the MPAA is determining what is excluded from the definition of 'a patented use of a composition of

---

138 MPAA s.287(c)(3)(B)(i).
139 MPAA s.287(c)(3)(B)(ii).
140 MPAA s.287(c)(3)(B)(iii).
141 MPAA s.287(c)(3)(A)(i).
142 MPAA s.287(c)(3)(B)(ii).

matter'. This was included as part of the two exceptions to the definition of medical activity found in section 287(c)(3)(B). This section excludes: (i) the use of a patented machine, manufacture or composition of matter in violation of such a patent; or (ii) the practice of a patented use of a composition of matter in violation of such a patent. In other words, a 'patented use of a composition of matter' and the practice of a patented use of composition of matter were not considered as medical activities. Section 287(c)(3)(D), therefore, limited the definition of a 'patented use of a composition of matter' by providing that it did not include a claim for a method of performing a medical or surgical procedure on a body that recited the use of a composition of matter, if the use of that composition of matter did not directly contribute to the achievement of the objective of the claimed method.[143]

The House Report explained that the use of a composition of matter in a claim 'will direct[ly] contribute to the achievement of the objective of the claimed method if it is itself novel or if it contributes to or is necessary to establish the non-obviousness of the claim as a whole'.[144] Therefore, to directly contribute to the achievement of the objective of the claimed method, the use of a composition of matter must either: (a) be novel; or (b)(i) contribute to, or (ii) be necessary to establish the non-obviousness of the claim as a whole. This meant that a claimed activity, which recited the use of a composition of matter, would not be considered as a medical activity unless it is novel or contributes to the objective of the claimed method.[145] Uses of compositions of matter included: novel uses for drugs; novel uses of chemical or biological reagents for diagnostic purposes; novel methods for scheduling or timing of the administration of drugs; novel methods of combining drug therapies; and, novel methods for providing genetic or biological materials to a patient (including gene therapies).[146]

A use claim would be considered as 'a patented use of a composition of matter' if it directly contributed to the objectives of the claimed method. In other words, the contribution of the use claim to the objective of the claimed method as a whole was *sine qua non* of patentability. This objective would be achieved either if the *use* was novel or if it contributed to or was necessary to establish the non-obviousness of the claim. It was strange that the determination of whether a claim was a method of medical treatment was made dependent on the novelty of the use claim and its overall impact

---

[143]   MPAA s.287(c)(3)(D).
[144]   HR Conf. Rep. No.104-863 (1996).
[145]   Ibid.
[146]   Ibid.

on the claimed method itself. The use of the word 'contribute' suggested that the threshold was a low one and, when juxtaposed with the requirement of 'necessity', it does indicate a real oddity. A claim where each method recited a 'use of a composition of matter', for example a novel use of a drug for the treatment of diabetes that involves the administration of a drug at a particular time of the day and/or at a dose and/or with a concomitant medicinal therapy, would not be construed as a medical activity. The novelty of the use claim was sufficient to overcome the exclusion of medical procedures from patent protection, which suggested that every new use of a pharmaceutical product could be tailored to come within the definition of 'medical activity', given the peculiar wording of this provision in section 287(c)(3)(D).

(d) Hybrid claims

Although not mentioned in the statute, the report identified what it termed a 'hybrid' claim, which exists when a claim consists of a step that recites the use of a composition of matter and at least another step that is not directed to the use of a composition of matter.[147] In such circumstances, the test to be applied is two-pronged. One must, first, determine *the objective of the claimed method*, taking into account all the process steps outlined in the claim and, then second, determine *whether the steps, involving the use of the composition of matter, alone or collectively, contribute to the achievement of the claimed method*.[148] For example, if the objective of the claimed method were to treat cancer, it would be necessary to determine whether the *steps* comprising the use of the anti-cancer drug would *contribute* to the achievement of that aim (treating cancer). On that basis, treatment regimes that involve a novel use of a substance or composition would, therefore, be patentable.[149] The report stated that where 'individual steps involving uses of one or more compositions of matter . . . are *not novel individually* or *in combination with each other*, these uses may directly contribute to the achievement of the objective of the claimed method if, in combination with the steps that collectively involve obvious medical or surgical techniques, they produce a novel and non-obvious method'.[150] In other words, novelty could be achieved if the old use of the composition of matter is combined with surgical or medical procedures that produce a novel and non-obvious method.

---

147   Ibid.
148   Ibid.
149   Ibid.
150   Ibid.

The example given by the conference report was of a heart transplant using a conventional anaesthetic (old use) in a claim for a non-conventional surgical procedure (new technique), which it claimed would exclude the claim from the definition of medical activity (section 287(c)(2)(B)(ii)).[151] A novel medical procedure, *simpliciter*, would not be patentable. However, when combined with an old use of a patented composition or matter, it would not be regarded as falling within the definition of medical activity, so patent protection would be available. This interpretation necessarily follows from an understanding of that subsection, when read in conjunction with subsection 287(c)(3)(D) (that the use should either be novel or contribute to the achievement of the non-obviousness of the claim), that a new procedure would confer novelty on a method that involved an old use of a composition of matter.

3   Infringement

The defendant, in order to claim immunity from infringement of the patented medical procedure, must prove that he is a registered medical practitioner or works for a related health care entity. Section 271(a) provides that anyone who 'without authority makes, uses, offers to sell or sells any patented invention ... infringes the patent'.[152] Similarly, too, a person who 'actively induces infringement of a patent shall be liable as infringer'.[153]

D   GENOMIC RESEARCH AND DIAGNOSTIC ACCESSIBILITY ACT (GRDA)

The aim of the then proposed and long buried GRDA[154] was 'to provide for non-infringing uses of patents on genetic sequence information for purposes of research and genetic diagnostic testing, and to require public disclosure of such information in certain patent applications'.[155] The GRDA was proposed because the 'interests of patients and the overall health care system in [the United States] will be far better served if

---

[151]   Ibid.

[152]   35 U.S.C. 271(a).

[153]   35 U.S.C. 271(b).

[154]   HR 3697 (2002). See also the proposed Genomic Science and Technology Innovation Act 2002. More recently, another version of the GRDA has been proposed: Genomic Research and Accessibility Act 2007.

[155]   HR 3697 (2002).

laboratories, universities, and the private sector are free to use patented information for the development of diagnostic tests'.[156] It may be argued that it has failed to achieve this because the proposed diagnostic immunity section relates only to genetic diagnosis and does not fall within the types of medical and surgical procedures usually associated with physicians. The latter are process patents and involve different arguments of policy and principle than those that are made for patents on the product, namely, diagnostic testing.

The GRDA would, first, provide immunity for infringers for research on genetic sequences.[157] Secondly, it deals with diagnostic testing by providing that section 287(c)(2) of title 35, United States Code, would be changed by amending subparagraph (A) to read as follows: '(A) the term "medical activity" means the performance of a genetic diagnostic, prognostic, or predictive test or a medical or surgical procedure'.[158] The GRDA would broaden the definition of medical activity to include a genetic diagnostic, prognostic or predictive test. The provision would not cover diagnostic methods that are not genetic in nature. It then defined the term 'genetic diagnostic, prognostic, or predictive test' to mean 'any test, designed to detect disease, to predict the potential for a medical disorder, or to predict the effectiveness of therapeutics, which uses either an ordered listing of nucleotides comprising a portion of a human or human pathogen genetic code or the proteins encoded by such nucleotides'.[159] This definition would be inserted into the MPAA as subparagraph (F) after section 287(c)(3)(E).

It would also repeal section 287(c)(3) so that persons engaged in the commercial development, manufacture, sale, importation or distribution of a machine, manufacture or composition of matter, or the provision of pharmacy or clinical laboratory services (other than clinical laboratory services provided in a physician's office), would now be granted immunity from patent infringement. However, these activities must be: (a) directly related to the commercial development, manufacture, sale, importation or distribution of a machine, manufacture or composition of matter or the

---

[156] Statement by Rep. Lynn Rivers, dated 14 March 2002, on the introduction of the GRDA into the United States House of Representatives.

[157] GDRA s.2(1). It shall not be an act of infringement for any individual or entity to use any patent for or patented use of genetic sequence information for purposes of research. This paragraph shall not apply to any individual or entity that is directly engaged in the commercial manufacture, commercial sale or commercial offer for sale of a drug, medical device, process or other product using such patent for or patented use of genetic sequence information.

[158] GRDA s.3(a)(1).

[159] GRDA s.3(a)(3).

provision of pharmacy or clinical laboratory services (other than clinical laboratory services provided in a physician's office), and (b) regulated under the Federal Food, Drug, and Cosmetic Act, the Public Health Service Act, or the Clinical Laboratories Improvement Act in order to get immunity from patent infringement.[160]

The GRDA would apply retrospectively. Section 287(c)(4) of the MPAA provided that the subsection shall not apply to any patent issued on or whose earliest effective filing date is before 30 September 1996. However, the GRDA provides that '[n]otwithstanding section 287(c)(4) of title 35, United States Code, the amendments made by subsection (a) shall not apply to any patent issued based on an application the earliest effective filing date of which is before the date of the enactment of this Act'.[161] The potential of this section for stifling research potential is vast and troubling. For example, this means that the BRCA1 gene patents (breast cancer gene patents) would not be available.[162] Not surprisingly, the biotechnology industry was vehemently opposed to the Bill.[163]

It seems clear that the GRDA is contrary to the spirit of the MPAA. The MPAA was a compromise Bill that followed the Ganske Amendment to House Bill 3814, which attempted to remove USPTO's funding for new medical procedures except as a necessary component of a patentable medical device or machine. The biotechnology industry made it clear that the Bill would 'undermine the patenting of gene therapy treatments'.[164] No intention to remove from patentability biotechnological processes or treatments derived from such processes could be found in the provisions of the MPAA. Indeed, the MPAA could be regarded as a classic case where industry lobbying had its greatest role because of the number of concessions made to the biotechnology industry. For example, section 287(c)(3)(B)(ii) provides that the term medical activity shall not include the practice of a process in violation of a biotechnology patent.

---

[160]   GRDA s.3(b).

[161]   GRDA s.3(c).

[162]   See generally S.J.R. Bostyn, 'The Critical Analysis of the (Non)-Patentability of Diagnostic Methods and the Consequences for BRCA1 Gene Type Patents in Europe' (2003) *Bio-Science L R* 111.

[163]   Letter to Rep. Lynn Rivers by the Biotechnology Industry Organization dated 21 March 2001 noting the chilling effect that HR 3967 would have on biotech research and development and the huge investments in research and development that are necessary for the continued development of innovative life-saving products.

[164]   142 Cong Rec H8278 (24 July 1996) (statement by Rep. Dooley).

E CONCLUSION

The legislators in the United States acted swiftly on the heels of the *Pallin v Singer* litigation to enact the MPAA. Procedural concerns aside, the MPAA did not affect the substantive issue of patent protection of medical treatment and diagnostic methods under section 101 of the Patents Act. What it did was provide immunity to physicians and related health care entities against suits for patent infringement. The public health considerations were at the forefront of the decision to enact the MPAA. As will be seen in Chapter 6, the Court in *Prometheus* eschewed any reliance on these public health and other policy considerations when deciding whether medical diagnostic methods were patentable under section 101. In rejecting these arguments, the Court concluded that it must, first, hesitate before departing from established general legal rules lest a new protective rule that seems to suit the needs of one field produce unforeseen results in another; and, second, recognise the role of Congress in crafting more finely tailored rules where necessary. The Court seems to have been keenly aware of section 287(c).

4. Patent-eligibility

A INTRODUCTION

The constitutional guarantee, by virtue of Article 1, Section 8, Clause 8, of the Constitution of the United States, provides that 'Congress shall have the power . . . To promote the Progress of Science and useful Arts, by securing for limited Times to Authors and Inventors the exclusive Right to their respective Writings and Discoveries.' In furtherance of this clause, Congress enacted the Patent Act and established the US Patent and Trademark Office (USPTO). To this end, section 101 of the Patent Act, 35 USC, relating to inventions patentable, provides that 'Whoever invents or discovers any new and useful process, machine, manufacture, or composition of matter, or any new and useful improvement thereof, may obtain a patent therefor, subject to the conditions and requirements of this title.' Since the claims at issue in this book are all methods or process claims, it is important to state the statutory definition of 'process' in section 100(b): 'The term "process" means process, art or method, and includes a new use of a known process, machine, manufacture, composition of matter, or material.'

The United States Supreme Court ('Court') and the United States Court of Appeals for the Federal Circuit ('Federal Circuit') have, in the past, attempted to determine the scope of this section. Although the Court in *Diamond v Chakrabarty*[1] endorsed the view that patent protection extends to 'anything under the sun made by man',[2] subsequent decisions of the Court have been more cautious, explaining, as it did in *Diamond v Diehr*,[3] that '[e]xcluded from such patent protection are laws of nature, natural phenomena, and abstract ideas'.[4]

In recent years, the Court has avoided decisions concerning the scope of section 101 of the Patent Act, presumably because it felt that its jurisprudence provided a clear statement of applicable legal principles or that the

---

[1]   *Diamond v Chakrabarty* 447 U.S. 303 (1980).
[2]   Ibid. at 308.
[3]   450 U.S. 175 (1981).
[4]   Ibid. at 185.

recent pronouncements of the Federal Circuit had not gone too far astray from that jurisprudence for them to be reined in. Patentees have filed patents on the basis of current understandings of the law and, if the Court were to step in without a significant reason to do so, it would unsettle the various patents that had been granted previously. Therefore, it is not surprising that in the last few years the Court has not only rejected a chance to review the scope of patent protection for diagnostic methods, but also recently took another opportunity to reconsider various Federal Circuit decisions relating to patentable subject matter. In *Laboratory Corporation v Metabolite Labs*,[5] not only did the Court refuse to consider the issue of the scope of patent protection for methods of medical treatments, in particular diagnostic methods, but also, importantly, it refused to give a definitive answer whether such patents are allowable, suggesting they might be, with its approval of the Federal Circuit's decision.

But before a view can be made on the patentability of medical or genetic diagnostic methods in Chapter 5, it is important that one returns to core principles of US patent law. As such, it will be necessary to re-examine, in this chapter, the leading Court decisions relating to patent-eligibility to see what light, if any, they throw on the question of whether the patents at issue in the spate of Federal Circuit decisions are patentable. This means that it will be necessary to revisit the trilogy of Court decisions in *Gottschalk v Benson*,[6] *Parker v. Flook*[7] and *Diamond v Diehr*.[8] Also important is the decision of the Court in *Bilski v Kappos*,[9] where it re-examined the issue of patent-eligibility under section 101 and its previous decisions in *Benson*, *Flook* and *Diehr*. The modest aim of this chapter is to revisit the seminal decisions of the Court on this issue, for it is the *Benson–Flook–Diehr* trilogy that the Court in *Bilski* claimed provided guidance as to the proper scope of section 101: first, to seek to investigate whether any first principles emerge from these decisions; second, to outline what they are and whether they are appropriate in light of advances in technology; and, third, to assess whether these principles can actually be applied to the issue of patenting medical and genetic diagnostic methods.

---

5   548 U.S. 926; 126 S. Ct. 2976; 165 L. Ed. 2d 990 (2006).
6   409 U.S. 63 (1972).
7   437 U.S. 584 (1978).
8   450 U.S. 175 (1981).
9   130 S. Ct. 3218; 177 L. Ed. 2d 792 (2010).

B FIRST PRINCIPLES

A clear starting point in any analysis of the approach of the Court in respect of patent-eligibility must be its seminal decision in *Benson*. In that decision, the Court had to consider whether a method for converting binary-coded decimal numerals into pure binary numerals was patent-eligible under section 101. More specifically, the invention related 'to the processing of data by program and more particularly to the programmed conversion of numerical information' in *general-purpose digital computers*.[10] Douglas J gave the unanimous decision of the Court. The direction in which the Court was heading was made very clear in the first paragraph of its decision. It then made two damning findings in respect of the claimed method at issue, namely: first, the 'claims were not limited to any particular art or technology, to any particular apparatus or machinery, or to any particular end use'; and, second, '[t]hey purported to cover any use of the claimed method in a general-purpose digital computer of any type'.[11] What do these two statements say about the Court's view of the claims? First, the Court was making it clear that the claimed method was not limited to any particular technology but could conceivably be used in most, if not all, related technologies. Second, it seemingly rejected the claimed method's purported limitation to 'general-purpose digital computers' as not narrow enough because there could possibly be other uses to which the claimed method could be put which owed nothing to the invention, *as such*. The Court's reasoning was yet to come but it was clear from these two statements that the claimed invention in *Benson* was doomed.

Before a firm view could be formed on whether the claimed method was patent-eligible, first it was necessary for the Court to construe the patent – in other words, what exactly did the patentee claim? As mentioned earlier, the claimed method, based on the actual wording in the patent specification, was for 'processing of data by program and more particularly to the programmed conversion of numerical information' in a computer. This, in the Court's opinion, was really a claim for 'method of programming a general-purpose digital computer to convert signals from binary-coded decimal form into pure binary form'.[12] At this juncture, the Court now had a better view about the actual scope of the claimed method: it was for a method of converting signals from one form to another, at the very least. In other words, the claimed method was for an 'algorithm', as the court

---

[10] *Benson* at 64.
[11] Ibid.
[12] Ibid. at 65.

explained: 'they are a *generalized* formulation for programs to solve mathematical problems of converting one form of numerical representation to another.'[13] The Court noted that the 'conversion of the [binary-coded decimal] numerals to pure binary numerals can be done *mentally* through use of [a] table'.[14] After examining how the method worked in practice, the Court ruled that '[t]he mathematical procedures can be carried out in existing computers long in use, no new machinery being necessary. And, as noted, they can also be performed *without* a computer.'[15]

With this understanding of the claims, and its scope, what principles should guide the Court in deciding whether the claimed method is patent-eligible? The Court then proceeded to examine principles from its previous judgments to guide it in resolving the issue at hand. After quoting two decisions, it noted that '[p]henomena of nature, though just discovered, mental processes, and abstract intellectual concepts are not patentable, as they are the basic tools of scientific and technological work'.[16] This is simple enough; it makes the statement that: phenomena of nature, mental processes and intellectual concepts are *not* patentable, *as such*. Nothing is said there about an invention that *includes* any of these three things. The answer was not too far off, for the Court then recited the following important point of principle from its previous decision of *Funk Bros. Seed Co. v Kalo Inoculant Co.*[17]: 'He who discovers a hitherto unknown phenomenon of nature has no claim to a monopoly of it which the law recognizes. If there is to be invention from such a discovery, it must come from the *application* of the law of nature to a new and useful end.'[18] In other words, although phenomena of nature, mental process and intellectual concepts are not patentable, if the patentee can apply any of these 'to a new and useful end', then his invention would be patent-eligible. The standard of patent-eligibility in relation to these things is whether the patentee can apply them to something new and useful; but this does not go far in spelling out the contours of how that application is to take place and how either of these things should be related to the invention for it to be patentable.

It held that the quotation above from *Funk* also applies to process claims and that, on the facts, 'the "process" claim is so abstract and sweeping as to cover both known and unknown uses of the [binary-coded decimal] to

---

13 Ibid. (emphasis added).
14 Ibid. at 67 (emphasis added).
15 Ibid. (emphasis added).
16 Ibid.
17 333 U.S. 127 (1948).
18 Ibid. at 130 (emphasis added).

pure binary conversion'.[19] This statement does not make it clear whether the claimed method was either a phenomenon of nature, mental process or an intellectual concept. The Court continued that the 'end use may (1) vary from the operation of a train to verification of drivers' licenses to researching the law books for precedents and (2) be performed through any existing machinery or future-devised machinery or without any apparatus'.[20] It then examined statements made by the Court in *Cochrane v Deener*,[21] specifically where it stated that '[a] process is a mode of treatment of certain materials to produce a given result. It is an act, or a series of acts, performed upon the subject-matter to be transformed and reduced to a different state or thing.'[22] The adoption by *Benson* of this statement in *Cochrane* is important as the Court is signalling the approach that should be adopted or used when the invention at issue is a process. To be patentable, the process must transform and reduce the subject matter of the invention to a different state or thing. Is this the test for patentability of a process/method patent? The Court responded that '[t]ransformation and reduction of an article "to a different state or thing" is the *clue* to the patentability of a process claim that does not include particular machines'.[23] Two points are worthy of note: first, the 'transformation' test is *a clue* to patentability and not a *sine qua non* of patentability; and, second, the 'transformation' test is applicable only where the process claim *does not* include particular machines.

If there was any doubt, even at that time, in 1972, as to whether the 'transformation' was the sole test for patent-eligibility, the Court in *Benson* answered that question, decisively rejecting that viewpoint. It noted that it was 'argued that a process patent must either be tied to a particular machine or apparatus or must operate to change articles or materials to a "different state or thing"'[24] – the so-called 'machine or transformation test'! The Court replied categorically that '[w]e *do not* hold that no process patent could ever qualify if it did not meet the requirements of our prior precedents'.[25] It is, indeed, surprising that the Federal Circuit held this test as the test for patent-eligibility under section 101 in later decisions in light of this clear statement of principle from the Court. The Court stated that '[i]t is said that the decision precludes a patent for any program servicing

19   *Benson* at 68.
20   Ibid.
21   94 U.S. 780 (1876).
22   Ibid. at 788.
23   *Benson* at 70 (emphasis added).
24   Ibid. at 71.
25   Ibid.

a computer. We do not so hold.'[26] In addition, it pointed out that '[i]t is said we freeze process patents to old technologies, leaving no room for the revelations of the new, onrushing technology. Such is *not* our purpose.'[27] In applying those principles to the facts, the Court reasoned, '[i]t is conceded that one may not patent an idea' but 'in practical effect that would be the result if the formula for converting [binary-coded decimal] numerals to pure binary numerals were patented in this case'.[28] The invention for which the applicant sought a patent, in the Court's opinion, was simply an 'idea'. This begs the critical question of whether an algorithm *is* an 'idea'. The Court claimed that the 'mathematical formula involved here has no substantial practical application except in connection with a digital computer, which means that if the judgment below is affirmed, the patent would wholly pre-empt the mathematical formula and in practical effect would be a patent on the algorithm itself'.[29] The invention was for a mathematical formula or algorithm and this, in the Court's view, was an 'idea', which could not be patented absent some practical application outside the claimed method. In other words, a patent on the algorithm itself would prevent others from using it, which would be overbroad. Whether such inventions should, as a matter of principle, be patented, the Court claimed, should be a matter for Congress and not the courts.[30] This was because 'considerable problems are raised which only committees of Congress can manage, for broad powers of investigation are needed, including hearings which canvass the wide variety of views which those operating in this field entertain'.[31]

Flook, the next decision in the trilogy, is a *difficult* decision. It was not surprising, therefore, that it divided the Court 6 to 3. There, the Court had to consider whether a method for updating alarm limits was patent-eligible under section 101.[32] More specifically, according to Stevens J, joined by Brennan, White, Marshall, Blackmun and Powell JJ, the method 'consists of three steps: an initial step which merely measures the present value of the process variable (e.g., the temperature); an intermediate step which uses an algorithm 1 to calculate an updated alarm-limit value; and a final step in which the actual alarm limit is adjusted to the updated value'.[33]

---

26   Ibid.
27   Ibid. (emphasis added).
28   Ibid.
29   Ibid. at 71–2.
30   Ibid. at 72.
31   Ibid. at 73.
32   *Flook* at 585.
33   Ibid.

There is no question that this method fell within the statutory definition of 'process' found in section 100(b). If it did, provided it met the requirement in *Benson*, it would be patent-eligible. It is only after the question of whether the invention is patent-eligible has been decided affirmatively that the question of whether it satisfied the other requirements of inventive step and novelty can be properly answered. This much is trite law. Not to the Court in *Flook*, because in the second sentence in its decision it made the bald assertion that '[t]he only *novel* feature of the method *is* a mathematical formula'.[34] It explained further that '[t]he only difference between the conventional methods of changing alarm limits and that described in respondent's application rests in the second step – the mathematical algorithm or formula'.[35]

After quoting *Benson* for the view that 'the discovery of a novel and useful mathematical formula may not be patented', the Court claimed that '[t]he question in this case is whether the identification of a limited category of useful, though conventional, post-solution applications of such a formula makes respondent's method eligible for patent protection'.[36] The usefulness of the mathematical algorithm or formula and the complexity of the invention was not lost on the Court as it explained that: using the formula, 'an operator can calculate an updated alarm limit once he knows the original alarm base, the appropriate margin of safety, the time interval that should elapse between each updating, the current temperature (or other process variable)' and 'the appropriate weighting factor to be used to average the original alarm base and the current temperature'.[37] It continued, noting that '[t]he patent claims cover *any use* of respondent's formula *for updating the value of an alarm limit* on any process variable *involved in a process comprising the catalytic chemical conversion of hydrocarbons*'.[38] The emphasised words clearly indicate the limited scope of the claims at issue. Claiming that, '[s]ince there are numerous processes of that kind in the petro-chemical and oil-refining industries, the claims cover a broad range of potential uses of the method'.[39] The approach in *Benson* was not whether the claimed invention could conceivably cover a 'broad range of potential uses' but, rather, whether it purported to cover any use of the claimed method. The Court understood this for it also stated that the claimed methods '*do not*, however, cover *every* conceivable application of

---

34   Ibid. (emphasis added).
35   Ibid. at 585–6.
36   Ibid. at 585.
37   Ibid. at 586.
38   Ibid. (emphasis added).
39   Ibid.

the formula'.[40] If this latter statement is correct, then it means that the claims in *Flook* were distinguishable from those in *Benson*, which 'were not limited to any particular art or technology, to any particular apparatus or machinery, or to any particular end use',[41] as was the case in *Flook*. Rather, '[t]hey purported to cover any use of the claimed method in a general-purpose digital computer of any type'.[42]

The Examiner had rejected the patent application on the basis that 'this method "would in practical effect be a patent on the formula or mathematics itself"' and the BOPA agreed;[43] however, its decision was reversed by the CCPA (Court of Customs and Patents Appeals), which 'read *Benson* as applying only to claims that entirely pre-empt a mathematical formula or algorithm, and noted that the respondent was only claiming on the use of his method to update alarm limits in a process comprising the catalytic chemical conversion of hydrocarbons'.[44] As a result, it held that 'since the mere solution of the algorithm would not constitute infringement of the claims, a patent on the method would not pre-empt the formula'.[45] The claimed method was simply for the use of the mathematical formula or algorithm in a specific way to achieve a particular purpose; others could apply the same formula to other new uses without any infringement. One cannot but agree with the CCPA that the claimed method would not pre-empt the formula – thereby satisfying the *Benson* requirement. The Court in *Flook* had now to explain how the principle emerging from *Benson*, and other leading Court decisions, was controlling precedent in respect of the claims at issue.

It pointed out, correctly, that the 'case turns entirely on the proper construction of [section] 101 of the Patent Act, which describes the subject matter that is eligible for patent protection' and 'does not involve the familiar issues of novelty and obviousness that routinely arise under [sections] 102 and 103 when the validity of a patent is challenged'.[46] But, arguably, it did involve the issue of whether the use of a mathematical formula or algorithm in an old method makes it novel. Additionally, and centrally in this case, the section 101 issue was whether the use of that mathematical formula or algorithm in the claimed methods pre-empted *all* uses whatsoever. Assuming that 'the formula [was] the only novel

---

40 Ibid. (emphasis added).
41 *Benson* at 64.
42 Ibid.
43 *Flook* at 587.
44 Ibid.
45 Ibid.
46 Ibid. at 588.

feature of respondent's method', the Court noted that '[t]he question [was] whether the discovery of this feature makes an otherwise conventional method eligible for patent protection'.[47] There is no question that '[t]he plain language of [section] 101 does not answer the question'[48] in *Flook*, as the Court readily admitted. Furthermore, '[r]easoning that an algorithm, or mathematical formula, is like a law of nature, *Benson* applied the established rule that a law of nature cannot be the subject of a patent'.[49] The question now for the Court in *Flook* was how to apply this principle of law to the facts with which it was there presented. In its view '[t]he line between a patentable "process" and an unpatentable "principle" is not always clear'.[50]

The respondent argued that its patent did 'not seek to "wholly pre-empt the mathematical formula," since there are uses of his formula outside the petrochemical and oil-refining industries that remain in the public domain'.[51] The Court disagreed with the respondent's view that 'the presence of specific "post-solution" activity – the adjustment of the alarm limit to the figure computed according to the formula – distinguishes this case from *Benson* and makes his process patentable'.[52] It claimed, '[t]he notion that post-solution activity, no matter how conventional or obvious in itself, can transform an unpatentable principle into a patentable process exalts form over substance' and that '[a] competent draftsman could attach some form of post-solution activity to almost any mathematical formula . . .'.[53] If this was the case, the Court continued, 'the Pythagorean theorem would not have been patentable, or partially patentable, because a patent application contained a final step indicating that the formula, when solved, could be usefully applied to existing surveying techniques'.[54] At footnote 11, it explained that 'in *Benson* there was a specific end use contemplated for the algorithm – utilization of the algorithm in computer programming'.[55] In addition, the Court noted that '[o]f course, as the Court [in *Benson*] pointed out, the formula had no other practical application; but it is not entirely clear why a process claim is any more or less patentable because the specific end use contemplated is the only one for which the algorithm has

---

[47] Ibid.
[48] Ibid.
[49] Ibid. at 589.
[50] Ibid.
[51] Ibid. at 589–90.
[52] Ibid. at 590.
[53] Ibid.
[54] Ibid.
[55] Ibid.

any practical application'.[56] The mention of 'obvious' and conventional steps in the claimed method comes close to blurring the lines between patentability under section 101 and obviousness under section 103. The failure to appreciate this distinction fully seems to permeate through most of the Court's jurisprudence under section 101. Also, more importantly, was the point made by the Court that it would prefer not to exalt form over substance and that the function of the courts is to determine what exactly has the patentee claimed, not merely what was contemplated by the draftsperson.

Having stated that, the Court then claimed, '[y]et it is equally clear that a process is not unpatentable simply because it contains a law of nature or a mathematical algorithm'.[57] It then cited *Mackay Radio & Telegraph Co. v Radio Corp. of America*[58] for the following proposition: '[w]hile a scientific truth, or the mathematical expression of it, is not patentable invention, a novel and useful structure created with the aid of knowledge of scientific truth may be'.[59] The Court also quoted the statement from *Funk Bros.*, which was quoted above in *Benson*.[60] In analysing the solution in the case, the Court explained that '*Mackay Radio* and *Funk Bros.* point to the proper analysis for this case: The process itself, not merely the mathematical algorithm, must be new and useful.'[61] Noting that 'the novelty of the mathematical algorithm is not a determining factor at all', the Court was of the opinion that '[w]hether the algorithm was in fact known or unknown at the time of the claimed invention, as one of the "basic tools of scientific and technological work" . . . it is treated as though it were a familiar part of the prior art'.[62] After citing from *O'Reilly v Morse*,[63] the Court asserted that 'this case must also be considered as if the principle or mathematical formula were well known'.[64] Again, the Court is making reference to novelty issues (under section 102) when discussing patentability under section 101.

But the question of the novelty of the invention has nothing at all to do with whether or not it satisfies section 101 and it is impermissible to dissect the patent between old parts and new parts for the purposes of novelty.

---

[56]   Ibid.
[57]   Ibid.
[58]   306 U.S. 86 (1939).
[59]   Ibid. at 97.
[60]   *Flook* at 591.
[61]   Ibid.
[62]   Ibid. at 591–2.
[63]   15 How. 62 (1853).
[64]   *Flook* at 592.

The method, it was accepted, was not new and the algorithm was part of the 'basic tools of scientific and technological work'; this did not mean that, consequently, the invention was not novel – novelty may very well lie in using this unpatentable formula in this old method to create something that did not exist before. This would be sufficient to satisfy the requirements of section 102. However, we are not here concerned with section 102, but only with the question of whether the patent as a whole was patent-eligible under section 101. It is this confusion that led the Court in *Flook* to arrive at its conclusion that the invention at issue was not patentable under section 101. The respondents also recognised this and argued that the Court's approach 'improperly imports into [section] 101 the considerations of "inventiveness" which are the proper concerns of [sections] 102 and 103'.[65]

The Court immediately replied that '[t]his argument is based on two fundamental misconceptions'.[66] The first was that the 'respondent incorrectly assumes that if a process application implements a principle in some specific fashion, it automatically falls within the patentable subject matter of [section] 101 and the substantive patentability of the particular process can then be determined by the conditions of [sections] 102 and 103'.[67] In its opinion, first, '[t]his assumption is based on [a] narrow reading of *Benson*, and is as untenable in the context of [section] 101 as it is in the context of that case'; and, second, '[i]t would make the determination of patentable subject matter depend simply on the draftsman's art and would ill serve the principles underlying the prohibition against patents for "ideas" or phenomena of nature'.[68] The Court explained the 'rule that the discovery of a law of nature cannot be patented rests, not on the notion that natural phenomena are not processes, but rather on the more fundamental understanding that they are not the kind of "discoveries" that the statute was enacted to protect'.[69] As a result, it stated that '[t]he obligation to determine what type of discovery is sought to be patented must precede the determination of whether that discovery is, in fact, new or obvious'.[70] That much is true; however, the Court's reference to section 102 and 103 issues in its discussion of patentability issues surely sowed the seeds for the confusion on this issue that is yet to be unravelled. It must be said that nothing in the respondent's arguments suggested that their arguments were at odds

---

[65] Ibid.
[66] Ibid.
[67] Ibid. at 593.
[68] Ibid.
[69] Ibid.
[70] Ibid.

with the principles enunciated by the Court. What they simply argued was that their invention was based on the *application* of the mathematical algorithm or formula to solve a specific problem and that, consequently, their invention was patent-eligible under section 101. The *use* of the mathematical algorithm or formula in the claimed method was the novel aspect of the invention; it was also what *constituted* the invention. It was the inability to appreciate that difference between the two which led the Court to err in its reasoning. Therefore, when the respondent argued that it was a 'new' use of the mathematical algorithm or formula in a method of updating alarm limits, the reference to 'new' was simply to: first, suggest that this was the first time this was being done; and, second, to show that it was the *use* of the mathematical algorithm or formula that was the subject matter of the invention. The Court was not convinced.

It continued that the second reason why the respondent's argument was a misconception was that the 'respondent assumes that the fatal objection to his application is the fact that one of its components – the mathematical formula – consists of unpatentable subject matter'.[71] The Court pointed out that its 'approach to respondent's application is, however, not at all inconsistent with the view that a patent claim must be considered as a whole'.[72] It ruled that the claimed 'process is unpatentable under [section] 101, not because it contains a mathematical algorithm as one component, but because once that algorithm is assumed to be within the prior art, the application, considered as a whole, contains no patentable invention'.[73] Surely, this is contrary to the Court's observation that 'a patent claim must be considered as a whole'. How, then, could the use of a mathematical algorithm 'as one component' of the application 'contain no patentable invention' when considered as a whole? The difficulty with which the Court was faced, as was mentioned above, was its inability to differentiate between the use of the mathematical algorithm or formula as the invention and as the inventive concept. The two concepts are different although they may refer to the same thing. Nonetheless, the Court continued that '[e]ven though a phenomenon of nature or mathematical formula may be well known, an inventive application of the principle may be patented. Conversely, the discovery of such a phenomenon cannot support a patent unless there is some *other inventive concept* in its application'.[74] The first sentence seems simply to restate the well-known principle that the

---

71 Ibid. at 593–4.
72 Ibid. at 594.
73 Ibid.
74 Ibid.

application of a *known* phenomenon of nature or mathematical formula *is* patentable, in principle. The Court's second sentence, too, restates the principle that the *discovery* alone of a phenomenon of nature or mathematical formula will not support a patent unless there is some other inventive concept, namely, its application in a way that was hitherto *unknown*. This is all trite law. Why, then, does its application to the claimed method in *Flook* lead to a split in the decision of the Court?

The Court was convinced that it was 'absolutely clear that respondent's application contains no claim of patentable invention'.[75] This, one might have thought, would indicate that the respondent's invention did not contain subject matter, barring any issue under sections 102 and 103, which would constitute an invention. However, it claimed that '[t]he chemical processes involved in catalytic conversion of hydrocarbons are well known, as are the practice of monitoring the chemical process variables, the use of alarm limits to trigger alarms, the notion that alarm limit values must be recomputed and readjusted, and the use of computers for "automatic monitoring-alarming"'.[76] But the question of whether any of the aspects of the invention are patent-eligible has nothing at all to do with whether any of them are well known or not – that inquiry properly belongs to section 102, not section 101, which deals with patent-eligibility. The Court stated that the '[r]espondent's application simply provides a new and presumably better method for calculating alarm limit values'.[77] The question, then, is why this invention was held ineligible for patent protection. It then immediately quotes the CCPA in *In re Richman*[78] for the view that 'if a claim is directed essentially to a method of calculating, using a mathematical formula, even if the solution is for a specific purpose, the claimed method is nonstatutory'.[79] However, it is at footnote 18 that some of the Court's reasoning is really revealed. While rejecting the respondent's argument concerning section 103, the Court explained that the respondent's 'argument confuses the issue of patentable subject matter under [section] 101 with that of obviousness under [section] 103'.[80] It emphasised that the respondent's 'process patent rests solely on the claim that his mathematical algorithm, when related to a computer program, will improve the existing process for updating alarm units'.[81] The Court then reiterated the essence

75   Ibid.
76   Ibid.
77   Ibid. at 594–5.
78   563 F.2d 1026 (CCPA 1977).
79   Ibid. at 1030.
80   *Flook* at 595.
81   Ibid.

of its decision stating that '[v]ery simply, our holding today is that a claim for an improved method of calculation, even when tied to a specific end use, is unpatentable subject matter under [section] 101'.[82]

Perhaps anticipating a negative outcry from its decision, the Court went on to explain that '[t]o a large extent our conclusion is based on reasoning derived from opinions written before the modern business of developing programs for computers was conceived'.[83] In any event, this matters little because the decision cited by the Court did not compel the result that it reached, as it reflected in the dissenting judgment of Stewart J. The Court continued that: first, '[t]he youth of the industry may explain the complete absence of precedent supporting patentability'; and, second, '[n]either the dearth of precedent, nor this decision, should therefore be interpreted as reflecting a judgment that patent protection of certain novel and useful computer programs will not promote the progress of science and the useful arts, or that such protection is undesirable as a matter of policy'.[84] Rather than answer the specific question of whether the claimed method was patent-eligible, which generally did not revolve around the patentability of computer programs per se, the Court simply claimed that '[d]ifficult questions of policy concerning the kinds of programs that may be appropriate for patent protection and the form and duration of such protection can be answered by Congress on the basis of current empirical data not equally available to this tribunal'.[85] Of course, this reply would have been appropriate in the context where the invention claimed a computer program as such, or the underlying mathematical algorithm or formula. The Court then concluded its judgment by stating that it was its 'duty to construe the patent statutes as they now read, in light of our prior precedents, and we must proceed cautiously when we are asked to extend patent rights into areas wholly unforeseen by Congress'.[86]

Stewart J, with whom Burger CJ and Rehnquist J agreed, opened his dissenting judgment with the statement that '[i]t is commonplace that laws of nature, physical phenomena, and abstract ideas are not patentable subject matter', which meant that '[a] patent could not issue, in other words, on the law of gravity, or the multiplication tables, or the phenomena of magnetism, or the fact that water at sea level boils at 100 degrees centigrade and freezes at zero – even though newly discovered'.[87] After

---

82 Ibid.
83 Ibid.
84 Ibid.
85 Ibid.
86 Ibid. at 596.
87 Ibid. at 598.

restating the principle, which emerged from *Benson*, Stewart J claimed that '[t]he present case is a far different one. The issue here is whether a claimed process loses its status of subject-matter patentability simply because *one step* in the process would not be patentable subject matter if considered in isolation.'[88] He then quoted from the decision of the CCPA in *In re Flook*, where it 'held that the process is patentable subject matter, *Benson* being inapplicable since "[the] present claims do not preempt the formula or algorithm contained therein, because solution of the algorithm, per se, would not infringe the claims"'.[89] In his view, '[t]hat decision seems to me wholly in conformity with basic principles of patent law'[90] and that 'thousands of processes and combinations have been patented that contained one or more steps or elements that themselves would have been unpatentable subject matter'.[91]

Stewart J was of the clear opinion that the Court 'says it does not turn its back on these well-settled precedents . . . but it strikes what seems to me an equally damaging blow at basic principles of patent law by importing into its inquiry under [section] 101 the criteria of novelty and inventiveness'.[92] In his view, '[s]ection 101 is concerned only with *subject-matter patentability*' and the question of '[w]hether a patent will actually issue depends upon the criteria of [sections] 102 and 103, which include novelty and inventiveness, among many others'.[93] Stewart J explained that '[i]t may well be that under the criteria of [sections] 102 and 103 no patent should issue on the process claimed in this case, because of anticipation, abandonment, obviousness, or for some other reason'.[94] However, he concluded by stating that: 'in my view the claimed process clearly meets the standards of subject-matter patentability of [section] 101.'[95]

Flook purported to apply the principles emerging from *Benson*, but it produced a split in the Court's decision. The majority in *Flook* felt that the claimed method was actually for *the* underlying mathematical algorithm or formula; whereas, the minority felt that it was the *application* of the underlying mathematical algorithm or formula. The question of whether the reasoning of the majority in *Flook* was correct was considered in the next leading case on patent-eligibility – *Diehr*. The dissenters in *Flook*,

---

[88]　Ibid. (emphasis in original).
[89]　*In re Flook*, 559 F.2d 21, 23 (CCPA 1977).
[90]　*Flook* at 599.
[91]　Ibid. at 599–600.
[92]　Ibid.
[93]　Ibid.
[94]　Ibid.
[95]　Ibid.

namely, Burger CJ, Stewart and Rehnquist JJ, along with two Justices from the minority in that decision, namely Powell and Blackmun JJ, formed the majority of five in *Diehr*. Four of the six Justices in the majority in *Flook*, namely Stevens, Brenan, White and Marshall JJ, formed the dissent in *Diehr*.

Rehnquist J delivered the opinion of the Court in *Diehr*, claiming that it 'granted *certiorari* to determine whether a process for curing synthetic rubber which includes in several of its steps the use of a mathematical formula and a programmed digital computer is patentable subject matter under [section] 101'.[96] Immediately, the context of the invention was made clear by the Court – it was simply for a method that uses a mathematical formula to achieve a particular objective. The Court claimed that '[t]he claimed invention is a process for molding raw, uncured synthetic rubber into cured precision products' and, in particular, the 'process uses a mold for precisely *shaping* the uncured material under heat and pressure and then *curing* the synthetic rubber in the mold so that the product will retain its shape and be functionally operative after the molding is completed'.[97] The impact of the claimed invention on the process is immediately apparent – the process underwent some form of change (or transformation) as a result of the contribution of the invention. The respondents claimed that 'their contribution to the art . . . reside[d] in the process of constantly measuring the actual temperature inside the mold'.[98] In other words, '[a]ccording to the respondents, the continuous measuring of the temperature inside the mold cavity, the feeding of this information to a digital computer which constantly recalculates the cure time, and the signalling by the computer to open the press, are all new in the art'.[99] Therefore, there was no question that the use of the algorithm or mathematical formula enabled the process to operate in a more efficient manner. The novelty, therefore, lay in the use of that mathematical formula to achieve the curing of rubber; and, as was mentioned before, the novel aspect of a claimed method *is* sometimes *the* invention itself. The Examiner, applying *Benson*, held the claims, which were 'carried out by a computer under control of a stored program',[100] unpatentable because they 'defined and sought protection of a computer program for operating a rubber-molding press'.[101] The problem with this decision was that the Examiner sought to exclude from the scope of section

---

[96] *Diehr* at 177.
[97] Ibid.
[98] Ibid. at 178.
[99] Ibid. at 179.
[100] Ibid. at 180.
[101] Ibid. at 181.

101 'computer programs', which conflicted with the Court's decisions that had limited the scope of section 101 only in respect of the laws of nature, physical phenomena and abstract ideas. The Examiner's decision was upheld by the BOPA but reversed by the CCPA.[102]

The Court, after examining the legislative history of section 101, and its previous decisions of *Benson* and *Cochrane*, among others, concluded that the 'physical and chemical process for molding precision synthetic rubber products falls within the [section] 101 categories of possibly patentable subject matter'.[103] In its view, that the 'claims involve the transformation of an article, in this case raw, uncured synthetic rubber, into a different state or thing cannot be disputed'.[104] One cannot but note that the Court used the 'transformation' test to determine that the claimed method was patentable under section 101. The Court asserted that '[i]ndustrial processes such as [the claimed method] are the types which have historically been eligible to receive the protection of our patent laws'.[105] It reiterated that: first, the 'conclusion regarding respondents' claims is not altered by the fact that in several steps of the process a mathematical equation and a programmed digital computer are used; and, second, the Court 'has undoubtedly recognized limits to [section] 101 and every discovery is not embraced within the statutory terms. Excluded from such patent protection are laws of nature, natural phenomena, and abstract ideas', citing *Flook* and *Benson*.[106] This statement merits further consideration. The Court was making it abundantly clear that it mattered little that, in the claimed method, there were several steps which mentioned or used a mathematical equation. It also made it clear that not every discovery would fall within the scope of section 101 – and the excluded discoveries are laws of nature, natural phenomena and abstract ideas. Therefore, to be unpatentable under section 101, the claimed method must fall within one or more of those defined categories. It follows that everything else should be patentable.

The Court explained that, in *Benson*, it 'held unpatentable claims for an algorithm used to convert binary code decimal numbers to equivalent pure binary numbers' because the 'sole practical application of the algorithm was in connection with the programming of a general purpose digital computer'.[107] By reading *Benson* in that restricted manner, the Court in *Diehr* was able to avoid the similarities in the claimed methods: the claims

---

[102]   *In re Diehr*, 602 F.2d 982 (CCPA 1979).
[103]   *Diehr* at 184.
[104]   Ibid.
[105]   Ibid.
[106]   Ibid.
[107]   Ibid. at 185–6.

in *Benson* pre-empted the use of the algorithm or mathematical formula in any general purpose digital computer, rather than for a specific purpose on a particular computer. It continued that, having 'defined "algorithm" as a "procedure for solving a given type of mathematical problem," [the Court in *Benson*] concluded that such an algorithm, or mathematical formula, is like a law of nature, which cannot be the subject of a patent'.[108] *Flook*, in the Court's view, 'presented a similar situation' to *Benson*.[109] The 'claims were drawn to a method for computing an "alarm limit"' which 'is simply a number and the Court concluded that the application sought to protect a formula for computing this number. Using this formula, the updated alarm limit could be calculated if several other variables were known.'[110] One might have thought the Court would have explained, in greater detail, why the claims at issue in *Flook* were materially different from the ones it considered in *Diehr*. That would have explained why it arrived at the opposite conclusion to the 'similar situation' as obtained in *Flook*.

On the facts, the Court held that, in contrast to *Benson* and *Flook*, the respondents did 'not seek to patent a mathematical formula. Instead, they seek patent protection for a process of curing synthetic rubber.'[111] By saying this, the Court, incorrectly, assumed that the decisions in *Benson* and *Flook* rested on the same jurisprudential grounds. It continued that '[t]heir process admittedly employs a well-known mathematical equation, but they do not seek to pre-empt the use of that equation. Rather, they seek only to foreclose from others the use of that equation in conjunction with all of the other steps in their claimed process.'[112] The Court was able to distinguish its decision in *Diehr* from those in *Benson* and *Flook* on the basis that the claimed method in *Diehr* did not pre-empt the use of the mathematical equation, as was the case in both *Benson* and *Flook*. That aspect was key to the Court's holding in *Diehr*. The Court explained it was obvious that 'one does not need a "computer" to cure natural or synthetic rubber, but if the computer use incorporated in the process patent significantly lessens the possibility of "overcuring" or "undercuring," the process as a whole does not thereby become unpatentable subject matter'.[113] The Court claimed that its 'earlier opinions lend support to our present conclusion that a claim drawn to subject matter otherwise statutory does not become nonstatutory simply because it uses a mathematical formula,

---

[108]   Ibid. at 186.
[109]   Ibid.
[110]   Ibid.
[111]   Ibid. at 187.
[112]   Ibid.
[113]   Ibid.

computer program, or digital computer'.[114] In other words, the involvement of a mathematical formula in a claimed method does not, by itself, mean that the claimed method does not fall within the scope of section 101. After citing statements from *Benson* and *Flook*, it also claimed that '[i]t is now commonplace that an application of a law of nature or mathematical formula to a known structure or process may well be deserving of patent protection'.[115] The basis of the reasoning in *Diehr* was that the *application* of the mathematical formula to solve the problem of curing rubber fell within the scope of section 101. This meant that the applicant did not seek to pre-empt the mathematical formula in all methods, or in all computers; it did so only in respect of its specific process for curing rubber. By so confining the application of the algorithm or mathematical formula, the applicant in *Diehr* was able to avoid the pitfalls that plagued the applicants in *Benson* and *Flook*. In addition, the Court explained, by way of example, that the 'Arrhenius equation is not patentable in isolation, but when a process for curing rubber is devised which incorporates in it a more efficient solution of the equation, that process is at the very least not barred at the threshold by [section] 101'.[116] In other words, the successful application of a known formula in a claimed method would be sufficient to overcome the threshold for patentability set forth in section 101.

The Court was of the opinion that: first, '[i]n determining the eligibility of respondents' claimed process for patent protection under [section] 101, their claims must be considered as a whole'; and, second, '[i]t is inappropriate to dissect the claims into old and new elements and then to ignore the presence of the old elements in the analysis'.[117] These two principles are critical as they underscore the importance of defining the claim as a whole, for it is the *invention* that must be ascertained from a reading of all the claims in the patent specification. That cannot properly be done if the claimed method is dissected into constituent parts that are either ignored or taken into account for the purpose of *defining the invention*. The Court continued that this was 'particularly true in a process claim because a new combination of steps in a process may be patentable even though all the constituents of the combination were well known and in common use before the combination was made'.[118] Again, if the purpose were to define the invention, there would be little utility in that exercise. The Court then concluded that '[t]he "novelty" of any element or steps in a process, or

---

[114]   Ibid.
[115]   Ibid.
[116]   Ibid. at 188.
[117]   Ibid.
[118]   Ibid.

even of the process itself, is of no relevance in determining whether the subject matter of a claim falls within the [section] 101 categories of possibly patentable subject matter'.[119] The question of whether some claims are old or new would not be necessary for two reasons: first, as mentioned before, the need to consider the claims as a whole; and, second, the novelty of the claimed method (even if it also defines the invention) is not relevant in determining whether the claim is patent-eligible. The Court then continued the discussion of this issue in footnote 12. The petitioner argued that: first, 'the procedure of dissecting a claim into old and new elements is mandated by ... *Flook*[,] which noted that a mathematical algorithm must be assumed to be within the "prior art"'; and, second, consequently, 'if everything other than the algorithm is determined to be old in the art, then the claim cannot recite statutory subject matter'.[120] The Court rejected that argument in no uncertain terms, asserting that '[t]he fallacy in this argument is that we did not hold in *Flook* that the mathematical algorithm could not be considered at all when making the [section] 101 determination'.[121] It continued that: first, '[t]o accept the analysis proffered by the petitioner would, if carried to its extreme, make all inventions unpatentable because all inventions can be reduced to underlying principles of nature which, once known, make their implementation obvious'; and, second, '[t]he analysis suggested by the petitioner would also undermine our earlier decisions regarding the criteria to consider in determining the eligibility of a process for patent protection'.[122]

Rejecting the argument 'that novelty is an appropriate consideration under [section] 101', the Court reiterated that that section, 'however, is a general statement of the type of subject matter that is eligible for patent protection "subject to the conditions and requirements of this title"', namely, novelty (section 102) and inventive step (section 103).[123] It then considered the legislative history of these sections which, in its view, confirmed its reading of section 101.[124] The Court explained that 'it may later be determined that the respondents' process is not deserving of patent protection because it fails to satisfy the statutory conditions of novelty under [section] 102 or nonobviousness under [section] 103' and that a 'rejection on either of these grounds does not affect the determination that respondents' claims recited subject matter which was eligible for patent protection

---

[119] Ibid. at 188–9.
[120] Ibid. at 189.
[121] Ibid.
[122] Ibid.
[123] Ibid.
[124] Ibid. at 190.

under [section] 101'.[125] Surely, this must be the appropriate analysis. Section 101 speaks to subject matter eligible for patent protection; so, based on the Court's precedents, the analysis first must focus on whether the claimed method falls within either of the excluded categories, namely, laws of nature, natural phenomena and abstract ideas. If the claimed method is for either of these, the analysis ends there, since the subject matter would be ineligible for patent protection. It is only if the claimed method surmounts the section 101 hurdle that the issue of whether the method is novel or non-obvious arises – not before!

The Court stated that 'the question [was] whether respondents' claims fell within the [section] 101 categories of possibly patentable subject matter', holding that it viewed the 'respondents' claims as nothing more than a process for molding rubber products and not as an attempt to patent a mathematical formula'.[126] In other words, the claimed method was for a process that used the mathematical formula, not for the formula itself. It explained that 'when a claim recites a mathematical formula (or scientific principle or phenomenon of nature), an inquiry must be made into whether the claim is seeking patent protection for *that formula in the abstract*'.[127] This is an important point as the Court is making a further limitation on the scope of patentable subject matter and its relationship with the judicially defined exclusions – the inquiry must be whether the claimed method is seeking patent protection for that 'scientific principle' or 'phenomenon of nature' 'in the abstract'. If so, then the claimed method is not patent-eligible. Admittedly, the Court provided no guidance on how lower courts, or even itself, would determine that question. The Court merely noted that: '[a] mathematical formula *as such* is not accorded the protection of our patent laws,' citing *Benson*; and 'this principle cannot be circumvented by attempting to limit the use of the formula to a particular technological environment', citing *Flook*.[128] The critical question, it seemed, was whether the claimed method attempted to patent the formula itself rather than the *application* of that formula in a series of steps. In addition, it stated that in the same way, 'insignificant postsolution activity will not transform an unpatentable principle into a patentable process', citing *Flook*; and that '[t]o hold otherwise would allow a competent draftsman to evade the recognized limitations on the type of subject matter eligible for patent protection'.[129] The claim, therefore, must be carefully scrutinised to

---

[125]   Ibid. at 191.
[126]   Ibid.
[127]   Ibid. (emphasis added).
[128]   Ibid.
[129]   Ibid. at 191–2.

determine if it claimed any of the actually excluded categories. The Court also stated that:

> when a claim containing a mathematical formula *implements* or *applies* that formula in a structure or process which, when considered as a whole, is performing a function which the patent laws were designed to protect (e.g., transforming or reducing an article to a different state or thing), then the claim satisfies the requirements of [section] 101.[130]

On the facts the Court concluded, affirming the decision of United States Court of Customs and Patent Appeals (CCPA), that the respondents' claims were not 'an attempt to patent a mathematical formula, but rather . . . drawn to an industrial process for the molding of rubber products'.[131]

Before one leaves the discussion of the majority judgment in *Diehr*, the Court engaged in some analysis of *Flook*, at footnote 14 of its opinion, which merits some consideration. It argued that 'the claims in *Flook* did more than present a mathematical formula'.[132] The Court noted that the claims: first, 'also solved the calculation in order to produce a new number or "alarm limit" and then replaced the old number with the number newly produced'; and, second, 'covered all uses of the formula in processes "comprising the catalytic chemical conversion of hydrocarbons"'.[133] It continued that since there were 'numerous such processes in the petrochemical and oil refinery industries', the claims, therefore, only 'covered a broad range of potential uses'; they 'did not cover every conceivable application of the formula'.[134] The Court claimed that it 'rejected in *Flook* the argument that because all possible uses of the mathematical formula were not pre-empted, the claim should be eligible for patent protection' and its 'reasoning in *Flook* is in no way inconsistent with our reasoning here'.[135] In its view, '[a] mathematical formula does not suddenly become patentable subject matter simply by having the applicant acquiesce to limiting the reach of the patent for the formula to a particular technological use'.[136] The Court explained that: first, '[a] mathematical formula in the abstract is nonstatutory subject matter regardless of whether the patent is intended to cover all uses of the formula or only limited uses'; and, second, '[s]imilarly, a mathematical formula does not become patentable subject matter merely

---

[130] Ibid. at 192 (emphasis added).
[131] Ibid. at 192–3.
[132] Ibid. at 193.
[133] Ibid.
[134] Ibid.
[135] Ibid.
[136] Ibid.

by including in the claim for the formula token postsolution activity such as the type claimed in *Flook*'.[137] The Court then concluded it was 'careful to note in *Flook* that the patent application did not purport to explain how the variables used in the formula were to be selected, nor did the application contain any disclosure relating to chemical processes at work or the means of setting off an alarm or adjusting the alarm limit'; and that '[a]ll the application provided was a "formula for computing an updated alarm limit"'.[138]

Not surprisingly, the dissenters in *Diehr* would rely on the Court's decision in *Flook* to justify their conclusion in that case. Stevens J, who wrote for the dissenters (and, incidentally, for the majority in *Flook*), commenced his judgment by stating that '[t]he starting point in the proper adjudication of patent litigation is an understanding of what the inventor claims to have discovered'.[139] This is trite law and it was asserted earlier that a proper interpretation of the claims is perhaps the most important step in determining whether a claimed method is patent-eligible under section 101. He claimed that '[t]he Court's decision in this case rests on a misreading of the Diehr and Lutton patent application' and that it had 'compounded its error by ignoring the critical distinction between the character of the subject matter that the inventor claims to be novel – the [section] 101 issue – and the question whether that subject matter is in fact novel – the [section] 102 issue'.[140] This is quite interesting because that was the same criticism that was levelled against the majority in *Flook* above. After examining exhaustively the history in the lower courts of patent protection (or lack thereof) for computer programs,[141] he claimed that, in *Benson*, the Court 'held that new mathematical procedures that can be conducted in old computers, like mental processes and abstract intellectual concepts . . . are not patentable processes within the meaning of [section] 101'.[142] In addition, Stevens J explained that '[i]n *Flook*, [the] Court clarified *Benson* in three significant respects'.[143] The first was that '*Flook* held that the *Benson* rule of unpatentable subject matter was not limited, as the lower court believed, to claims which wholly pre-empted an algorithm or amounted to a patent on the algorithm itself'.[144] The second related to the

---

[137]   Ibid.
[138]   Ibid.
[139]   Ibid. at 193–4.
[140]   Ibid. at 194.
[141]   Ibid. at 194–201.
[142]   Ibid. at 201.
[143]   Ibid. at 204.
[144]   Ibid.

statement that 'the Court made it clear that an improved method of calculation, even when employed as part of a physical process, is not patentable subject matter under [section] 101'.[145] In respect of the third, he noted that, in *Benson*, 'the Court explained the correct procedure for analyzing a patent claim employing a mathematical algorithm. Under this procedure, the algorithm is treated for [section] 101 purposes as though it were a familiar part of the prior art; the claim is then examined to determine whether it discloses "some other inventive concept"'.[146] Stevens J then considered the decisions of the CCPA that were critical of the Court's decision in *Flook*, concluding that its 'reading of *Flook* – although entirely consistent with the lower court's expansive approach to [section] 101 during the past 12 years – trivializes the holding in *Flook*, the principle that underlies *Benson*, and the settled line of authority reviewed in those opinions'.[147]

He then rejected the Court's characterisation of the issue in *Diehr* as 'whether a process for curing synthetic rubber ... is patentable subject matter', claiming that the respondents 'do not claim to have discovered anything new about the process for curing synthetic rubber'.[148] In his view, the Court read 'the inventors' discovery [as] a method of constantly measuring the actual temperature inside a rubber molding press'[149] but stated, rather, 'their discovery is an improved method of calculating the time that the mold should remain closed during the curing process'.[150] Stevens J claimed that, if the Court's reading of the claims were correct, he would agree that they be disclosed patentable subject matter; and that, if the Court accepted his reading, he felt confident that the case would have been decided differently.[151]

In addition, Stevens J claimed that '[t]here are three reasons why [he] cannot accept the Court's conclusion that Diehr and Lutton claim to have discovered a new method of constantly measuring the temperature inside a mold'.[152] He claimed that: first, 'there is not a word in the patent application that suggests that there is anything unusual about the temperature-reading devices used in this process – or indeed that any particular species of temperature-reading device should be used in it'.[153]

---

145 Ibid.
146 Ibid.
147 Ibid. at 205.
148 Ibid. at 206.
149 Ibid.
150 Ibid. at 206–7.
151 Ibid.
152 Ibid. at 207.
153 Ibid.

Secondly, he claimed that, 'since devices for constantly measuring actual temperatures – on a back porch, for example – have been familiar articles for quite some time, [he found] it difficult to believe that a patent application filed in 1975 was premised on the notion that a "process of constantly measuring the actual temperature" had just been discovered'.[154] In respect of the third, Stevens J noted that 'the [BOPA] expressly found that "the only difference between the conventional methods of operating a molding press and that claimed in [the] application rests in those steps of the claims which relate to the calculation incident to the solution of the mathematical problem or formula used to control the mold heater and the automatic opening of the press"', concluding that '[t]his finding was not disturbed by the [CCPA] and is clearly correct'.[155] All these points are of no significance in respect of an inquiry of whether the claims were patent-eligible under section 101, because they related to the reason why, in his opinion, the claimed method was not novel, which is required by section 102, and completely irrelevant to the inquiry under section 101. He claimed that '[a] fair reading of the entire patent application, as well as the specific claims, makes it perfectly clear that what [the respondents] claim to have discovered is a method of using a digital computer to determine the amount of time that a rubber molding press should remain closed during the synthetic rubber-curing process' and that '[t]heir method of updating the curing time calculation is strikingly reminiscent of the method of updating alarm limits that Dale Flook sought to patent'.[156]

Stevens J claimed that, in *Flook*, the claims 'involved the use of a digital computer in connection with a catalytic conversion process'.[157] He continued that, '[i]n *Flook*, the digital computer repetitively recalculated the "alarm limit" – a number that might signal the need to terminate or modify the catalytic conversion process; in this case, the digital computer repetitively recalculates the correct curing time – a number that signals the time when the synthetic rubber molding press should open'.[158] Stevens J argued that '[t]he essence of the claimed discovery in both cases was an algorithm that could be programmed on a digital computer'.[159] In comparing both decisions, he claimed: first, '[i]n *Flook*, the algorithm made use of multiple process variables; [whereas in *Diehr*], it makes use of only one'; and, second, '[i]n *Flook*, the algorithm was expressed in a newly developed mathematical

---

[154] Ibid. at 207–8.
[155] Ibid. at 208.
[156] Ibid. at 209.
[157] Ibid.
[158] Ibid.
[159] Ibid.

formula; [whereas in *Diehr*], the algorithm makes use of a well-known mathematical formula'.[160] In addition, he claimed that '[n]either of these differences can explain [the Court's] holding',[161] which, in his view, rested on 'a misunderstanding of the applicants' claimed invention and a failure to recognize the critical difference between the "discovery" requirement in [section] 101 and the "novelty" requirement in [section] 102'.[162] Stevens J also mentioned that 'the most significant distinction between the invention at issue in *Flook* and that at issue in [*Diehr*] lies not in the characteristics of the inventions themselves, but rather in the drafting of the claims'.[163]

Stevens J was of the opinion that '[t]he Court misapplies [*Flook*] because . . . it fails to understand or completely disregards the distinction between the subject matter of what the inventor claims to have discovered – the [section] 101 issue – and the question [of] whether that claimed discovery is in fact novel – the [section] 102 issue'.[164] He continued that 'as was true in *Flook*, if the only concept that the inventor claims to have discovered is not patentable subject matter, [section] 101 requires that the application be rejected without reaching any issue under [section] 102; for it is irrelevant that unpatentable subject matter – in that case a formula for updating alarm limits – may in fact be novel'.[165] Stevens J. argued that a '[p]roper analysis, therefore, must start with an understanding of what the inventor claims to have discovered – or phrased somewhat differently – what he considers his inventive concept to be'.[166] At footnote 34, he claimed that: first, '[r]ather than directing its attention to the applicants' claimed discovery, the Court instead focuses upon the general industrial context in which the applicants intend their discovery to be used'; and, second, '[i]mplicit in this interpretation of the patent application is the assumption that, as long as the claims describe a specific implication of the applicants' discovery, patentable subject matter is defined'.[167] 'This assumption was expressly rejected in *Flook*.'[168] He was of the opinion that the respondents 'claim to have developed a new method of programming a digital computer in order to calculate – promptly and repeatedly – the correct curing time in a

---

[160]   Ibid. at 210.
[161]   Ibid.
[162]   Ibid. at 211.
[163]   Ibid. at 211 (footnote 32).
[164]   Ibid.
[165]   Ibid. at 212.
[166]   Ibid.
[167]   Ibid. at 213.
[168]   Ibid.

familiar process'.[169] Therefore, '[i]n the [section] 101 analysis, [the Court] must assume that the sequence of steps in this programming method is novel, unobvious, and useful'; however, '[t]he threshold question of whether such a method is patentable subject matter remains'.[170]

Stevens J stated, '[i]f that method is regarded as an "algorithm" as that term was used in [*Benson*], and [*Flook*], and if no other inventive concept is disclosed in the patent application, the question must be answered in the negative'.[171] He explained that '[i]n both *Benson* and *Flook*, the parties apparently agreed that the inventor's discovery was properly regarded as an algorithm; the holding that an algorithm was a "law of nature" that could not be patented therefore determined that those discoveries were not patentable processes within the meaning of [section] 101'.[172] Stevens J also claimed that, '[a]s the Court recognizes . . ., *Flook* also rejected the argument that patent protection was available if the inventor did not claim a monopoly on every conceivable use of the algorithm but instead limited his claims by describing a specific postsolution activity – in that case setting off an alarm in a catalytic conversion process'.[173] He noted that, '[a]s a practical matter, however, the postsolution activity described in the *Flook* application was no less significant than the automatic opening of the curing mold involved in this case'.[174] Stevens J explained that, in both *Benson* and *Flook*, 'the postsolution activity is a significant part of the industrial process', '[b]ut in neither case should that activity have any *legal* significance because it does not constitute a part of the inventive concept that the applicants claimed to have discovered'.[175]

Stevens J also pointed out that, in *Benson*, the Court 'held that a program for the solution by a digital computer of a mathematical problem was not a patentable process within the meaning of [section] 101'[176] and that, in *Flook*, the Court 'further held that such a computer program could not be transformed into a patentable process by the addition of postsolution activity that was not claimed to be novel'.[177] That holding, he continued, 'plainly requires the rejection of [the applicant's claims]'.[178] Stevens J

---

169   Ibid. at 212–13.
170   Ibid. at 213.
171   Ibid. at 213–14.
172   Ibid. at 214–15.
173   Ibid. at 215.
174   Ibid.
175   Ibid. (emphasis in original).
176   Ibid. at 215–16.
177   Ibid. at 216.
178   Ibid.

concluded, citing *Benson* and *Flook*, that '[t]he broad question [of] whether computer programs should be given patent protection involves policy considerations that this Court is not authorized to address'.[179]

Although *Benson* was a unanimous decision of the Court, *Flook* was decided with a majority of six and *Diehr* with only a majority of one. With this division of the Court, it was surprising that the Court did not reconsider the issue of patent eligibility for another 30 years.

C RECONSIDERATION

The Court had left the Federal Circuit free rein to interpret its decisions in *Benson*, *Flook* and *Diehr* to solve issues of patent eligibility under section 101. For almost 30 years the Court did not intervene in determining patent eligibility, allowing the Federal Circuit to adopt various tests, including the 'useful, concrete, and tangible result' test accepted in *State Street Bank & Trust Co. v Signature Financial Group, Inc*,[180] and the 'machine-or-transformation test' accepted in *In re Bilski*.[181] This, however, changed in June 2010 when the Court decided the case of *Bilski v Kappos*,[182] where it had to clarify the standard of patentability under section 101. In *In re Bilski*, the Federal Circuit had held that a process was patentable *only* if it was, first, tied to a particular machine or apparatus or, second, if it transformed a particular article into a different state or thing. It then reversed its previous decision in *State Street Bank* and, moreover, asserted that *this* test – the 'machine or transformation test' – was the *sole* test for determining patentability under section 101. In *State Street Bank*, it had also held that claims to a process were eligible for patent protection as long as they produced a 'useful, concrete and tangible result'.[183] *That* test, the Federal Circuit in *In Re Bilski* held, was 'insufficient to determine whether a claim is patent-eligible under section 101',[184] preferring the 'machine or transformation test'.[185]

The Court in *Bilski* had to consider the deceptively simple question of whether a patent can be issued for a claimed invention designed for the

---

[179] Ibid. at 216–17.

[180] 149 F.3d 1368 (Fed. Cir. 1998), cert. denied, 525 U.S. 1093 (1999). See also *AT&T Corp. v Excel Communications Inc*. 172 F.3d 1352 (Fed. Cir. 1999).

[181] 545 F.3d 943 (Fed. Cir. 2008).

[182] 130 S. Ct. 3218; 177 L. Ed. 2d 792.

[183] *State Street Bank* at 1373.

[184] *In re Bilski*, 545 F.3d 943 at 960.

[185] Ibid.

business world.[186] Kennedy J, who delivered the opinion of the Court, noted that the patent application claimed a procedure for instructing buyers and sellers how to protect against the risk of price fluctuations in a discrete section of the economy.[187] For three reasons, it was argued that the claimed invention was outside the scope of patent law, namely: (a) it was not tied to a machine and did not transform an article; (b) it involved a method of conducting business; and (c) it was merely an abstract idea.[188] The applicant sought patent protection for a claimed invention that explains how buyers and sellers of commodities in the energy market can protect, or hedge, against the risk of price changes. The Court noted that the Examiner rejected that application on the basis that it was 'not implemented on a specific apparatus and merely manipulates [an] abstract idea and solves a purely mathematical problem without any limitation to a practical application[;] therefore, the invention is not directed to the technological arts'. The BOPA affirmed that decision, 'concluding that the application involved only mental steps that do not transform physical matter and was directed to an abstract idea'.[189] The Federal Circuit *en banc*, with a 9–3 majority, affirmed both decisions.

In answering the central question before it, the Court also had to consider whether the Federal Circuit was correct in ruling that the 'machine or transformation test' was the *sole* test to be used for determining the patentability of a 'process' under section 101.[190] Applying that test, the Federal Circuit had held that the petitioners' application was not patent-eligible. The Court began its analysis with section 101, stating it specifies four independent categories of inventions or discoveries that are eligible for protection: processes, machines, manufactures and compositions of matter.[191] Citing *Chakrabarty*, the Court observed that: first, '[i]n choosing such expansive terms . . . modified by the comprehensive "any," Congress plainly contemplated that the patent laws would be given wide scope';[192] and, second 'its precedents provide three specific exceptions to section 101's broad patent-eligibility principles, namely, "laws of nature, physical phenomena, and abstract ideas"'.[193] The Court explained that '[w]hile these exceptions are not required by the statutory text, they are consistent

---

186   177 L. Ed. 2d 792 at 799.
187   Ibid.
188   Ibid.
189   Ibid. at 799–800.
190   Ibid.
191   Ibid. at 800.
192   Ibid.
193   Ibid. at 801.

with the notion that a patentable process must be "new and useful"'.[194]
The Court continued, in any case, that these exceptions have defined the
reach of the statute as a matter of statutory *stare decisis* going back 150
years. Even if the requirements of section 101 were satisfied, the Court
accepted that the matter did not end there but that, in order to receive the
Patent Act's protection, the claimed invention must also satisfy 'the conditions and requirements of this title', namely, novelty (section 102), non-
obvious (section 103) and full and particular description (section 112).
Since the claim was a 'process', the Court opined that section 101 must be
read in light of section 100(b), which defines a 'process' as: 'process, art
or method, and includes a new use of a known process, machine, manufacture, composition of matter, or material'.[195] In its view, the section 101
patent-eligibility inquiry is only a threshold test – even if an invention may
qualify as a process, machine, manufacture or composition of matter, it
would still need to satisfy the other above-mentioned requirements. The
Court then went on to consider the 'two proposed categorical limitations
on "process" patents under [section] 101 that would, if adopted, bar petitioners' application in the present case: the machine-or-transformation test
and the categorical exclusion of business method patents'.[196]

In respect of the Federal Circuit's view that 'an invention is a "process"
only if: "(1) it is tied to a particular machine or apparatus, or (2) it transforms a particular article into a different state or thing"', the Court,
quoting *Diehr*, reiterated that it has 'more than once cautioned that lower
courts "should not read into the patent laws limitations and conditions
which the legislature has not expressed"'.[197] In other words, the exceptions
recognised by the Court in *Benson*, *Flook* and *Diehr* are the only exceptions and limitations to section 101 patentability and, unless the invention fell within either of these, it should be patent-eligible. It observed
that the words in the Patent Act, unless otherwise defined, should be
given their ordinary, contemporary, common meaning.[198] In addition,
the Court claimed that '[a]ny suggestion in this Court's case law that the
Patent Act's terms deviate from their ordinary meaning has only been an
explanation for the exceptions for laws of nature, physical phenomena,
and abstract ideas'.[199] It explained it had 'not indicated that the existence
of the well-established exceptions to patentability, namely, laws of nature,

---

194   Ibid.
195   Ibid.
196   Ibid.
197   Ibid.
198   Ibid., citing *Diehr*.
199   *Bilski* at 802.

physical phenomena, and abstract ideas, gives the Judiciary *carte blanche* to impose other limitations that are inconsistent with the text and the statute's purpose and design'.[200] The Court continued, stating that '[c]oncerns about attempts to call any form of human activity a "process" can be met by making sure the claim meets the requirements of [section] 101'.[201]

By adopting the 'machine or transformation test' as the sole test for what constitutes a 'process' (as opposed to just an important and useful clue), the Court held that the Federal Circuit violated the relevant statutory interpretation principles[202] and that it incorrectly concluded the Court had endorsed the 'machine or transformation test' as the exclusive test.[203] It noted that it was unaware of any 'ordinary, contemporary, common meaning' of the terms 'process, art or method' that would require these terms to be tied to a machine or to transform an article.[204] After citing statements from its decisions in *Cochrane*, *Benson* and *Flook*, the Court concluded that its precedents establish that 'the machine-or-transformation test is *a useful and important clue, an investigative tool*, for determining whether some claimed inventions are processes under section 101 and that the machine-or-transformation test is *not the sole test* for deciding whether an invention is a patent-eligible "process"'.[205]

The Court explained that '[i]t is true that patents for inventions that did not satisfy the machine-or-transformation test were rarely granted in earlier eras, especially in the Industrial Age. . . . But times change. Technology and other innovations progress in unexpected ways.'[206] This is significant as the Court is emphasising that as technology develops, so too should the tests used by the Court in determining patent-eligibility, especially where a particular test is technology specific and not easily applied in other contexts. This must be correct in so far as a test designed for the Industrial Age might prevent the patenting of inventions that may well deserve patent protection. Further, it would run contrary to the constitutional mandate of Congress to promote the useful arts if the Court were to adopt a test to interpret Congress's words in section 101, which denies patent protection to inventions merely because they fall outside an outmoded test. The Court also explained that this fact does not mean unforeseen innovations such as computer programs are always unpatentable. It then castigated the

---

200   Ibid.
201   Ibid.
202   Ibid.
203   Ibid.
204   Ibid.
205   Ibid. at 803 (emphasis added).
206   Ibid.

'machine or transformation test' as a relic of the Industrial Age (where the inventions were grounded in a physical or other tangible form) and argued it was doubtful whether that test should be the sole criterion for determining the patentability of inventions in the Information Age.[207] The Court, agreeing with numerous amicus, asserted that 'the machine-or-transformation test would create uncertainty as to the patentability of software, *advanced diagnostic medicine techniques*, and inventions based on linear programming, data compression, and the manipulation of digital signals'.[208] In its view, in the course of applying the 'machine or transformation test' to emerging technologies, courts may pose questions of such intricacy and refinement that they risk obscuring the larger object of securing patents for valuable inventions without transgressing the public domain. Consequently, the Court held that, in deciding whether previously unforeseen inventions qualify as patentable 'processes', it may not make sense to require lower courts to confine themselves to asking the questions posed by the 'machine or transformation test', adding that section 101's terms suggest that new technologies may call for new inquiries.[209]

It explained that it was 'important to emphasize that its decision was not commenting on the patentability of any particular invention, let alone holding that any of the above-mentioned technologies from the Information Age should or should not receive patent protection'.[210] The Court continued that '[t]his Age puts the possibility of innovation in the hands of more people and raises new difficulties for the patent law';[211] and, further, '[w]ith ever more people trying to innovate and thus seeking patent protections for their inventions, the patent law faces a great challenge in striking the balance between protecting inventors and not granting monopolies over procedures that others would discover by independent, creative application of general principles'.[212] The Court then concluded that '[n]othing in this opinion should be read to take a position on where that balance ought to be struck'.[213] This was to be achieved on a case-by-case basis by the Federal Circuit as issues come before it to be resolved.

In relation to the issue of whether there was a categorical exclusion of business methods from the scope of section 101, the Court claimed that it 'similarly precludes the broad contention that the term "process"

[207] Ibid.
[208] Ibid. (emphasis added).
[209] Ibid. at 803–4.
[210] Ibid. at 804.
[211] Ibid.
[212] Ibid.
[213] Ibid.

categorically excludes business methods' and that the '[t]erm "method," which is within [section] 100(b)'s definition of "process," at least as a textual matter and before consulting other limitations in the Patent Act and this Court's precedents, may include at least some methods of doing business'.[214] In addition, the Court explained that it was unaware of any argument that the 'ordinary, contemporary, common meaning' of 'method' excludes business methods.[215] It noted, '[t]he argument that business methods are categorically outside of [section] 101's scope is further undermined by the fact that federal law [section 273(b)(1)] explicitly contemplates the existence of at least some business method patents'.[216] The Court argued that, '[i]n searching for a limiting principle, this Court's precedents on the unpatentability of abstract ideas provide useful tools' and that if the Federal Circuit 'were to succeed in defining a narrower category or class of patent applications that claim to instruct how business should be conducted, and then rule that the category is unpatentable because, for instance, it represents an attempt to patent abstract ideas, this conclusion might well be in accord with controlling precedent'.[217] It continued, '[b]ut beyond this or some other limitation consistent with the statutory text, the Patent Act leaves open the possibility that there are at least some processes that can be fairly described as business methods that are within patentable subject matter under [section] 101'.[218]

With all of this, the Court then proceeded to examine its precedents relating to patent-eligibility. The Court claimed that the '[p]etitioners seek to patent both the *concept* of hedging risk and the *application* of that *concept* to energy markets'.[219] It continued that, rather than adopting categorical rules that might have wide-ranging and unforeseen impacts, it resolved the instant case narrowly on the basis of its previous decisions in *Benson*, *Flook* and *Diehr*, which showed the petitioners' claims were not patentable processes, because they attempted to patent *abstract ideas*.[220] All the nine Justices agreed with this conclusion. After examining *Benson* and *Flook*, the Court stated that 'in *Diehr*, the Court established a limitation on the principles articulated in *Benson* and *Flook*' and '*Diehr* explained that while an abstract idea, law of nature, or mathematical formula could not be patented, "an application of a law of nature or

---

[214]   Ibid.
[215]   Ibid.
[216]   Ibid.
[217]   Ibid. at 805.
[218]   Ibid.
[219]   Ibid. at 806 (emphasis added).
[220]   Ibid. at 806.

mathematical formula to a known structure or process may well be deserving of patent protection"'.[221] On the facts of the case the Court, applying its previous precedents of *Benson*, *Flook* and *Diehr*, held that the claimed method was not a patentable 'process' but merely an explanation of the basic concept of hedging, or protecting against risk.[222] It then concluded '[t]he concept of hedging, described in claim 1 and reduced to a mathematical formula in claim 4, was an unpatentable abstract idea, just like the algorithms at issue in *Benson* and *Flook*'; and that '[a]llowing petitioners to patent risk hedging would pre-empt use of this approach in all fields, and would effectively grant a monopoly over an abstract idea'.[223] The Court continued that the 'remaining claims are broad examples of how hedging can be used in commodities and energy markets' but that '*Flook* established that limiting an abstract idea to one field of use or adding token postsolution components did not make the concept patentable'.[224] In its view, '[t]hat is exactly what the remaining claims in petitioners' application do. These claims attempt to patent the use of the abstract idea of hedging risk in the energy market and then instruct the use of well-known random analysis techniques to help establish some of the inputs into the equation.'[225] Interestingly, the Court noted that the claims at issue 'add even less to the underlying abstract principle than the invention in *Flook* did, for the *Flook* invention was at least directed to the narrower domain of signaling dangers in operating a catalytic converter'.[226] The main point is that the invention must *apply* the abstract principle for it to be patentable; otherwise it would be a claim to the laws of nature and would not be patent-eligible.

In conclusion, the Court emphasised that it 'once again declines to impose limitations on the Patent Act that are inconsistent with the Act's text' and that '[t]he patent application here can be rejected under our precedents on the unpatentability of abstract ideas'.[227] Therefore, it noted that it 'need not define further what constitutes a patentable "process," beyond pointing to the definition of that term provided in [section] 100(b) and looking to the guideposts in *Benson*, *Flook*, and *Diehr*'.[228] The Court then stated that: first, 'nothing in [its] opinion should be read

---

[221]   Ibid. at 807.
[222]   Ibid.
[223]   Ibid.
[224]   Ibid.
[225]   Ibid.
[226]   Ibid.
[227]   Ibid.
[228]   Ibid.

as endorsing interpretations of [section] 101 that the [Federal Circuit] has used in the past', citing *State Street* and *AT&T Corp*;[229] second, '[i]t may be that the [Federal Circuit] thought it needed to make the machine-or-transformation test exclusive precisely because its case law had not adequately identified less extreme means of restricting business method patents, including (but not limited to) application of our opinions in *Benson*, *Flook*, and *Diehr*';[230] and third, '[i]n disapproving an exclusive machine-or-transformation test, we by no means foreclose the Federal Circuit's development of other limiting criteria that further the purposes of the Patent Act and are not inconsistent with its text'.[231] As will be seen in the next section, the Federal Circuit has attempted to follow the Court's mandate with limited success.

Stevens J, with whom Ginsburg, Breyer and Sotomayor JJ agreed, concurred with the judgment of the Court. He argued that in the area of patents, it is especially important that the law remains stable and clear and that the only question presented was whether the so-called 'machine or transformation test' was the exclusive test for what constitutes a patentable 'process' under section 101.[232] Stevens J argued that it would be possible to answer that question simply by holding, as the entire Court agreed, that although the 'machine or transformation test' was reliable in most cases, it was not the exclusive test for patentability under section 101. Although accepting the Court's view that, in light of the uncertainty that currently pervades this field, it was prudent to provide further guidance for lower courts, he thought it was necessary for him to take a different approach.[233] Stevens J claimed that, rather than making any broad statements about how to define the term 'process' in section 101 or tinkering with the bounds of the category of unpatentable, abstract ideas, he would restore patent law to its historical and constitutional moorings. He held that the Court was wrong to suggest that any series of steps that is not itself an abstract idea or law of nature may constitute a 'process' within the meaning of section 101.[234] Stevens J thought that the wiser course would have been to hold that the petitioners' method was not a 'process' because it described only a general method of engaging in business transactions – and business methods are not patentable. In other words, he argued that although a process is not patent-ineligible simply because it is useful for conducting

---

[229]   Ibid. at 807–8.
[230]   Ibid. at 808.
[231]   Ibid.
[232]   Ibid.
[233]   Ibid.
[234]   Ibid. at 809.

business, a claim that merely describes a method of doing business does not qualify as a 'process' under section 101.[235]

Stevens J took issue with some language used by the Court that seemed inconsistent with the Court's centuries-old reliance on the machine-or-transformation criteria as clues to patentability.[236] He claimed that the opinion for a plurality suggested that these criteria might operate differently when addressing technologies of a recent vintage, in particular, that the 'machine or transformation test' is useful 'for evaluating processes similar to those in the Industrial Age', but is less useful 'for determining the patentability of inventions in the Information Age'.[237] Stevens J continued that in moments of caution, however, the Court explained – correctly – that it was merely restoring the law to its historical state of rest; explaining that, notwithstanding this internal tension, he understood the Court's opinion to hold only that the 'machine or transformation test' remained an important test for patentability, few, if any, processes cannot effectively be evaluated using these criteria.

He also criticised the Court's discussion of an issue which he claimed was not contained in the questions presented – whether the particular series of steps in the petitioners' application was an abstract idea, noting that the Court used language that could suggest a shift in the Court's approach to that issue.[238] Stevens J, although agreeing that the petitioners sought to patent an abstract idea, argued that the Court did not show how this conclusion follows 'clearly' from the Court's case law. He claimed that the patent at issue was not for '[a] principle, in the abstract', or a 'fundamental truth'; and neither did it claim the sort of phenomenon of nature or abstract idea that was embodied by the mathematical formula at issue in *Benson* and in *Flook*.[239] In addition, Stevens J claimed that the Court never provided a satisfying account of what constituted an unpatentable abstract idea, and did not even explain if it was using the machine-or-transformation criteria; but it essentially asserted its conclusion that the petitioners' application claimed an abstract idea.[240] Therefore, he held that this mode of analysis (or lack thereof) might have led to the correct outcome in this case, but it also meant that the Court's musings on this issue stood for very little. After an exhaustive survey of the limited textual, historical and functional clues, particularly in the absence of any clear

---

[235]   Ibid.
[236]   Ibid. at 811–12.
[237]   Ibid. at 812.
[238]   Ibid.
[239]   Ibid.
[240]   Ibid. at 813.

guidance from Congress, Stevens J concluded they all pointed toward the same result that the claim at issue was not a 'process' within the meaning of section 101 because methods of doing business were not, in themselves, covered by the statute.[241]

Breyer J wrote a separate opinion in order to highlight the substantial agreement by the Justices on many of the fundamental issues of patent law raised by the case, particularly, in light of the need for clarity and settled law in this highly technical area.[242] He claimed that, in addition to the Court's unanimous agreement that the claims at issue were unpatentable abstract ideas, it was his view that the following four points were consistent with both the opinion of the Court and the opinion of Stevens J: first, although the text of section 101 is broad, it is not without limit (citing *Benson*, *Diehr* and *Chakrabarty*); second, in a series of cases that extend over a century, the Court has stated that transformation and reduction of an article to a different state or thing is the clue to the patentability of a process claim that does not include particular machines (citing *Benson*, *Flook* and *Diehr*); third, while the 'machine or transformation test' has always been a 'useful and important clue', it has never been the 'sole test' for determining patentability (citing *Benson* and *Diehr*);[243] and, fourth, although the 'machine or transformation test' is not the only test for patentability, this by no means indicates that anything which produces a 'useful, concrete, and tangible result' (as in *State Street Bank*) is patentable.[244] Therefore, he concluded it was his view that, in re-emphasising the 'machine or transformation test' was not necessarily the sole test of patentability, the Court neither intended to de-emphasise the test's usefulness nor to suggest that many patentable processes lie beyond its reach.

D   MAKING SENSE OF *BILSKI*

The Court in *Bilski* explained that '[i]n disapproving an exclusive "machine or transformation test," we by no means foreclose the Federal Circuit's development of other limiting criteria that further the purposes of the Patent Act and are not inconsistent with its text'.[245] The Federal Circuit lost no time in making sense of the Court's decision in *Bilski*, since a mere six months later it was already attempting to do so in *Research Corp.*

---

[241]   Ibid. at 835.
[242]   Ibid. at 836.
[243]   Ibid. at 836–7.
[244]   Ibid. at 837.
[245]   Ibid. at 808.

Technologies Inc. v Microsoft Corp.[246] In that decision, the Federal Circuit, in an opinion written by Rader CJ, with whom Newman and Plager JJ agreed, had to determine whether the following claims were patent-eligible under section 101: (a) a method for the half-toning of grey-scale images by utilising a pixel-by-pixel comparison of the image against a blue noise mask in which the blue noise mask comprises a random non-deterministic, non-white noise single-valued function which is designed to produce visually pleasing dot profiles when thresholded at any level of said grey-scale images; (b) the method of claim 1, wherein said blue noise mask is used to halftone a colour image ('310 patent); and (c) a method for the half-toning of colour images, comprising the steps of utilising, in turn, a pixel-by-pixel comparison of each of a plurality of colour planes of said colour image against a blue noise mask in which the blue noise mask comprises a random non-deterministic, non-white noise single-valued function which is designed to provide visually pleasing dot profiles when thresholded at any level of said colour images, wherein a plurality of blue noise masks are separately utilised to perform said pixel-by-pixel comparison and in which at least one of said blue noise masks is independent and uncorrelated with the other blue noise masks ('228 patent).

After reciting the text of section 101, the Federal Circuit claimed section 101 'emphasizes that "any" subject matter in the four independent categories and "any" improvement in that subject matter qualify for protection', noting, further, that the Court had 'recently reemphasized the significance of these broad statutory categories with the broadening double "any" exhortation as well' in *Bilski*.[247] The Federal Circuit cited from the Court decisions in *Chakrabarty*, *Diehr*, *Flook* and *Bilski* and then claimed that 'section 101 does not permit a court to reject subject matter categorically because it finds that a claim is not worthy of a patent'.[248] It then noted that '[i]n this case, the subject matter is a "process" for rendering a halftone image' and that '[a]s a process, the subject matter qualifies under both the categorical language of section 101 and the process definition in section 100'.[249] Therefore, it proceeded 'to examine the Supreme Court's three exceptions', claiming that the 'parties do not dispute, and this [it] agrees, that the inventors do not purport to have invented laws of nature or physical phenomena'.[250] As a result, the Federal Circuit turned to abstractness, noting that the Court in *Bilski* 'refocused [the Federal Circuit's] inquiry

---

[246] 627 F.3d 859 (Fed. Cir. 2010).
[247] Ibid. at 867.
[248] Ibid. at 868.
[249] Ibid.
[250] Ibid.

into processes on the question of whether the subject matter of the invention is abstract', but the Court 'did not presume to provide a rigid formula or definition for abstractness', citing Stevens J, dissenting, in *Bilski*.[251]

The Federal Circuit explained that it 'also will not presume to define "abstract" beyond the recognition that this disqualifying characteristic should exhibit itself so manifestly as to override the broad statutory categories of eligible subject matter and the statutory context that directs primary attention on the patentability criteria of the rest of the Patent Act'.[252] It noted that: first, the subject matter is a 'process' for rendering a half tone image; and, second, as a process, the subject matter qualified under both the categorical language of section 101 and the process definition in section 100. Therefore, the Federal Circuit proceeded to examine the Court's three exceptions.[253] It observed, agreeing, that the parties did not dispute that the inventors did not purport to have invented laws of nature or physical phenomena, continuing that it must now turn to abstractness. The Federal Circuit reasoned that the Court in *Bilski* refocused the Federal Circuit's inquiry into processes on the question of whether the subject matter of the invention is abstract.[254] However, it made clear that the Court did not presume to provide a rigid formula or definition for abstractness, noting that even Stevens J, concurring, in *Bilski*, admonished the Court by observing that the Court 'never provide[d] a satisfying account of what constitutes an unpatentable abstract idea'. In any event, it decided to follow the invitation by the Court to the Federal Circuit to develop 'other limiting criteria that further the purposes of the Patent Act and are not inconsistent with its text'.[255]

In following this invitation, the Federal Circuit noted that it would also not presume to define 'abstract' beyond the recognition that this disqualifying characteristic should exhibit itself so manifestly as to override the broad statutory categories of eligible subject matter and the statutory context that directed primary attention on the patentability criteria of the rest of the Patent Act.[256] In applying this test to the patents at issue, it claimed that: first, it 'perceives nothing abstract in the subject matter of the processes claimed in the '310 and '228 patents'; and, second, '[t]he '310 and '228 patents claim methods (statutory "processes") for rendering a halftone image of a digital image by comparing, pixel by pixel, the digital

---

[251]   Ibid.
[252]   Ibid.
[253]   Ibid.
[254]   Ibid.
[255]   Ibid.
[256]   Ibid.

image against a blue noise mask'.[257] In addition, it noted '[t]he fact that some claims in the '310 and '228 patents require a "high contrast film," "a film printer," "a memory," and "printer and display devices" also confirm this court's holding that the invention is not abstract'.[258] The Federal Circuit stated that '[t]he invention presents functional and palpable applications in the field of computer technology' and emphasised that 'inventions with specific applications or improvements to technologies in the marketplace are not likely to be so abstract that they override the statutory language and framework of the Patent Act'.[259] It also noted that, although 'the claimed methods incorporate algorithms and formulas that control the masks and halftoning', 'even though admittedly a significant part of the claimed combination', these 'do not bring this invention even close to abstractness that would override the statutory categories and context'.[260] Relying principally on the reasoning of the Court in *Diehr*, the Federal Circuit observed that: first, the patentees did not seek to patent a mathematical formula; instead, they sought patent protection for a process of half toning in computer applications; and, second, 'because the inventions claimed in the '310 and '228 patents are directed to patent-eligible subject matter, the process claims at issue, which claim aspects and applications of the same subject matter, are also patent-eligible'.[261] The Federal Circuit noted that 'an invention which is not so manifestly abstract as to override the statutory language of section 101 may nonetheless lack sufficient concrete disclosure to warrant a patent' and accepted that section 112 'provides powerful tools to weed out claims that may present a vague or indefinite disclosure of the invention'.[262] As a result, it reversed the District Court's opinion, finding that the '310 and '228 patents were patent-eligible under section 101.

In late summer of 2011, the Federal Circuit revisited the jurisprudence of the Court under section 101, including its recent pronouncements on that section. In *Cyber Source Corporation v Retail Decisions Inc*,[263] the Federal Circuit, in an opinion written by Dyk J, with whom Bryson and Prost JJ agreed, had to consider a patent for a method and system for detecting fraud in a credit card transaction between a consumer and a merchant

---

[257] Ibid.
[258] Ibid.
[259] Ibid. at 869.
[260] Ibid.
[261] Ibid.
[262] Ibid.
[263] 654 F.3d 1366 (Fed. Cir. 2011).

over the Internet.[264] The '154 patent used Internet address information (IP addresses, MAC addresses, email addresses, etc.) to determine whether an Internet address relating to a particular transaction is consistent with other Internet addresses that have been used in transactions utilising the same credit card.[265] Claim 3, the main claim at issue, was for a method for verifying the validity of a credit card transaction over the Internet comprising the steps of: (a) obtaining information about other transactions that have utilised an Internet address is identified with the credit card transaction; (b) constructing a map of credit card numbers based upon the other transactions; and (c) utilising the map of credit card numbers to determine if the credit card transaction is valid. The District Court ruled that: first, claim 3 was an unpatentable mental process for collecting data and weighing values which did not become patentable by tossing in references to Internet commerce; and, second, with respect to claim 2, simply appending '[a] computer readable media including program instructions . . .' to an otherwise non-statutory process claim is insufficient to make it statutory. After referring to its decisions that led ultimately to the Court's decision in *Bilski* that rejected use of the 'machine or transformation test' as the exclusive test for the patentability of a claimed process, the Federal Circuit went on to explore the Court's mandate, as mentioned above, for the Federal Circuit to develop further limiting criteria for patentability under section 101 that further the purposes of the Patent Act and are not inconsistent with its text.[266]

The Federal Circuit held that the method of claim 3 simply required one to 'obtain and compare intangible data pertinent to business risks'. In its view, the mere collection and organisation of data regarding credit card numbers and Internet addresses were insufficient to meet the transformation prong of the test, and the plain language of claim 3 did not require the method to be performed by a particular machine, or even a machine at all.[267] It also rejected the appellant's argument that the claimed method was tied to a particular machine because it 'would not be necessary or possible without the Internet', clarifying that: first, regardless of whether 'the Internet' could be viewed as a machine, it was clear that the Internet could not perform the fraud detection steps of the claimed method; second, moreover, while claim 3 described a method of analysing data regarding Internet credit card transactions, nothing in claim 3 required an infringer

---

264   Ibid. at 1367.
265   Ibid. at 1367–8.
266   Ibid. at 1370.
267   Ibid.

to use the Internet to obtain that data (as opposed to obtaining the data from a pre-compiled database).[268] Since the Internet was merely described as the source of the data, the Federal Circuit held that this offended the well-established principle from the case law that mere data-gathering steps could not make an otherwise non-statutory claim statutory. As a result, it held that the District Court did not err in holding that claim 3 fails to meet the 'machine or transformation test'.[269]

However, the Federal Circuit observed that its analysis did not end there, noting that although the Court in *Bilski* held that the 'machine or transformation test' was not the sole test for deciding whether an invention is a patent-eligible process, the Court also made clear that a patent claim's failure to satisfy the 'machine or transformation test' was not dispositive of the section 101 inquiry.[270] However, it found that claim 3 of the '154 patent failed to recite patent-eligible subject matter because it was drawn to an unpatentable mental process – a subcategory of unpatentable abstract ideas. After examining the Court's cases of *Benson*, *Flook* and *Bilski*, and its own decision in *In re Comiskey*,[271] the Federal Circuit reiterated what it said in the latter case:[272]

> [T]he patent statute does not allow patents on particular systems that depend for their operation on human intelligence alone, a field of endeavor that both the framers and Congress intended to be beyond the reach of patentable subject matter . . .. [I]t is established that the application of human intelligence to the solution of practical problems is not in and of itself patentable.

Appling this reasoning, it held that it was clear that unpatentable mental processes were the subject matter of claim 3, adding that: first, all of claim 3's method steps could be performed in the human mind, or by a human using a pen and paper; second, claim 3 did not limit its scope to any particular fraud detection algorithm, and no algorithms were disclosed in the '154 patent's specification; and, third, the broad scope of claim 3 extended to essentially any method of detecting credit card fraud based on information relating past transactions to a particular 'Internet address', even methods that can be performed in the human mind.[273]

The Federal Circuit held that, first, the step (a) in claim 3 which required

---

268   Ibid.
269   Ibid.
270   Ibid. at 1371.
271   554 F.3d 967 (Fed. Cir. 2009).
272   Ibid. at 980.
273   *CyberSource* at 1371.

'obtaining information about other transactions that have utilized an Internet address that is identified with the credit card transaction', could be performed by a human who simply reads records of Internet credit card transactions from a pre-existing database.[274] It continued that even if some physical steps were required to obtain information from the database, for example, entering a query via a keyboard, clicking a mouse, such data-gathering steps could not alone confer patentability. Second, the requirement in step (b) of claim 3 that a person may 'construct a map of credit card numbers' could be achieved by writing down a list of credit card transactions made from a particular Internet protocol (IP), and that nothing in the language in claim 3, or in the specification, required the constructed 'map' to consist of anything more than a list of a few credit card transactions.[275] Third, step (c) of claim 3, which required 'utilizing the map of credit card numbers to determine if the credit card transaction is valid', was so broadly worded that it encompassed literally any method for detecting fraud based on the gathered transaction and Internet address data.

The Federal Circuit held that this necessarily included even logical reasoning that could be performed entirely in the human mind; for example, a person could literally infringe step (c) by identifying a likely instance of fraud based on the simple observation that numerous transactions using different credit cards, having different user names and billing addresses, all originated from the same IP address.[276] It, therefore, concluded that all the steps in claim 3 could be performed in the human mind and that such a method that could be performed by human thought alone was merely an abstract idea and was not patent-eligible under section 101. In addition, the Federal Circuit explained that methods which could be performed entirely in the human mind were unpatentable not because there was anything wrong with claiming mental method steps as part of a process containing non-mental steps, but rather because computational methods which could be performed entirely in the human mind were the types of methods that embody the 'basic tools of scientific and technological work' that were free to all men and reserved exclusively to none.[277]

In relation to claim 2 of the '154 patent, held the Federal Circuit, apart from containing somewhat redundant language, it was clear that the claim recited nothing more than a computer-readable medium contain-

---

[274] Ibid. at 1372.
[275] Ibid.
[276] Ibid. at 1373.
[277] Ibid.

ing program instructions for executing the method of claim 3.[278] It noted that the method underlying claim 2 was clearly the same method of fraud detection recited in claim 3, which was found to be unpatentable because it was drawn to a mental process – i.e., an abstract idea. The Federal Circuit emphasised that, irrespective of what statutory category (process, machine, manufacture or composition of matter) a claim's language was crafted to literally invoke, it would look to the underlying invention for patent-eligibility purposes.[279] In the instant case, it held it was clear that the invention underlying both claims 2 and 3 was a method for detecting credit card fraud, not a manufacture for storing computer-readable information. After examining the decision of the CCPA in *In re Abele*,[280] the Federal Circuit, following its decision *In re Alappat*,[281] noted it held that, as a general matter, programming a general-purpose computer to perform an algorithm 'creates a new machine, because a general-purpose computer in effect becomes a special-purpose computer once it is programmed to perform particular functions pursuant to instructions from program software'.[282] However, it cautioned that the Federal Circuit had never suggested that simply reciting the use of a computer to execute an algorithm that could be performed entirely in the human mind falls within the *Alappat* rule. As a result, the Federal Circuit concluded that, despite its *Beauregard*[283] claim format, under *Abele*, it treated claim 2 as a process claim for patent-eligibility purposes. It claimed *Abele* made clear that claiming only its performance by computers, or by claiming the process did not change the basic character of a process claim drawn to an abstract idea embodied in program instructions on a computer-readable medium.[284]

The Federal Circuit agreed with the District Court that the claimed process manipulated data which organised it in a logical way such that additional fraud tests might be performed, adding that the mere manipulation or reorganisation of data, however, did not satisfy the transformation prong; therefore, claim 2 failed to meet the transformation test.[285] Following *Bilski*'s requirement that to impart patent-eligibility to an

---

[278]   Ibid. at 1374.
[279]   Ibid.
[280]   684 F.2d 902 (CCPA 1982).
[281]   33 F.3d 1526 (Fed. Cir. 1994).
[282]   Ibid. at 1545.
[283]   (Named after *In re Beauregard*, 53 F.3d 1583 (Fed. Cir. 1995) – a claim to a computer-readable medium (e.g., a disk, hard drive or other data storage device) containing program instructions for a computer to perform a particular process) *CyberSource* at 1373.
[284]   *CyberSource* at 1375.
[285]   Ibid.

otherwise unpatentable process under the theory that the process was linked to a machine, and the use of the machine 'must impose meaningful limits on the claim's scope', it held that the incidental use of a computer to perform the mental process of claim 3 did not impose a sufficiently meaningful limit on the claim's scope. Therefore, it held that the 'computer readable medium' limitation of claim 2 did not make the otherwise unpatentable method patent-eligible under section 101.[286] The Federal Circuit also held that merely claiming a software implementation of a purely mental process that could otherwise be performed without the use of a computer did not satisfy the machine prong of the 'machine or transformation test'.[287]

It claimed that purely mental processes can be unpatentable, even when performed by a computer, which was precisely the holding of the Court in *Benson*. The Federal Circuit held, following *Benson*,[288] the Court in *Flook* and *Bilski* found other method claims invalid under section 101 for being drawn to abstract ideas.[289] This was because, in *Benson*, the Court held that, although claim 8 specifically recited the use of a computer-readable medium, including steps such as 'storing the BCD signals in a re-entrant shift register' – a physical computer memory component – the Court nonetheless found that the claim was drawn to an unpatentable abstract idea.[290] It continued that, in so holding, the Court did not indicate that those claims could have avoided invalidity under section 101 by merely requiring a computer to perform the method, or by reciting a computer-readable medium containing program instructions for performing the method. This, the Federal Circuit emphasised, was entirely unlike cases where, as a practical matter, the use of a computer was required to perform the claimed method.[291] In an interesting discussion in footnote 4, the Federal Circuit observed that the Court in *Diehr* characterised *Flook* as a case involving the use of a mathematical formula in the abstract, regardless of whether the patent was 'intended to cover all uses of the formula or only limited uses'.[292] It continued that the analogy with the claims in the instant case

---

[286]   Ibid.
[287]   Ibid.
[288]   Where a claim to a method of programming a general-purpose computer to convert BCD numbers into pure binary was unpatentable because the conversion of BCD numerals to pure binary numerals could be done mentally, and because the process was 'so abstract and sweeping as to cover both known and unknown uses of the BCD to pure binary conversion'.
[289]   Ibid. at 1376.
[290]   Ibid.
[291]   Ibid.
[292]   Ibid. at 1376.

was a close one: here, the claims contained no hint as to how the information regarding the Internet transactions would be sorted, weighed and ultimately converted into a useable conclusion that a particular transaction was fraudulent, adding that the claims in the instant case were, therefore, even more abstract than the claims in *Flook*.[293]

The Federal Circuit distinguished *Research Corp* on the basis that, because the method in that case required the manipulation of computer data structures (e.g., the pixels of a digital image and a two-dimensional array known as a mask) and the output of a modified computer data structure (a half toned digital image), the method could not, as a practical matter, be performed entirely in a human's mind. In the instant case, however, the Federal Circuit was of the opinion it was clear that one could mentally perform the fraud detection method that underlay both claims 2 and 3 of the '154 patent, as the method consisted of only the general approach of obtaining information about credit card transactions utilising an Internet address and then using that information in some undefined manner to determine if the credit card transaction was valid.[294] It therefore concluded that since claims 2 and 3 attempted to capture unpatentable mental processes (i.e., abstract ideas), they were invalid under section 101.[295]

In another recent decision, the Federal Circuit had to consider the scope of section 101 in the post-*Bilski* era. In *Ultramercial LLC v Hulu LLC*,[296] it examined the '545 patent, which claimed a method for distributing copyrighted products (e.g., songs, movies, books) over the Internet, where the consumer receives a copyrighted product for free in exchange for viewing an advertisement and the advertiser pays for the copyrighted content.[297] Chief Judge Rader, with whom Lourie and O'Malley JJ agreed, noted that: first, a definition of the invention via claim construction could clarify the basic character of the subject matter of the invention; second, claim meaning may clarify the actual subject matter at stake in the invention and can enlighten, or even answer, questions about subject-matter abstractness; and, third, in the instant case, the subject matter at stake and its eligibility did not require claim construction.[298] The Federal Circuit then made reference to the Court's decisions of *Chakrabarty*, *Bilski* and the Federal Circuit's decision in *Classen*, which pointed out the difference between

---

[293] Ibid.
[294] Ibid.
[295] Ibid. at 1376–7.
[296] 657 F.3d 1323 (Fed. Cir. 2011).
[297] Ibid. at 1324.
[298] Ibid. at 1325.

the threshold inquiry of patent-eligibility and the substantive conditions of patentability.[299] After citing from its own decision in *Research Corp*, the Federal Circuit claimed that title 35 did not list a single ineligible category, suggesting that any new, non-obvious and fully disclosed technical advance was eligible for protection, subject to the following limited judicially created exceptions: laws of nature, physical phenomena and abstract ideas.[300] It continued that: first, laws of nature and physical phenomena cannot be invented; and, second, abstractness, however, had presented a different set of interpretive problems, particularly for the section 101 'process' category. The Federal Circuit, following the Court's examination in *Bilski* of the definition of process of section 100(b) (finding that the ordinary, contemporary, common meaning of 'method' may include even methods of doing business), held that the Federal Circuit itself detected no limitations or conditions on subject-matter eligibility expressed in statutory language.[301]

It reiterated that both the Court in *Bilski* and the Federal Circuit in *Research Corp* had recognised the difficulty of providing a precise formula or definition for the judge-made ineligible category of abstractness.[302] The Federal Circuit continued that, because technology is ever-changing and evolves in unforeseeable ways, the Federal Circuit gives substantial weight to the statutory reluctance to list any new, non-obvious and fully disclosed subject matter as beyond the reach of section 101. After examining the definition of abstractness found in *Research Corp*, it opined that, although abstract principles were not eligible for patent protection, an application of an abstract idea might well be deserving of patent protection.[303] In the Federal Circuit's view, the application of an abstract idea to a 'new and useful end' was the type of invention that the Court in *Benson* had described as deserving of patent protection, continuing that, after all, unlike the Copyright Act, which divides idea from expression, the Patent Act covered and protected any new and useful technical advance, including applied ideas.

In respect of the claimed invention for a method for monetising and distributing copyrighted products over the Internet, the Federal Circuit held that, as a method, since the claim satisfied section 100's definition of 'process' and thus fell within a section 101 category of patent-eligible subject matter, the Federal Circuit should focus its inquiry on

---

[299]   Ibid. at 1326.
[300]   Ibid.
[301]   Ibid.
[302]   Ibid. at 1327.
[303]   Ibid.

the abstractness of the subject matter claimed by the '545 patent.[304] It claimed, in relation to the subject matter of the '545 patent, the mere idea that advertising could be used as a form of currency was abstract, just as the vague, unapplied concept of hedging that proved patent-ineligible in *Bilski*. However, it also noted that the '545 patent did not simply claim the age-old idea that advertising can serve as currency – instead it disclosed a practical application of this idea.[305] The Federal Circuit observed that the '545 patent claimed a particular method for monetising copyrighted products, which consisted of the following steps: (1) receiving media products from a copyright holder; (2) selecting an advertisement to be associated with each media product; (3) providing said media products for sale on an Internet website; (4) restricting general public access to the media products; (5) offering free access to said media products on the condition that the consumer view the advertising; (6) receiving a request from a consumer to view the advertising; (7) facilitating the display of advertising and any required interaction with the advertising; (8) allowing the consumer access to the associated media product after such display and interaction, if any; (9) recording this transaction in an activity log; and (10) receiving payment from the advertiser. In its view, many of these steps were likely to require intricate and complex computer programming and that, in addition, certain of these steps clearly required specific application to the Internet and a cyber-market environment.[306]

The Federal Circuit stated that, viewing the subject matter as a whole, the invention involved an extensive computer interface, noting that: first, the Federal Circuit did not define the level of programming complexity required before a computer-implemented method can be patent-eligible; second, nor did the Federal Circuit hold that use of an Internet website to practise such a method was either necessary or sufficient in every case to satisfy section 101; and, third, the Federal Circuit simply found the claims at issue to be patent-eligible, in part because of these factors.

It also examined the contention that the software programming necessary to facilitate the invention deserved no patent protection or amounted to abstract subject matter or, in the confusing terminology of machines and physical transformations, failed to satisfy the 'particular machine' requirement.[307] Applying its decision in *In re Alappat*, the Federal Circuit, observing that, far from abstract, advances in computer technology – both

---

[304] Ibid. at 1327–8.
[305] Ibid. at 1328.
[306] Ibid.
[307] Ibid.

hardware and software – drove innovation in every area of scientific and technical endeavour, held it understood that the broadly claimed method in the '545 patent did not specify a particular mechanism for delivering media content to the consumer (i.e., FTP downloads, email or real-time streaming).[308] It emphasised the breadth and lack of specificity did not render the claimed subject matter impermissibly abstract, noting that the 'coarse eligibility filter' of section 101 should not be used to invalidate patents based on concerns about vagueness, indefinite disclosure or lack of enablement, as these infirmities are expressly addressed by section 112. In addition, the Federal Circuit opined that the '545 patent did not claim a mathematical algorithm, a series of purely mental steps, or any similarly abstract concept it claimed a particular method for collecting revenue from the distribution of media products over the Internet.[309]

It distinguished *CyberSource Corp* on the basis that the Federal Circuit therein discerned that an invention claimed an 'unpatentable mental process', adding that the eligibility exclusion for purely mental steps was particularly narrow.[310] However, unlike the claims in *CyberSource*, the Federal Circuit held that the claims in the instant case required, among other things, controlled interaction with a consumer via an Internet website, something far removed from purely mental steps.[311] Consequently, it held that, as a practical application of the general concept of advertising as currency and an improvement to prior art technology, the claimed invention was not 'so manifestly abstract as to override the statutory language of section 101'.[312] After deciding *Prometheus*, the Court granted *certiorari*, vacated the judgment of the Federal Circuit in this decision and remanded the case back to the Federal Circuit for reconsideration in light of the Court's decision in *Prometheus*.[313]

The Federal Circuit again had to consider the scope of section 101 of the Patent Act in *Fuzzysharp Tech Inc v 3DLABS*.[314] Claim 12 of the '047 patent was for a method of reducing a step of visibility computations in 3-D computer graphics from a perspective of a viewpoint. The District Court invalidated all the asserted claims based on its conclusion that they do not satisfy the 'machine or transformation test', i.e., they do not involve

---

[308]   Ibid. at 1329.

[309]   Ibid.

[310]   Ibid. at 1329–30.

[311]   Ibid. at 1330.

[312]   Ibid.

[313]   *WildTangent Inc. v Ultramercial LLC* 32 S. Ct. 2431; 182 L. Ed. 2d 1059 (2012).

[314]   447 Fed. Appx. 182 (Fed. Cir. 2011).

the use of a particular machine, and they do not result in the transformation of an article to a different state. In a non-precedential opinion, the Federal Circuit agreed with the District Court's analysis, although it recognised that, since the Court's decision in *Bilski*, a failure to satisfy the 'machine or transformation test' no longer ensured that the subject matter of a claim would be deemed unpatentable.[315] It claimed that the references to a computer in claim 12 imposed only two limitations: the machine must be able to compute; and it must be able to store data. Citing *Benson*, the Federal Circuit held that the recitation of computer functions in the claim did not confine the pre-emptive effect of the claim because the underlying method had 'no substantial practical application except in connection with a digital computer'.[316] In its view, those limitations were, therefore, not 'meaningful limits' on the claim's scope.

The appellant argued that some of its unasserted claims are tied to particular hardware in the form of z-buffers and other specific pieces of computer hardware, and that those claims 'confirm that the methods of the Asserted Claims operate on and in the environment of computer graphics hardware systems'.[317] The Federal Circuit argued that, in addressing questions of patentable subject matter, it must assess each claim independently – there was no basis for looking to other claims except to the extent that they inform the meaning of the challenged claims through claim differentiation.[318] Nonetheless, the appellant claimed the Federal Circuit looked to elements recited in unasserted claims in *Research Corp*. However, the Federal Circuit in the instant case was of the view that the Federal Circuit in *Research Corp* concluded that the asserted claims were patent-eligible without looking to unasserted claims and then simply noted that elements recited in unasserted claims 'confirm [its] holding that the invention is not abstract'.[319] It continued that that statement did not change the long-standing rule that each claim must be limited to patentable subject matter, adding that, if it were sufficient to satisfy section 101 that some claims in the patent were patent-eligible, independent claims could avoid section 101's scrutiny altogether as long as they were paired with dependent claims that were patent-eligible.[320] The Federal Circuit then concluded that, based on the Court's decision in *Bilski* and its own more recent precedents, the patent-eligibility of at least one of the asserted claims turned on questions

---

[315] Ibid. at 184.
[316] Ibid. at 185.
[317] Ibid.
[318] Ibid.
[319] Ibid.
[320] Ibid. at 185–6.

of claim construction which the District Court did not have the opportunity to address. Therefore, it vacated the judgment of the District Court and remanded to it for further proceedings.[321]

In *Dealertrack Inc v Huber*,[322] the Federal Circuit had to consider the patentability of claims in the '841 and '427 patents, which were directed to a computer-aided method and system respectively for processing credit applications over electronic networks.[323] In respect of whether claim 1 of the '427 patent offended section 101 of the Patent Act, Linn J, with whom Dyk J agreed, after citing the Court's decision in *Bilski* and the Federal Circuit's decision in *Research Corp*, accepted that, therefore, it generally follows that any invention within the broad statutory categories of section 101 which is made by man, not directed to a law of nature or physical phenomenon, and not so manifestly abstract as to pre-empt a fundamental concept or idea, is patent-eligible.[324] Claim 1 was directed to a computer-aided method of managing a credit application. Again, after citing the test for patentability recently adopted by the Federal Circuit in *Research Corp*, the Federal Circuit stated that, in the instant case, however, it was compelled to conclude that the claims were invalid as being directed to an abstract idea pre-emptive of a fundamental concept or idea that would foreclose innovation in this area.[325]

It continued that the appellant's claimed process, in its simplest form, included three steps: receiving data from one source (step A), selectively forwarding the data (step B, performed according to step D), and forwarding reply data to the first source (step C). In the Federal Circuit's opinion: first, the claim explained the basic concept of processing information through a clearinghouse, just as claim 1 in *Bilski* explained the basic concept of hedging; second, steps that constituted the method did not impose meaningful limits on the claim's scope.[326] It then concluded that neither the appellant nor any other entity was entitled to wholly pre-empt the clearinghouse concept.[327] Nonetheless, the appellant argued that the 'computer-aided' limitation in the preamble of the specification sufficiently limited the claims to an application of an idea. The Federal Circuit disagreed, arguing that, first, the claims were silent as to how a computer aided the method, the extent to which a computer aided the method or the

---

[321] Ibid. at 186.
[322] 674 F.3d 1315 (Fed. Cir. 2012).
[323] Ibid. at 6.
[324] Ibid. at 39–40.
[325] Ibid. at 47.
[326] Ibid. at 47–8.
[327] Ibid. at 48.

significance of a computer to the performance of the method; and, second, the undefined phrase 'computer aided' was no less abstract than the idea of a clearinghouse itself.[328] Citing *CyberSource*, it observed that, because the computer could be programmed to perform very different tasks in very different ways, it did not play a significant part in permitting the claimed method to be performed, adding that simply adding a 'computer aided' limitation to a claim covering an abstract concept, without more, was insufficient to render the claim patent-eligible.[329]

The Federal Circuit noted that the claims did not require a specific application, nor were they tied to a particular machine, and that the computer did no more than the computer in *Benson* to limit the scope of the claim. It continued that the claims were also not analogous to those in *Ultramercial LLC*.[330] Distinguishing *Ultramercial LLC*, where the Federal Circuit found that the patent claimed a practical application with concrete steps requiring an extensive computer interface, the Federal Circuit, in the instant case, held the claims at issue recited only that the method was 'computer aided' without specifying any level of involvement or detail. It added that considering patent-eligibility under section 101, one must focus on the claims, and that the claims of the '427 patent were construed by the District Court not to be limited to any particular algorithm.[331] The appellant argued that the claim was patent-eligible because it covered the use of a clearinghouse only in the car loan application process, and not all uses thereof – although directed to a particular use, it nonetheless covered a broad idea. The Federal Circuit rejected this reasoning, citing *Bilski* for the view that the dependent claims were not patent-eligible though they limited an abstract idea to one field of use or added token post-solution components.[332] It also explained that the restriction in the instant case was precisely the kind of limitation held to be insufficient to confer patent-eligibility by the Court in *Bilski*, clarifying that the notion of using a clearinghouse generally, and using a clearinghouse specifically to apply for car loans, like the relationship between hedging in the energy market in *Bilski*, was of no consequence without more. As a result, the Federal Circuit affirmed the decision of the District Court that claims 1, 3, and 4 of the '427 patent were patent-ineligible abstract ideas under section 101.[333]

Plager J dissented from the part of the Federal Circuit's opinion

---

[328] Ibid.
[329] Ibid. at 49.
[330] Ibid. at 50.
[331] Ibid.
[332] Ibid. at 51.
[333] Ibid. at 52.

regarding the '427 patent and its validity under section 101 on the basis that the Federal Circuit should exercise its inherent power to control the processes of litigation, and insist that litigants, and trial courts, initially address patent invalidity issues in infringement suits in terms of the defences provided in the statute, 'conditions of patentability', specifically sections 102 and 103, and in addition sections 112 and 251, and not foray into the jurisprudential morass of section 101 unless absolutely necessary.[334]

Fort Properties Inc v American Master Lease LLC[335] concerned the '788 patent, which disclosed an investment tool designed to enable property owners to buy and sell properties without incurring tax liability, in particular claim 1, which comprised a method of creating a real estate investment instrument adapted for performing tax-deferred exchanges.[336] The decision of the Federal Circuit was given by Prost J, with whom Schall and Moore JJ agreed. The District Court, applying the 'machine or transformation test', invalidated each of the 41 claims in the '788 patent for failing to claim patent-eligible subject matter under section 101.[337] The issue for the Federal Circuit was whether the real estate investment tool disclosed in the '788 patent fell under the 'process' category of section 101.[338] In its opinion, four seminal Court precedents, namely, *Diehr*, *Benson*, *Flook* and *Bilski*, provided guidance regarding when an invention qualified as a patent-eligible process as opposed to an abstract idea. After examining each decision, the Federal Circuit concluded that the claims of the '788 patent did not satisfy the patent-eligibility requirements of section 101 because: first, the claims, like the invention in *Bilski*, disclosed an investment tool not requiring the use of a computer; second, specifically, claims 1–10 and 22–31 involve aggregating real property into a real estate portfolio, dividing the interests in the portfolio into a number of deed-shares and subjecting those shares to a master agreement; and, third, claims 11–21 then described how property can be bought and sold under this arrangement in a manner that permits a tax-deferred exchange.[339]

The respondent argued that the claims constituted a patentable process and not an abstract idea because they required a series of steps to take place in the real world that involve real property, deeds and contracts, and that, more specifically, the deeds removed the invention from the realm of the abstract because they were physical legal documents signifying

---

[334]   Ibid. at 53.
[335]   671 F.3d 1317 (Fed. Cir. 2012).
[336]   Ibid. at 1319.
[337]   Ibid. at 1319.
[338]   Ibid. at 1320.
[339]   Ibid. at 1322.

real property ownership that must be publicly recorded.[340] The appellant countered that the claimed method of aggregating property, making it subject to an agreement, and then issuing ownership interests to multiple parties consists entirely of mental processes and abstract intellectual concepts, adding that, under *Bilski*, the invention's intertwinement with deeds, contracts and real property did not transform the abstract method into a patentable process. The Federal Circuit agreed with the appellant, observing that the claims in *Bilski* were tied to the physical world through at least two tangible means: commodities and money.[341] However, in its view, these ties were insufficient to render the abstract concept of hedging patentable, adding that it viewed the instant case as similar to *Bilski*. The Federal Circuit reasoned that, like the invention in *Bilski*, claims 1–31 of the '788 patent disclosed an investment tool, particularly a real estate investment tool, designed to enable tax-free exchanges of property. In its opinion, this was an abstract concept which, under *Bilski*, could not be transformed into patentable subject matter merely because of connections to the physical world through deeds, contracts and real property.[342] The Federal Circuit also held that its reasoning was further supported by the fact that the claimed algorithm in *Flook* also had ties to the physical world since the invention involved the 'catalytic chemical conversion of hydrocarbons', yet the Court still characterised that invention as unpatentable. Therefore, it concluded that claims 1–31 of the '788 patent did not disclose patent-eligible subject matter.[343]

In relation to claims 32–41, the Federal Circuit noted that they had the same ties to deeds, contracts and real property as claims 1–31 and that, consequently, these physical connections were insufficient to qualify claims 32–41 for patent-eligibility under section 101. It further noted that these contained an additional limitation which required a computer to 'generate a plurality of deedshares'.[344] The Federal Circuit explained that it had recently provided guidance on how claim limitations involving computers apply in the section 101 analysis, namely, *CyberSource*, where it held that the basic character of a process claim drawn to an abstract idea was not changed by claiming only its performance by computers, or by claiming the process embodied in program instructions on a computer-readable medium. To be patentable, in its opinion, the use of the machine must impose meaningful limits on the claim's scope. For example, in *Ultramercial*

---

[340] Ibid.
[341] Ibid.
[342] Ibid.
[343] Ibid.
[344] Ibid. at 1323.

LLC, the claimed invention required intricate and complex computer programming and specific application to the Internet and a cyber-market environment.[345] The Federal Circuit opined that, in that decision, the addition of the computer to the claims was not merely insignificant post-solution activity; rather, the invention itself involved advances in computer technology which were sufficient to qualify the claims for patent-eligibility under section 101.

However, it noted that, in *Dealertrack*, the Federal Circuit concluded that claims to a method of applying for credit did not satisfy section 101 even though the claims contained a limitation requiring the invention to be 'computer aided'.[346] It continued that in *Dealertrack*, the Federal Circuit held: first, the claims were silent as to how a computer aided the method, the extent to which a computer aided the method or the significance of a computer to the performance of the method; and, second, simply adding a 'computer aided' limitation to a claim covering an abstract concept, without more, was insufficient to render the claim patent-eligible. The Federal Circuit observed that the Federal Circuit in *Dealertrack* distinguished *Ultramercial* on the grounds that its claims recited only that the method was 'computer aided' without specifying any level of involvement or detail, while the *Ultramercial* claims required 'an extensive computer interface'.[347]

Applying these precedents, the Federal Circuit in the instant case held that the computer limitation in claims 32–41 of the '788 patent, like the computer limitation in *Dealertrack*, did not 'play a significant part in permitting the claimed method to be performed', and that, more specifically, claims 32–41 only required the computer to 'generate a plurality of deed-shares'. In its view, the respondents simply added a computer limitation to claims covering an abstract concept – that is, the computer limitation was simply insignificant post-solution activity, holding that, without more, claims 32–41 could not qualify as patent-eligible.[348] As a result, the Federal Circuit, agreeing with the District Court, concluded that, since claims 1–41 of the '788 patent attempted to capture unpatentable abstract subject matter, they were invalid under section 101.[349]

In the most recent decision of the Federal Circuit in *MySpace v GraphOn Corp*[350] a sharp split in the opinion of the court occurred as to the proper

---

[345]   Ibid.
[346]   Ibid.
[347]   Ibid.
[348]   Ibid. at 1323–4.
[349]   Ibid. at 1324.
[350]   672 F.3d 1250 (Fed. Cir. 2012).

approach when considering challenges to patent-eligibility under section 101 of the Patent Act. The majority, Plager and Newman JJ, were of the view that the matter should be disposed of under sections 102 and 103 of the Patent Act, rather than section 101. Mayer J dissented. The Federal Circuit, via majority, with Plager J writing the judgment, with whom Newman J agreed, noted that the position of the minority, for the subject-matter eligibility requirements contained in section 101 to be an 'antecedent question' which must be addressed before the court could reach the sections 102 and 103 issues, was not unique to the dissent; it added that one could find support for it, as the dissent noted in the literature and in the language found in some cases (namely, the Federal Circuit's decision in *Dealertrack* and the Court's decision in *Bilski*).[351] However, it noted that others have urged judicial restraint in the face of what has become a plethora of opinions adding to the Federal Circuit's section 101 jurisprudence (namely, the additional views of Rader CJ and Newman J in the Federal Circuit's decision in *Classen*). The views of the Federal Circuit in this case were not surprising since Plager J had expressed a similar opinion in his dissenting opinion in *Dealertrack*.

The Federal Circuit argued that, even assuming it could reach out for the section 101 issue without having it raised by the parties or decided by the trial court, there was an even more basic problem with the dissent's position; namely, the problem with addressing section 101 initially every time it was presented as a defence was that the answer in each case required the search for a universal truth: in the broad sweep of modern innovative technologies, does this invention fall outside the breadth of human endeavour that possibly could be patented under section 101?[352] The Federal Circuit accepted that, while the Court recognised Congress intended in this general provision that the patent laws should be given wide scope, it had established, again in broad terms, three areas of activity that are excepted, namely, laws of nature, physical phenomena and abstract ideas. Noting that, over the years, the Court and the Federal Circuit have found dealing with 'laws of nature' and 'physical phenomena' reasonably manageable, it observed that, when it came to explaining what was to be understood by 'abstract ideas' in terms that were something less than abstract, the courts have been less successful.[353] The Federal Circuit argued that: first, the effort had become particularly problematic in recent times when applied to that class of claimed inventions loosely described as business method

---

[351] Ibid. at 1258.
[352] Ibid.
[353] Ibid. at 1259.

patents; and, second, if indeterminacy of the law governing patents was a problem in the past, it surely was becoming an even greater problem now, as the current plethora of Federal Circuit cases had shown.

It continued that, even with its recent pronouncement in *Research Corp* concerning 'abstract' idea, the opinions of the Federal Circuit spent page after page revisiting its own case law and those of the Court, and still the Federal Circuit continued to disagree vigorously over what is or is not patentable subject matter.[354] The Federal Circuit noted that this effort to descriptively cabin section 101 jurisprudence was reminiscent of the oenologists trying to describe a new wine, adding that they had an abundance of adjectives – earthy, fruity, grassy, nutty, tart, woody, to name just a few – but picking and choosing in a given circumstance which ones applied and in what combination depended less on the assumed content of the words than on the taste of the tongue pronouncing them. It explained that: first, rather than taking the path the dissent urged, courts could avoid the swamp of verbiage that is section 101 by exercising their inherent power to control the processes of litigation, and insist that litigants initially address patent invalidity issues in terms of the conditions of patentability defences as the statute provides, specifically sections 102, 103 and 112; and, second, if that were done in the typical patent case, litigation over the question of validity of the patent would be concluded under these provisions, and it would be unnecessary to enter the murky morass that is section 101 jurisprudence.[355] This, in the Federal Circuit's opinion, would make patent litigation more efficient, conserve judicial resources and bring a degree of certainty to the interests of both patentees and their competitors in the marketplace. It claimed that the District Courts and the Federal Circuit should follow the Court's lead and should avoid reaching for interpretations of broad provisions, such as section 101, when more specific statutes, such as sections 102, 103 and 112, could decide the case.[356]

Pointing out that the *Prometheus* litigation – a long-running section 101 dispute – had two trips to the Court from the Federal Circuit, the Federal Circuit remarked what a waste of time and resources it would prove to be if the dispute between the *Prometheus* parties was eventually resolved on the grounds the government predicted, namely, the likelihood that the disputed claims were invalid under sections 102 or 103. It was of the opinion that adopting this practice would also preclude section 101 claims from becoming the next toss-in for every defendant's response to a patent

---

[354]   Ibid.
[355]   Ibid. at 1260.
[356]   Ibid. at 1261.

infringement suit, particularly in business method patent litigation.[357] The Federal Circuit then questioned whether this meant that section 101 could never be raised initially in a patent infringement suit. It responded in the negative, stating that: first, in certain technology fields, and particularly when laws of nature or physical phenomena were the issue, efficiency might dictate applying the coarse filter of section 101 first to address legitimate questions of patent eligibility; and, second, even when the patent invoked the abstractness issue, such as in a business method patent, if it was clear and convincing beyond peradventure – that is, under virtually any meaning of 'abstract' – that the claim at issue was well over the line, a case could be made for initially addressing the section 101 issue in the infringement context.[358] However, the Federal Circuit opined that the latter patent would be a rather unusual and infrequent circumstance and that, more often, when the question of abstractness is presented in its usual abstract terms, the trial court could, as a matter of case management, summarily put aside the section 101 defence on whatever grounds seem applicable in the case.[359] It continued that litigants would then be left to address the invalidity defences of sections 102, 103 and 112, as the statute provides, and the litigants, the trial court and the Federal Circuit on review would have some semblance of a chance at arriving at a predictable and understandable result. In the result, the Federal Circuit held the proper course of action, in the instant case, was the one that the District Court and the majority had followed: decide the case on the question of compliance with sections 102 and 103 as Congress has instructed, and decline the dissent's invitation to put the parties and this court in the swamp that is section 101 jurisprudence.[360]

Mayer J, dissenting, took another approach, correctly arguing that issue of whether a claimed method met the subject-matter eligibility requirements contained in section 101 was an 'antecedent question' that must be addressed before the Federal Circuit could consider whether particular claims were invalid as obvious or anticipated.[361] This approach, he conceded, was adopted by the Court in *Flook* and *Bilski*. In respect of the claims at issue, he stated that they were significantly broader in scope and had the potential to wield far greater pre-emptive power than those at issue in *Bilski*.[362] Mayer J continued that: first, the potential scope of the patents was staggering; second, they arguably covered any online system in which

---

357   Ibid.
358   Ibid.
359   Ibid. at 1262.
360   Ibid.
361   Ibid. at 1264.
362   Ibid. at 1264–5.

users controlled the content and categorisation of their own communications; and, third, the claims thus cut across vast swathes of the Internet and potentially extended to most online advertising and social networking sites. Like the claims considered by the Court in *Bilski*, he claimed that the ones at issue were likewise directed to a fundamental and widely understood concept, namely, the idea that information could be stored in a computer database by one person and then accessed, in an unedited form, by another person, a fundamental tenet of network computing that was likely to be taught in any basic computer science course.[363]

Mayer J reasoned that the methods disclosed in Bilski's application and those in the case were not unpatentable because they lacked any practical utility – rather, they fell outside the ambit of section 101 because they were too useful and too widely applied to possibly form the basis of any patentable invention. The claimed method in *Bilski*, in his opinion, was rejected because avoiding excessive economic risk had long been a cornerstone of commercial enterprise.[364] Likewise, in the instant case, Mayer J explained that the concept of allowing users to control the content of their online communications was 'abstract' because free and unrestricted Internet communication has become a staple of contemporary life; and that permitting the appellant to exert monopoly power over any online system that allowed users to control the content of their own communications would pre-empt use of one of the 'basic tools' of modern social and commercial interaction.[365] The requirements of section 101 could not be avoided simply because the claimed method disclosed very specific steps for allowing users to create and modify database entries. Mayer J opined that a patentee would not uphold his end of the 'bargain' of the patent system (disclosure for exclusive monopoly for a limited time) if he sought broad monopoly rights over a basic concept or fundamental principle without a concomitant contribution to the existing body of scientific and technological knowledge.[366] In his view, this principle explained the decisions of the Court in *Flook* and *Bilski*.

In respect of the use of computer technology in many of those patents, Mayer J claimed that, while running a particular process on a computer undeniably improved efficiency and accuracy, cloaking an otherwise abstract idea in the guise of a computer-implemented claim was insufficient to bring it within section 101, citing the Court's decision in *Flook*

---

[363]   Ibid. at 1265.
[364]   Ibid.
[365]   Ibid. at 1265–6.
[366]   Ibid. at 1266.

and *Benson*.[367] He also referred to decisions of the Federal Circuit, namely, *CyberSource Corp* and *Dealertrack* for the same proposition. In rejecting the argument that, instead of 101, sections 102, 103 and 112 should be used to weed out patents of dubious quality, Mayer J claimed that there were several insurmountable problems with this approach.[368] The first was that, as a practical matter, it had proved woefully inadequate in preventing a deluge of very poor-quality patents. Second, there was nothing in *Bilski* to suggest that section 101 could be subverted by a misplaced reliance on sections 102, 103 or 112.[369] He continued that a robust application of section 101 was required to ensure that the patent laws comported with their constitutionally defined objective of promoting the progress of the useful arts.[370]

E CONCLUSION

The decisions of the Court in *Benson*, *Flook* and *Diehr* are the foundational cases on patent-eligibility under section 101 of the Patents Act. These decisions, as applied and expanded upon by the Court's most recent pronouncements in *Bilski*, make it plain that, first, section 101 of the Patent Act contains an important implicit exception for the laws of nature, natural phenomena and abstract ideas. The rationale for this implicit exception was that the monopolisation of those tools through the grant of a patent might tend to impede innovation more than it would tend to promote it. Second, it is the application of the implicit exceptions to patentability that matters for patent-eligibility under section 101. Third, the 'machine or transformation test' has always been a 'useful and important clue'; it has never been the 'sole test' for determining patentability. The decisions of the Federal Circuit post-*Bilski* have adopted a new test to determine patent-eligibility under section 101, namely, whether the invention was not 'so manifestly abstract as to override the statutory language of section 101'. If the Court decides to hear the *Classen* or the *AMP v USPTO* cases on appeal from the Federal Circuit, it might have to pronounce on this new test devised by the Federal Circuit.

---

[367] Ibid. at 1267.
[368] Ibid. at 1268.
[369] Ibid.
[370] Ibid. at 1269.

5. Consideration by the Federal Circuit

A   INTRODUCTION

As was seen in Chapter 2, in the early period, before the decisions of the Court in *Benson*, *Flook* and *Diehr*, the Federal Circuit opined on the issue of whether medical and diagnostic patents were patentable in the early period. In the 1980s, it produced some of its more direct decisions that centred on that question; however, it was in the period after the decision of the Court in *Laboratory Corporation* that the plethora of decisions of the Federal Circuit in relation to medical patents commenced. It is important to consider these cases because the majority of decisions on this area were considered in the Federal Circuit and its views on the patent eligibility of medical and diagnostic methods have certainly influenced the Court when it finally decided the issue in *Prometheus*. This chapter considers in detail the decision of the Federal Circuit before and after it became active in delineating the issues at the heart of patent-eligibility of medical and diagnostic methods – which it did in no less than five decisions handed down in 2010 and 2011. These decisions directly provide the backdrop against which the patentability of medical patents must be assessed subject, of course, to the definitive statement of the Court in *Prometheus*.

B   THE INITIAL PERIOD

In the 1980s, the United States Court of Customs and Patent Appeals (CCPA), the predecessor to the Federal Circuit, considered the issue of whether patent protection should be provided for medical, diagnostic and related methods. In *In re Meyer*,[1] the invention was for a process and an apparatus for carrying out the process of testing a complex system and analysing the results of these tests. The process included:

---

[1]   688 F.2d 789 (CCPA 1982). See also *In re Abele* 684 F.2d 902 (CCPA 1982).

(a) dividing the complex system into a plurality of 'elements' and (b) associating a factor of function or malfunction with each of these elements.[2] The claims in full were for: a process for identifying locations of probable malfunction in a complex system, said process comprising the steps of: (a) *selecting* a plurality of elements in the complex system, said elements having known locations; (b) *initializing* a factor associated with each of said elements; (c) *testing* the complex system for a response, which response, if effective, requires proper functioning of certain said elements, the probable identity or at least some of these certain elements being known; (d) *determining* whether said response of the complex system was at least partially effective or ineffective; (e) *modifying* the factor associated with at least some of said elements known to be possibly involved in the response in accordance with the effectiveness of the response; and (f) *repeating* steps (c), (d) and (e) for further responses of the complex system to obtain resultant factors for at least some of said elements, whereby said resultant factors are indicative of probable malfunction of their associated elements and thereby indicative of probable malfunction at the locations of these elements.[3]

In *In re Bilski*, the Federal Circuit characterised the claim in *In re Meyer* as a claim for a computerised method for aiding a neurologist in diagnosing patients.[4] The Examiner rejected the claim because, in its view, the claimed method was patent-ineligible, citing the decisions of the Court in *Benson* and *Flook*. This was because it claimed a mathematical algorithm and the BOPA affirmed that decision, reasoning as follows: that the first step of *selecting* 'relates to nothing more than the selection of a source for the accumulation of data to be used in the analysis' and *initialising* 'is a factor which relates to the probability that the particular element is malfunctioning. At the beginning of the test procedure a proper factor would be zero.'[5] The CCPA claimed the *testing* step was 'nothing more than a data gathering step. Such a step cannot make an otherwise nonstatutory claim statutory.'[6] Additionally, it noted that the *determining* step is merely 'information that is read into the computer' and the *modifying* step 'takes place in the computer by a comparison process in which test outcomes are compared with stored data'.[7] In the latter step, the 'computer infers from this comparison that certain elements are functioning or not functioning'.[8] In its view, the 'process recited is an attempt to patent a mathematical algorithm rather than a process for producing a product as in' *Diehr*.[9]

---

[2] *In re Meyer* at 790.
[3] Ibid. at 792–3.
[4] *In re Bilski* 545 F.3d 943 at 1002 (Fed. Cir. 2008) (*en banc*).
[5] *In re Meyer* at 794.
[6] Ibid.
[7] Ibid.
[8] Ibid.
[9] Ibid.

The question for the CCPA in *In re Meyer* was whether the claimed method at issue was patentable under section 101. It claimed that the invention was mainly concerned with replacing, in part, the thinking (mental) processes of a neurologist with a computer, continuing that the decisive question was whether that mental process was applied to physical elements or process steps in an otherwise statutory process, machine, manufacture or composition of matter, in accordance with section 101.[10] It was, therefore, the application of the mental step that was key to patentability under section 101. By doing so, the claimed method would transform the idea, or mental step, from the arena of abstractness to the field of practical application, which is primarily what section 101 is concerned with. The claimed method, although a type of diagnostic method, was complicated by the use of the computer to carry out the comparison step. This, however, does not diminish the CCPA's recognition that the step was, in fact, a mental step which would ordinarily be done by a medical practitioner. Since the method contained a mathematical algorithm the CCPA had to consider whether the inclusion of that step meant that the claimed method, as a whole, was not patentable under section 101. It noted that '[o]nce a mathematical algorithm has been found, the claim as a whole must be further analyzed', adding that '[i]f it appears that the mathematical algorithm is implemented in a specific manner to define structural relationships between the physical elements of the claim (in apparatus claims) or to refine or limit claim steps (in process claims), the claim being otherwise statutory, the claim passes muster under [section] 101'.[11]

Observing that, in answering the question before it, 'the claims are to be given their broadest reasonable interpretation consistent with the specification', the CCPA held that the 'claims are to a mathematical algorithm representing a mental process that has not been applied to physical elements or process steps and is, therefore, not limited to any otherwise statutory process, machine, manufacture, or composition of matter'.[12] Again, the application of the mental element was being emphasised by the court. The claimed method was, therefore, not patentable. The CCPA, however, was preoccupied with the issue of whether the replacement of the mental step of determining whether certain elements were functioning or not functioning by a computer was an excluded method on the basis of the exclusion accepted in *Benson*, *Flook* and *Diehr*, that a claimed method to a mathematical algorithm was unpatentable. Importantly, the CCPA did

---

[10]   Ibid. at 795–6.
[11]   Ibid. at 796.
[12]   Ibid.

accept that, in the modifying step, the comparison takes place in the computer and it is the computer that determined whether certain elements were functioning or not functioning. It would seem that, if that 'mental' element is replaced by a computer, it would no longer be relevant to ask the question since it would no longer exist; and, in the instant case, its replacement by a computer meant that the question then was whether it was patent-eligible because it included a mathematical algorithm.

In *In re Grams*,[13] the Federal Circuit had to consider whether a claim for method of diagnosing an abnormal condition in an individual was patentable under section 101.[14] In its view, the invention provided for a method of testing a complex system to determine whether the system condition was normal or abnormal and, if it was abnormal, to determine the cause of the abnormality.[15] The claim, in full, was as follows:

A method of diagnosing an abnormal condition in an individual, the individual being characterized by a plurality of correlated parameters of a set of such parameters that is representative of the individual's condition, the parameters comprising data resulting from a plurality of clinical laboratory tests which measure the levels of chemical and biological constituents of the individual and each parameter having a reference range of values, *the method comprising* [a] *performing* said plurality of clinical laboratory tests on the individual to measure the values of the set of parameters; [b] *producing* from the set of measured parameter values and the reference ranges of values a first quantity representative of the condition of the individual; [c] *comparing* the first quantity to a first predetermined value to determine whether the individual's condition is abnormal; [d] upon *determining* from said comparing that the individual's condition is abnormal, successively testing a plurality of different combinations of the constituents of the individual by eliminating parameters from the set to form subsets corresponding to said combinations, producing for each subset a second quantity, and comparing said second quantity with a second predetermined value to detect a non-significant deviation from a normal condition; and [e] *identifying* as a result of said testing a complementary subset of parameters corresponding to a combination of constituents responsible for the abnormal condition, said complementary subset comprising the parameters eliminated from the set so as to produce a subset having said non-significant deviation from a normal condition.[16]

The claimed method, in essence, consisted of comparing and then measuring the levels of chemical and biological constituents in an individual to those of a normal set of parameters to determine whether the individual's

13 888 F.2d 835 (Fed. Cir. 1989).
14 Ibid. at 836.
15 Ibid.
16 Ibid. at 836–7.

condition was normal. This was a clear diagnostic method of treatment of a human or animal body. The Federal Circuit noted that the performing step 'requires the performance of clinical laboratory tests on an individual to obtain data for the parameters (e.g., sodium content)'.[17] In its view, the other steps 'analyze that data to ascertain the existence and identity of an abnormality, and possible causes thereof' and that they were 'in essence a mathematical algorithm'.[18] The claimed method was complicated by the addition of the mathematical algorithm.

The issue for the Federal Circuit was whether the claims, which included an algorithm for measuring the values, were excluded from patent protection.[19] It noted, quoting *In re Walter*,[20] that once a mathematical algorithm was extant in the claimed method, the claim as a whole must be analysed and, if the mathematical algorithm was implemented in a specific manner to define structural relationships between the physical elements of the claim or to refine or limit claim steps, it would be patentable under section 101.[21] The Federal Circuit also noted that the sole physical process step in the claimed method was step [a], *performing* the clinical tests on individuals to obtain data, but that 'it focuses on the algorithm itself, although it briefly refers to, without describing, the clinical tests that provide data'.[22] As a result, it held, citing *Benson*, that the claims were unpatentable under section 101 as being related to a non-statutory mathematical algorithm, and upheld the rejection of the patent by the District Court.[23] The Federal Circuit did not have to pronounce on the issue of whether the extant diagnostic method was patentable under section 101 (which never arose for discussion) since the claims included a subject matter ineligible for patent protection, namely, a mathematical method; and, therefore, the claim was rejected on that basis alone.

In the process of reasoning, the Federal Circuit in *In re Grams*[24] noted that the claim it had considered was similar to the ones considered by the CCPA in *In re Meyer*. It explained that the claims in *In re Meyer* were for a process and apparatus for identifying probable malfunction in a complex system and that '[i]n a sense, the objective there of identifying malfunction

---

17   Ibid. at 837.
18   Ibid.
19   Ibid.
20   618 F.2d 758, 205 USPQ 397 (CCPA 1980).
21   *In re Grams* at 837.
22   Ibid. at 840.
23   Ibid. at 841.
24   888 F.2d 835, 840 (Fed. Cir. 1989).

is similar to the objective here of identifying abnormality'.[25] The Federal Circuit claimed that the BOPA in *In re Meyer* held that 'the claim included an algorithm and a data-gathering step' and rejected it as 'an attempt to patent a mathematical algorithm rather than a process for producing a product' and that this was affirmed by the CCPA.[26] As a result, it concluded that, in the instant case, the BOPA 'made similar determinations' so it would affirm it.[27]

In *In re Griffin*,[28] the claim was for a method for diagnosing an increased risk for thrombosis or a genetic defect causing thrombosis in the human body.[29] The full claims were as follows:

A method for diagnosing an increased risk for thrombosis or a genetic defect causing thrombosis comprising the steps of: (A) *obtaining*, from a test subject, test nucleic acid comprising codon 506 within EXON 10 of the human Factor V gene; and (B) *assaying* for the presence of a point mutation in the nucleotides of codon 506 within EXON 10 of the human Factor V gene, *wherein* said point mutation *correlates* to a decrease in the degree of inactivation of human Factor V and/or human Factor Va by activated protein C, wherein the presence of said point mutation in said test nucleic acid indicates an increased risk for thrombosis or a genetic defect causing thrombosis.

Although the issue in this decision was not whether the claimed method was patentable under section 101, but, rather, whether it was invalid under section 102(g) of the Patent Act, the Federal Circuit still considered the meaning of such diagnostic claims. It simply noted that the preamble was directed to 'diagnosing an increased risk for thrombosis of a genetic defect causing thrombosis'.[30] The diagnostic method was indicated in the following: 'wherein the presence of said point mutation in said test nucleic acid indicates an increased risk for thrombosis or a genetic defect causing thrombosis'. Consequently, the Federal Circuit held that diagnosis is thus the essence of this invention; its appearance in the count gives 'life and meaning' to the manipulative steps.[31]

---

[25]   Ibid. at 840.
[26]   Ibid.
[27]   Ibid. at 840–41.
[28]   285 F.3d 1029 (Fed. Cir. 2002).
[29]   Ibid. at 1031.
[30]   Ibid. at 1033.
[31]   Ibid.

C   THE FEDERAL CIRCUIT DISCUSSES *LABORATORY CORPORATION*

The majority opinion of the Federal Circuit in *In re Bilski*[32] explained, at footnote 27, that several Justices of the Court, in a dissent to a dismissal of a writ of *certiorari*, expressed their view that a similar claim in *Laboratory Corporation* was drawn to unpatentable subject matter.[33] The majority continued that there the claimed process only comprised the steps of: (a) 'assaying a body fluid for an elevated level of total homocysteine'; and (b) 'correlating an elevated level of total homocysteine in said body fluid with a deficiency of cobalamin or folate'.[34]

Rader J, in dissent, pointed out that the Federal Circuit's 'willingness to venture away from the statute follows on the heels of an oft-discussed dissent from the Supreme Court's dismissal of its grant of *certiorari* in [*Laboratory Corporation*]'.[35] He noted that the dissent was 'premised on a fundamental misapprehension of the distinction between a natural phenomenon and a patentable process'.[36] Rader J claimed that the distinction between 'phenomena of nature', 'mental processes' and 'abstract intellectual concepts' was not difficult to draw. He claimed that the fundamental error in the dissent in *Laboratory Corporation* was its 'failure to recognize the difference between a patent ineligible relationship – i.e., that between high homocysteine levels and folate and cobalamin deficiencies – and a patent eligible process for applying that relationship to achieve a useful, tangible, and concrete result – i.e., diagnosis of potentially fatal conditions in patients'.[37] He noted that there was nothing abstract in that claimed method, asserting that testing blood for a dangerous condition was not a natural phenomenon but a human invention.[38]

Further, Rader J explained that the distinction was simple but critical, noting that a patient may suffer from the unpatentable phenomenon of nature, namely high homocysteine levels and low folate.[39] The invention, in his opinion, 'did not attempt to claim that natural phenomenon; but instead claimed a process for assaying a patient's blood and then analyzing

---

[32]   545 F.3d 943 (Fed. Cir. 2008) (*en banc*).
[33]   Ibid. at 965.
[34]   Ibid.
[35]   Ibid. at 1014.
[36]   Ibid.
[37]   Ibid.
[38]   Ibid.
[39]   Ibid.

the results with a new process that detects the life-threatening condition'.[40] Rader J said that 'the sick patient did not practice the patented invention, but instead the patent covered a process for testing blood that produces a useful, concrete, and tangible result: incontrovertible diagnostic evidence to save lives'.[41] In his opinion, the 'patent did not claim the patent ineligible relationship between folate and homocysteine, nor did it foreclose future inventors from using that relationship to devise better or different processes'.[42] Consequently, Rader J held that, contrary to the language of the dissent, it was the sick patient who embodied only the correlation between homocysteine and vitamin deficiency, not the claimed process.[43]

He claimed that, from the standpoint of policy, the dissent in *Laboratory Corporation* avoided the same fundamental question that the Federal Circuit did not ask or answer in *In re Bilski*, namely: '[i]s this entire field of subject matter undeserving of incentives for invention? If so, why?'[44] In the context of the decision in *Laboratory Corporation*, he claimed that that question was very telling: 'the natural condition diagnosed by the invention was debilitating and even deadly'.[45] Rader J pointed out that, before the invention featured in *Laboratory Corporation*, medical science lacked an affordable, reliable and fast means to detect this debilitating condition. Consequently, he claimed, 'denial of patent protection for this innovation – precisely because of its elegance and simplicity (the chief aims of all good science) – would undermine and discourage future research for diagnostic tools'.[46] In other words, he asked: 'does not Patent Law wish to encourage researchers to find simple blood tests or urine tests that predict and diagnose breast cancers or immunodeficiency diseases?' In that context, he explained, the Federal Circuit might profitably ask whether its decisions incentivise research for cures and other important technical advances.[47] He cautioned that, with such attention, the Federal Circuit inadvertently advised investors that 'they should divert their unprotectable investments away from discovery of "scientific relationships" within the

---

[40]   Ibid.

[41]   Ibid.

[42]   Ibid.

[43]   Ibid.

[44]   Ibid.

[45]   See U.S. Patent No. 4,940,658, col. 1, ll. 32–40 ('Accurate and early diagnosis of cobalamin and folate deficiencies . . . is important because these deficiencies can lead to life-threatening hematologic abnormalities . . . . Accurate and early diagnosis of cobalamin deficiency is especially important because it can also lead to incapacitating and life-threatening neuropsychiatric abnormalities').

[46]   545 F.3d 943 at 1014 (Fed. Cir. 2008) (*en banc*).

[47]   Ibid.

body that diagnose breast cancer or Lou Gehrig's disease or Parkinson's or whatever'.[48]

D   RECENT MEDICAL PATENT JURISPRUDENCE

1   *Prometheus Laboratories Inc. v Mayo Collaborative Services*

(a)   The District Court

In *Prometheus Laboratories Inc. v Mayo Collaborative Services*,[49] the claim was for a method of optimising therapeutic efficacy for treatment of an immune-mediated gastrointestinal disorder.[50] The main claim of the invention was that the blood levels of certain metabolites of some thiopurine drugs used for treatment of immune-mediated gastrointestinal disorders correlate with toxic side effects of the thiopurine drugs.[51] The claims under consideration in this decision, at first blush, seem to be in similar terms to the ones considered by the Court in *Laboratory Corporation*, in so far as they both related to finding a correlation between two things. But the result of that correlation differs – whereas in *Laboratory Corporation*, the correlation enabled the medical practitioner to make a diagnosis, in *Prometheus*, it provided information to the medical practitioner suggesting whether a more efficient dose should be used for the patient. Thus, the claim in *Laboratory Corporation* was to a diagnostic method; whereas, the claim in *Prometheus* was to a method of finding out the optimum dosage regime for a patient.

The District Court in *Classen* held that the patents claimed the correlations between certain thiopurine drug metabolite levels and therapeutic efficacy and toxicity. It reasoned that the claims contained three steps, namely: (1) administration of the drug to a subject; (2) determination of the metabolite levels; and (3) a warning that an adjustment in dosage may be required.[52] The District Court explained the fact that the inventors framed the claims as treatment methods only did not render them patentable; rather, it found that 'the "administering" and "determining" steps were merely necessary data-gathering steps for any use of the correlations' and that 'as construed, the final step – the "warning" step (i.e. the "wherein" clause) – is

---

48   Ibid.
49   581 F.3d 1336 (Fed. Cir. 2009).
50   Ibid. at 1340.
51   Ibid.
52   Invalidity Opinion, 2008 WL 878910 at 9.

only a mental step'.[53] It noted that the 'warning step' did not require any *actual* change in dosage and that it was 'the metabolite levels themselves that "warn" the doctor that an adjustment in dosage *may* be required'.[54] It explained the claims included 'only two active steps: "administering" the drug and "determining" metabolite levels, which are merely data-gathering steps; plus the additional mental step that the doctor be warned (by the metabolite levels) that an adjustment in dosage may be required. Therefore, the claims recite the correlations themselves.'[55] With this understanding of the claims, the District Court concluded that the claims recited the correlations between particular concentrations of 6-TG and 6-MMP and therapeutic efficacy or toxicity in patients taking AZA drugs.[56]

The District Court also held that there was little doubt that the claimed correlations were 'natural phenomena'.[57] It explained that the inventors did not 'create' the correlation between thiopurine drug metabolite levels and therapeutic efficacy and toxicity; rather, the correlation resulted from a natural body process, which the inventors conceded was found in the patient population.[58] It stated that the correlation between particular 6-TG and 6-MMP metabolite levels and therapeutic efficacy and toxicity was not an 'invention'; rather, '6-TG and 6-MMP are products of the natural metabolizing of thiopurine drugs, and the inventors merely observed the relationship between these naturally produced metabolites and therapeutic efficacy and toxicity'.[59] As a result, the District Court found that those correlations were natural phenomena and not patentable inventions because the correlations resulted from a natural body process.[60] In addition, the District Court held that '[b]ecause the claims cover the correlations themselves, it follows that the claims "wholly pre-empt" the correlations'.[61] It also held that the claims recited a natural phenomenon – the correlations between thiopurine drug metabolite levels and therapeutic efficacy and/ or toxicity – and that they 'wholly pre-empt' use of those correlations. Therefore, the District Court concluded that the claims were invalid under section 101.[62]

---

[53] Ibid.
[54] Ibid. (emphasis added).
[55] Ibid. at 9–10.
[56] Ibid. at 10.
[57] Ibid.
[58] Ibid. at 11.
[59] Ibid. at 15.
[60] Ibid. at 11.
[61] Ibid. at 17.
[62] Ibid.

In the course of reasoning, the District Court also examined the dissenting judgment of Breyer J in *Laboratory Corporation*. It observed that the facts of the instant case were similar to those of *Laboratory Corporation*, namely, that the patent claimed a method of measuring the level of an amino acid in the blood, called homocysteine, which correlated with a deficiency in two vitamins, cobalamin and folate.[63] The District Court claimed that, although the dissent in *Laboratory Corporation* did not have precedential value, it found Breyer J's reasoning persuasive, noting that the claims in the patents under consideration were clearly analogous to the claim in *Laboratory Corporation*. It explained that the claim in *Laboratory Corporation* comprised two steps, namely: first, assaying a body fluid for an elevated level of total homocysteine; and, second, correlating an elevated level of total homocysteine in said body fluid with deficiency of cobalamin or folate.[64] The District Court reasoned that: first, the 'assaying' step in *Laboratory Corporation* was akin to the 'administering' and 'determining' steps in the claims under consideration as both were necessary steps for any use of the correlations; and, second, *Laboratory Corporation*'s 'correlating' step was akin to the 'wherein' clause in the claims under consideration as both recite the claimed correlation.[65] Therefore, it claimed that the same reasoning which led Breyer J to conclude the correlation between elevated homocysteine levels and deficiency of cobalamin or folate was a natural phenomenon supported the finding that the correlation between thiopurine drug metabolite levels and therapeutic efficacy and toxicity was also a natural phenomenon.[66]

(b)   The Federal Circuit: first judgment

On appeal, the Federal Circuit explained that the issue before it was whether the claims met the requirements of section 101.[67] While noting it had also been established that 'while a claim drawn to a fundamental principle – i.e., a law of nature, natural phenomenon, or abstract idea – is unpatentable', it accepted that 'an application of a law of nature or mathematical formula to a known structure or process may well be deserving of patent protection'.[68] The key issue for patentability, the Federal Circuit observed, was whether a claim was drawn to a fundamental principle or an

---

[63]   Ibid. at 11–12.
[64]   Ibid. at 12–13.
[65]   Ibid. at 13.
[66]   Ibid.
[67]   *Prometheus* 581 F.3d 1336 at 1341 (Fed. Cir. 2009).
[68]   Ibid. at 1342, citing *In re Bilski* at 953.

application of a fundamental principle.[69] After examining the argument of the appellants, Prometheus, and the respondents, Mayo, the Federal Circuit ruled that it agreed with Prometheus that the asserted claims were drawn to statutory subject matter and, therefore, reversed the District Court's decision.[70] It observed that the proper inquiry under section 101 was whether these methods met the Court's 'machine or transformation test' articulated in *Benson* and *Diehr*, and applied in *Bilski*, and, if so, whether the machine or the transformation was central to the purpose of the claims.[71]

The Federal Circuit concluded that the methods of treatment claimed in the patent fell within the realm of patentable subject matter because they 'transform an article into a different state or thing', and this transformation was 'central to the purpose of the claimed process'.[72] The transformation, it explained, 'was of the human body following administration of a drug and the various chemical and physical changes of the drug's metabolites that enabled their concentrations to be determined'.[73] The Federal Circuit continued that, since the claimed methods met the transformation prong under *In re Bilski*, it was not necessary for it to consider whether they also met the machine prong test.[74] It also stated that claims were methods of treatment that were always transformative when a defined group of drugs was administered to the human body to remedy the effects of the illness.[75]

The Federal Circuit then distinguished *In re Grams* on the basis that, in that decision, the Federal Circuit had found the process was not patentable, because the invention essentially claimed a mathematical algorithm rather than any transformation of the tested individuals. In other words, the process was unpatentable because 'it was merely an algorithm combined with a data-gathering step', i.e., performing a clinical test.[76] The Federal Circuit noted that the claims in *In re Grams* did not require the performing of clinical tests on individuals that were transformative – thus rendering the entire process patentable subject matter – because the tests were just to 'obtain data'. In its opinion, the Federal Circuit focused only on the algorithm rather than the clinical tests purported to be covered by the

---

[69] *Prometheus* at 1342.

[70] Ibid.

[71] Ibid. at 1345.

[72] Ibid.

[73] Ibid.

[74] Ibid. at 1346.

[75] Ibid.

[76] Ibid.

claims.[77] The Federal Circuit asserted that, unlike the clinical test recited in *In re Grams*, the administering and determining steps in Prometheus's claimed methods were not 'merely' data-gathering steps or 'insignificant extra-solution activity'; they were part of treatment regimes for various diseases using thiopurine drugs.[78] As a result, it concluded the claims were, therefore, not drawn merely to correlations between metabolite levels and toxicity or efficacy.[79]

The Federal Circuit held that the steps preceding the 'warning' steps provided useful information to the physician for possible dosage adjustments to the method of treatment using the drugs for a particular patient.[80] Consequently, it held that the claims were directed to therapeutic methods of treatment which determined the optimal dosage level for a course of treatment, and that the claimed method comprised a series of transformative steps that optimised efficacy and reduced toxicity of a method of treatment for particular diseases using particular drugs.[81] In addition, the Federal Circuit held that the claims covered transformative methods of treatment, not correlations; that they covered a particular application of natural processes to treat various diseases; and, that transformative steps utilising natural processes were not unpatentable subject matter.[82] It must be noted that the Federal Circuit mentioned 'transformation' but it did not specify exactly what was to be transformed in the claimed method. Moreover, it reiterated, first, the claims did not pre-empt natural processes – they merely utilised them in a series of specific steps; and, second, because the claims met the 'machine or transformation test', they did not pre-empt a fundamental principle or all uses of these natural processes.[83] The Federal Circuit therefore concluded the claimed methods of treatment were patentable subject matter, which satisfied the requirements under *In re Bilski's* transformation prong for patent-eligible subject matter under section 101.[84]

---

[77]   Ibid.
[78]   Ibid.
[79]   Ibid.
[80]   Ibid. at 1349.
[81]   Ibid.
[82]   Ibid.
[83]   Ibid.
[84]   Ibid. at 1350. *Ariad Pharmaceuticals Inc. v Eli Lilly and Co* 560 F.3d 1366 (Fed. Cir. 2009), which related to diagnostic methods, but the decision focused on the requirement for sufficiency.

(c)   The Federal Circuit: judgment on remand

(i)   Relevance of the machine or transformation test   Responding to the Court's request for it to reconsider its first decision in *Prometheus* in light of the Court's decision in *Bilski*, the Federal Circuit reconsidered the issue of patenting treatment or dosage regimes in its second decision in *Prometheus*.[85] The first thing the Federal Circuit pointed out was that the Court did not 'reject the machine-or-transformation test, but rather characterized the test as "a useful and important clue, an investigative tool, for determining whether some claimed inventions are processes under [section] 101"'.[86] In addition, it stated that the Court's decision in *Bilski* 'did not undermine our pre-emption analysis of Prometheus's claims and it rejected the machine-or-transformation test only as a definitive test'.[87] In other words, the Court did not 'disavow the machine-or-transformation test'.[88] This paved the way for the Federal Circuit in *Prometheus* to use the reasoning in its first *Prometheus* decision which was based on the 'machine or transformation test'. It claimed that, in light of the Court's decision in *Bilski*, 'patent eligibility in this case turns on whether Prometheus's asserted claims are drawn to a natural phenomenon, the patenting of which would entirely pre-empt its use as in *Benson* or *Flook*, or whether the claims are drawn only to a particular application of that phenomenon as in *Diehr*'.[89]

(ii)   Interpreting the claims   Before examining the decision of the Federal Circuit in *Prometheus*, it is necessary to have a firm understanding of what exactly Prometheus claimed in the patent specification. Three of the claims make it clear that the patent claimed a 'method of optimizing therapeutic efficacy' for treatment of a particular disease; others claimed a 'method of optimizing therapeutic efficacy and reducing toxicity' associated with treatment of a particular disease. Both claims related to a method of medical treatment but were not claims to actual methods of medical treatment. A method of treating a particular disease by using some drugs would be a method of medical treatment because the claimed method would be for *treating* the patient *using* that particular drug. This is not the case here, where the claims concerned, not the actual treatment

---

[85]   *Prometheus Laboratories Inc. v Mayo Collaborative Services* 628 F.3d 1347 (Fed. Cir. 2010).

[86]   Ibid. at 10.

[87]   Ibid. at 14.

[88]   Ibid. at 15.

[89]   Ibid. at 12.

of the patient using 6-thioguanine, but, rather, a method of determining the optimal treatment of the patient by administering drugs to the patient, observing certain conditions, and then comparing those results with standard values. That information would then enable the physician to know whether to increase or decrease the dosage of the drug.

The Federal Circuit in *Prometheus* seemed confused as to the exact scope of the claims. That question, arguably, was the most important one because only after you determine what the claims cover could you sensibly entertain a discussion of whether it fell within the scope of section 101. The Federal Circuit noted that the claimed method related to 'the treatment of a specific disease by administering specific drugs and measuring specific metabolites'.[90] It then spoke of 'the treatment methods claimed in Prometheus's patents'.[91] Confusingly, the Federal Circuit pointed out that the 'asserted claims are in effect claims to *methods of treatment*' but then, later on in the same paragraph, said that 'Prometheus here claimed *methods for optimizing efficacy and reducing toxicity of treatment regimes* for gastrointestinal and non-gastrointestinal autoimmune diseases that utilize drugs providing 6-TG by administering a drug to a subject'.[92] More important, however, is its assertion that the 'invention's purpose to *treat the human body* is made clear in the specification and the preambles of the asserted claims'.[93] Although novelty is not a question to be considered when determining patent-eligibility under section 101, it is instructive to note that if the claims were actually for a method of treating the human body using those drugs, then it would not be novel because the method was already known. What the patentee invented was a method of finding out how to make that medical treatment (treatment using particular drugs) more efficient by, first, increasing its chances of success and, second, reducing the associated side effects. It is clear that, when the wording of the claims is read in the context of what the patentee sought to achieve, there was no intention to claim merely a method of medical treatment.

The Federal Circuit claimed that, 'unlike the clinical test recited in *Grams*, the administering and determining steps in Prometheus's claimed methods are not "merely" data-gathering steps or "insignificant extra-solution activity"; they are part of *treatment regimes for various diseases* using thiopurine drugs'.[94] This cannot be correct, because the claimed method was not directed to a treatment regime at all – it merely provided a method

---

[90]   Ibid. at 15.
[91]   Ibid. at 16.
[92]   Ibid. (emphasis added).
[93]   Ibid. at 17.
[94]   Ibid. at 21 (emphasis added).

by which that treatment regime could be *ascertained*. The treatment regime is the actual dosage that the patient would have to take. This was not found in the claims because it was not directed to a particular dosage regime, but to the method by which each individual dosage regime may be ascertained. In the last paragraph of its 23-page opinion, the Federal Circuit asked what it thought was the critical question, namely: what did the applicant invent? It replied by saying it was 'a series of transformative steps that optimizes efficacy and reduces toxicity of a method of treatment for particular diseases using particular drugs'.[95] This is not in line with its previous assertions that the claimed methods were for treating the human body or were methods of medical treatment. Moreover, this wording correctly puts the *invention* in its proper context – it related to a method of medical treatment but was not actually a method of medical treatment.

(iii) Applying the machine or transformation test The Federal Circuit in *Prometheus* held that the 'machine or transformation test', 'as applied to the [Prometheus] claims . . . leads to a clear and compelling conclusion, viz., that [they] pass muster under [section] 101. They do not encompass laws of nature or preempt natural correlations.'[96] It also held that 'Prometheus's asserted method claims recite a patent-eligible application of naturally occurring correlations between metabolite levels and efficacy or toxicity, and thus do not wholly preempt all uses of the recited correlations'.[97] It continued that: first, the 'steps involve a particular application of the natural correlations' and, second, the 'claims do not preempt all uses of the natural correlations; they utilize them in a series of specific steps.'[98] In addition, the Federal Circuit claimed that the 'inventive nature of the claimed methods stems not from preemption of all use of these natural processes, but from the application of a natural phenomenon in a series of steps comprising particular methods of treatment'.[99] Importantly, it held that '[o]ther drugs might be administered to optimize the therapeutic efficacy of the claimed treatment'.[100]

The Federal Circuit therefore reaffirmed its previous view that the treatment methods claimed in Prometheus's patents satisfied the transformation prong of the 'machine or transformation test', as they transformed an article into a different state or thing and this transformation was central

---

95   Ibid. at 23.
96   Ibid. at 15.
97   Ibid.
98   Ibid.
99   Ibid. at 15–16.
100 Ibid. at 16.

to the purpose of the claimed process.[101] The most crucial part of the reasoning of the Federal Circuit was its opinion that the transformation that occurred in the claimed method was 'of the human body and of its components following the administration of a specific class of drugs and the various chemical and physical changes of the drugs' metabolites that enable their concentrations to be determined'.[102] As a result, it held that there was no need for it to separately determine whether the claims also satisfied the machine prong of the test.[103] What, therefore, is the nature of this so-called transformation? If the claimed method was for a method of medical treatment, then the transformation identified by the Federal Circuit would have been correct because the transformation would be the effect in the human body that cures the patient. The invention, however, was not for the method of treatment – it was for a method of finding the optimum treatment for a particular patient. The so-called transformation, if it existed, was not at all a central feature of the claimed method. The chemical reaction which took place in the human body did not transform anything worthy of patent protection under section 101 because the claimed method was not directed to that aspect of the drug – its ability to treat patients.

The Federal Circuit continued that, after administration of a drug such as AZA or 6-MP, 'the human body necessarily undergoes a transformation. The drugs do not pass through the body untouched without affecting it.'[104] It claimed that the transformation was, in fact, the actual effect on the body after metabolising the artificially administered drugs, which was the sole purpose of administering the drugs. In other words, the drugs were administered to a patient, providing 6-TG, which was thought to be the drugs' active metabolite in the treatment of a disease.[105] This would have been correct if the claimed method was for a method of medical treatment whereby the patient was to take certain drugs to treat a particular ailment. That was not the object of the claimed method – for if it were, the claim would lack novelty because, as mentioned above, that fact was already known. What researchers sought to do, and Prometheus did successfully, was to find a way of determining the optimum dosage level of the drug. Usually, this would be applicable generally to everyone and the claimed method would indicate that a particular dosage would have the effect of increasing efficacy and decreasing the toxic side effects. However, in this

---

[101]   Ibid.
[102]   Ibid.
[103]   Ibid.
[104]   Ibid. at 17.
[105]   Ibid.

case, there was not a particular dosage that would apply universally (and the patent did not claim a dosage regime) but the dosage would be patient-specific after analysing the information derived from carrying out the claimed method. Contrary to this view, the Federal Circuit held that the administering step was not merely data-gathering but a significant trans-formative element of Prometheus's claimed methods of treatment that was sufficiently definite to confine the patent monopoly within rather definite bounds.[106] The administering step did not amount to a transformation as it related to a process by which the subject matter of the claimed method was to be achieved. It was a means to an end, not the end in itself!

After noting that not all the claimed methods contained the adminis-tering step, the Federal Circuit explained that this did not diminish the patentability of the claimed methods because the determining step was also transformative and central to the claimed methods. In other words, '[d]etermining the levels of 6-TG or 6-MMP in a subject necessarily involves a transformation'.[107] It seems incredulous, to say the least, that a step, directed at the reader of the specification or the person carrying out the invention, could amount to a transformation. The Federal Circuit did not show how the trick is done! It continued by noting that 'this transfor-mation is central to the purpose of the claims, since the determining step is, like the administering step, a significant part of the claimed method'.[108] What is puzzling about this statement is why the importance of a step to a claimed method should mean that it is transformative. Should not that transformation be shown to exist irrespective of the nature or significance of the step in question? It is true that '[m]easuring the levels of 6-TG and 6-MMP is what enables possible adjustments to thiopurine drug dosage to be detected for optimizing efficacy or reducing toxicity during a course of treatment', but this involves no transformation in the ordinary sense of the word.

In respect of the requirement in *Flook*, as noted above, that the steps must not merely amount to insignificant extra-solution activity, the Federal Circuit held that the 'administering and determining steps are transforma-tive and are central to the claims rather than merely insignificant extra-solution activity'.[109] It continued that the 'crucial error the district court made in reaching the opposite conclusion was failing to recognize that the first two steps of the asserted claims are not merely data-gathering

---

[106] Ibid. at 18.
[107] Ibid.
[108] Ibid. at 19.
[109] Ibid.

steps'.[110] The Federal Circuit agreed with the District Court that the administering and determining steps gather useful data but claimed 'it is also clear that the presence of those two steps in the claimed processes is not "merely" for the purpose of gathering data'.[111] The question then is what really was the function of those two steps in the claimed method? The Federal Circuit replied that the two steps 'are part of a treatment protocol, and they are transformative', claiming 'the administering step provides thiopurine drugs for the purpose of treating disease, and the determining step measures the drugs' metabolite levels for the purpose of assessing the drugs' dosage during the course of treatment'.[112] By the Federal Circuit's own admission, it is clear that the role of the two steps in the claimed method, although important, did not mean that they were transformative.

It then claimed that '[g]iven the integral involvement of the administering and determining steps in Prometheus's therapeutic methods, this case is easily distinguishable from prior cases that found asserted method claims to be unpatentable for claiming data-gathering steps and a fundamental principle',[113] citing *In re Grams*. I am not altogether sure how *In re Grams* was distinguishable from the claims at issue. Both decisions considered the same type of claims. The Federal Circuit noted that in *In re Grams*, '[t]he claims did not require the performing of clinical tests on individuals that were transformative – and thus rendering the entire process patentable subject matter – because the tests were just to "obtain data"'.[114] On the contrary, the claimed method in *In re Grams* was to determine whether a patient suffered from a particular abnormality – i.e., a classic diagnostic method. From the information gathered, a conclusion could, therefore, be made as to whether the patient was suffering from a particular abnormality. However, in the instant case, the claim was to determine whether an increase or decrease in the dosage was appropriate for a particular patient. The claimed method did not determine the actual dosage required by the patient – that was to be done by the physician after analysing the information gathered from the claimed method. In the end, the Federal Circuit held that Prometheus's asserted method claims satisfied the pre-emption test as well as the transformation prong of the 'machine or transformation test'.[115]

---

[110] Ibid.
[111] Ibid.
[112] Ibid. at 19–20.
[113] Ibid. at 20.
[114] Ibid.
[115] Ibid. at 23.

(iv)   Natural phenomena   The Federal Circuit was quick to point out, as noted above, that the claimed methods did not encompass laws of nature or pre-empt natural correlations – they involved a particular application of the natural correlations.[116] In other words, the 'method claims recite a patent-eligible application of naturally occurring correlations between metabolite levels and efficacy or toxicity, and thus do not wholly preempt all uses of the recited correlations'.[117] It was of the opinion that it did 'not view the disputed claims as merely claiming natural correlations and data-gathering steps'.[118] The Federal Circuit claimed that 'the administering and determining steps are not insignificant extra-solution activity, and the claims are therefore not drawn merely to correlations between metabolite levels and toxicity or efficacy'.[119] The essence of the claims was that the metabolite level, ascertained through carrying out the claimed method, correlated to the efficacy of the drugs and the toxic side effects of using the drugs. It is that correlation that enabled the physician to determine whether an increase or decrease in the dosage of the drug was needed for a particular patient.

(v)   Mental step   In addition, the Federal Circuit agreed with the District Court that the final 'wherein' clauses were mental steps and, therefore, not patent-eligible per se.[120] It argued that the claims at issue were not 'simply to the mental steps' and that those subsequent mental steps did not, by themselves, 'negate the transformative nature of prior steps'.[121] The difficulty here was that, as was seen above, a critical element of the claimed method was the correlation that enabled the physician to determine, in respect of information derived from carrying out the test for each patient, whether an upwards or downwards change in the dosage was needed for that particular patient. More importantly, and in addition to this, was the part of the claimed method where the physician is to make a judgement, based on the results, as to whether the dosage for that particular patient should be increased or decreased. This was the basis of the claimed method – i.e., a method of finding the dosage for each patient tested by: first, administering the drug to the patient; and, second, determining the level of 6-thioguanine in the patient. This information is then processed by a physician (the mental step) based on the correlation (part of the laws of nature).

---

[116]   Ibid. at 15.
[117]   Ibid.
[118]   Ibid. at 16.
[119]   Ibid. at 21.
[120]   Ibid.
[121]   Ibid.

The Federal Circuit argued that, when viewed in the proper context, the final step of providing a warning based on the results of the prior steps did not detract from the patentability of Prometheus's claimed methods as a whole.[122] What then would be patentable? Based on the reasoning of the Federal Circuit, it would be the administration and determining aspect of the claim which, as stated above, are, by their nature, hardly, if ever, transformative. The Federal Circuit claimed that, 'contrary to Mayo's assertions, a physician who only evaluates the result of the claimed methods, without carrying out the administering and/or determining steps that are present in all the claims, cannot infringe any claim that requires such steps'.[123] Arguably, the essence of the invention was the ability of the physician, based on the information provided, to be able to determine what alterations, consequently, should be made to the patient's dosage regime. This is not transformation, plain and simple.

The Federal Circuit was of the opinion that, because the 'wherein clauses describe the mental processes used to determine the need to change the dosage levels of the drugs, each asserted claim as a whole was drawn to patentable subject matter'.[124] Contrary to the view of the Federal Circuit, this is but one reason why the claimed method was not drawn to a patentable subject matter; the other was that the claimed method embraced the correlation which was a natural phenomenon. Importantly, the Federal Circuit accepted that, '[a]lthough a physician is not required to make any upward or downward adjustment in dosage during the "warning" step, the prior steps provide useful information for possible dosage adjustments to the method of treatment using thiopurine drugs for a particular subject'.[125] This statement implicitly accepts the point made above that the real purpose of the claimed method was to determine whether a particular patient needed an adjustment in the drugs administered. Notwithstanding this, the Federal Circuit said that '[v]iewing the treatment methods as a whole, Prometheus has claimed therapeutic methods that determine the optimal dosage level for a course of treatment'.[126] If, as argued above, the claimed methods related to a method of determining whether adjustments were needed for specific patients, then the Federal Circuit cannot be correct in saying that they were 'treatment methods'.

---

[122]   Ibid.
[123]   Ibid.
[124]   Ibid. at 22.
[125]   Ibid.
[126]   Ibid.

2 *Association of Molecular Pathology v U.S. Patent and Trademark Office*

(a) The District Court

In *AMP v USPTO*,[127] one of the claimed methods was, essentially, for the identification of a predisposition to breast cancer based on 'analyzing' or 'comparing' the BRCA1 and BRCA2 gene sequences.[128] The District Court pointed out that the claimed process was not limited to any particular method of analysis and did not specify any further action beyond the act of 'analyzing'.[129] The District Court distinguished the first decision of the Federal Circuit in *Prometheus* on the basis that the determining step in that decision was found to be transformative because the action of determining the metabolite levels was itself construed to include the extraction and measurement of metabolite concentrations.[130] However, it argued that, in the instant case, the language of the claims was plain and that the ordinary meanings of 'analyzing' and 'comparing' established that the claimed method was directed to 'the abstract mental processes of "comparing" and "analyzing" gene sequences'.[131] The purpose of the claimed method, it continued, was to detect the germline alteration in the BRCA1 gene. The District Court held that the Federal Circuit in *Prometheus* did not suggest that preparatory physical transformation required for the performance of, but not included in, claims directed to mental processes should be incorporated into the claim for the purpose of the section 101 analysis.[132] As a result, it held that the preparatory transformations relating to obtaining the DNA sequences could not be relied on to satisfy the requirements of section 101[133] and, even if the claims could be construed to include those transformations, it would still not satisfy the 'machine or transformation test' in *In re Bilski*.[134] Applying the reasoning of the decision of the Federal Circuit in *In re Grams*, the District Court held that the isolation and sequencing of DNA from a human sample, even if incorporated in the claimed method, represented nothing more than

---

[127] *Association of Molecular Pathology v U.S. Patent and Trademark Office* (*AMP v USPTO*) US District Court, Southern District of New York, 09 Civ 415, 29 March 2010.

[128] Ibid. at 146.

[129] Ibid. at 137.

[130] Ibid. at 141.

[131] Ibid.

[132] Ibid. at 144–5.

[133] Ibid. at 145.

[134] Ibid. at 147.

data-gathering steps to obtain the DNA sequence information on which to perform the claimed comparison or analysis.[135]

In regard to the claim relating to comparing the growth rate of cells in the absence of a potential cancer therapeutic, the District Court held that it, arguably, recited certain transformative steps, such as the administration of the test compound.[136] However, it further held, the essence of the claim was that it embraced an act of comparing cell growth rates and coming to the conclusion that a slower growth rate of the host cells was indicative of a cancer therapeutic.[137] This, the District Court held, was the scientific method itself for which the claimed method sought patent protection.[138] As such, it held the transformative steps represented nothing more than preparatory, data-gathering steps to obtain growth rate information, which did not render the claimed mental process patentable under section 101.[139]

(b) The Federal Circuit

In relation to the claims to methods of 'comparing' or 'analyzing' BRCA sequences, Lourie J, with whom Moore and Bryson JJ agreed, speaking for the Federal Circuit, concluded that Myriad's claims to 'comparing' or 'analyzing' two gene sequences fell outside the scope of section 101 because they claimed only abstract mental processes.[140] In its view, all but one of Myriad's method claims were directed to patent-ineligible, abstract mental processes, and failed the 'machine or transformation test'.[141] The Federal Circuit noted that the claims recited, for example, a 'method for screening a tumor sample', by 'comparing' a first BRCA1 sequence from a tumour sample and a second BRCA1 sequence from a non-tumour sample, wherein a difference in sequence indicates an altera-tion in the tumour sample.[142] In its view, the claims recited nothing more than the abstract mental steps necessary to compare two different nucleo-tide sequences: look at the first position in a first sequence; determine the nucleotide sequence at that first position; look at the first position in a second sequence; determine the nucleotide sequence at that first position;

---

[135]   Ibid. at 146.
[136]   Ibid. at 148.
[137]   Ibid.
[138]   Ibid. at 149.
[139]   Ibid.
[140]   653 F.3d 1329 (Fed. Cir. 2011). The ideas in this section have been derived, in part, from E. Ventose, 'Patent Protection for the BRCA1 gene and Genetic Diagnostic Methods in the United States' (2012) *Journal of Intellectual Property Law and Practice* 7.
[141]   Ibid. at 1355.
[142]   Ibid. at 1356.

determine if the nucleotide at the first position in the first sequence and the first position in the second sequence are the same or different, wherein the latter indicated an alternation; and repeat for the next position.[143] After citing from the Court's decisions of *Flook, Diehr* and *Bilski*, the Federal Circuit argued that, although the application of a formula or abstract idea in a process might describe patentable subject matter, Myriad's claims did not *apply* the step of comparing two nucleotide sequences in a process; rather, the step of comparing two DNA sequences was the entire process claimed.[144] The Federal Circuit was again pointing out the need for the claims to provide evidence of a practical application in order for it to traverse the patent-eligibility requirement in section 101.

The Federal Circuit held that the method claims, in the instant case, were distinguishable from the claims upheld by the Federal Circuit under section 101 in *Prometheus*, noting that, in that decision, the patents claimed methods for optimising the dosage of thiopurine drugs administered to patients with gastrointestinal disorders.[145] It noted that, in *Prometheus*, the claimed methods included the steps of: (a) 'administering' a thiopurine drug to a subject, and/or (b) 'determining' the drug's metabolite levels in the subject, wherein the measured metabolite levels were compared with predetermined levels to optimise drug dosage. The Federal Circuit claimed that *Prometheus*: first, held that, in addition to the 'administering' step being transformative, the 'determining' step was both transformative and central to the purpose of the claims; second, specifically held that, because the metabolite levels could not be determined by mere inspection, the determining step necessarily required a transformation; and, third, this transformation was not just insignificant extra-solution activity or necessary data-gathering steps, but was central to the claims, because determining the metabolite levels was what enabled the optimisation of drug dosage.[146] However, in its view, the Myriad claims did not include the step of 'determining' the sequence of BRCA genes by, for example, isolating the genes from a blood sample and sequencing them, or any other necessarily transformative step; rather, the comparison between the two sequences could be accomplished by mere inspection alone.[147] As a result, the Federal Circuit held that Myriad's claimed methods of comparing or analysing nucleotide sequences failed to satisfy the 'machine or transformation test', and were instead directed to the abstract mental process of comparing

---

143 Ibid.
144 Ibid.
145 Ibid. at 1357.
146 Ibid.
147 Ibid.

two nucleotide sequences. Therefore, it concluded a patent-eligible process under section 101 could not be claimed.[148]

The plaintiffs argued that the claim for a method of screening a potential cancer therapeutic was directed to the abstract idea of comparing the growth rates of two cell populations and pre-empted a basic scientific principle – that a slower growth rate in the presence of a potential therapeutic compound suggested that the compound was a cancer therapeutic.[149] The Federal Circuit, taking as its starting point the 'machine or transformation test', concluded that the claim included transformative steps, an 'important clue' that it was drawn to a patent-eligible process. It noted that the claim recited a method that comprised the steps of: (1) 'growing' host cells transformed with an altered BRCA1 gene in the presence or absence of a potential cancer therapeutic; (2) 'determining' the growth rate of the host cells with or without the potential therapeutic; and (3) 'comparing' the growth rate of the host cells. The Federal Circuit argued that the claim included more than the abstract mental step of looking at two numbers and 'comparing' two host cells' growth rates.[150] In its view, the claim included: first, the steps of 'growing' transformed cells in the presence or absence of a potential cancer therapeutic, an inherently transformative step involving the manipulation of the cells and their growth medium; and, second, the step of 'determining' the cells' growth rates, a step that also necessarily involved physical manipulation of the cells. It concluded these steps were central to the purpose of the claimed process.[151] The Federal Circuit added that the 'goal of the claim is to assess a compound's potential as a cancer therapeutic, and growing the cells and determining their growth rate is what achieves that goal'.[152]

In addition, the Federal Circuit held that the claim was not so 'manifestly abstract' as to claim only a scientific principle, and not a patent-eligible process, in accordance with the learning in *Research Corp.*[153] In its view the claim did not cover all cells, all compounds or all methods of determining the therapeutic effect of a compound; rather, it was tied to specific host cells transformed with specific genes and grown in the presence or absence of a specific type of therapeutic. Observing that the claim was tied to measuring a therapeutic effect on the cells solely by changes in the cells' growth rate, it concluded that it represented 'functional and

---

[148]   Ibid.
[149]   Ibid.
[150]   Ibid.
[151]   Ibid.
[152]   Ibid. at 1358.
[153]   Ibid.

palpable applications' in the field of biotechnology, thereby satisfying the requirement of patentable subject matter under section 101.[154]

In light of the Court's decision in *Prometheus*, the Court granted *certiorari*, vacated the judgment of the Federal Circuit and remanded the case back to the Federal Circuit for reconsideration.[155]

3   *Classen Immunotherapies, Inc. v Biogen Idec*

(a)   The District Court

The claim in *Classen Immunotherapies Inc. v Biogen Idec*[156] related to a method of determining whether an immunisation schedule affected the incidence or severity of a chronic immune-mediated disorder in a treatment group of mammals, relative to a control group of mammals.[157] In the District Court,[158] Merck argued that the claimed methods were unpatentable because they involved 'thinking about' whether a vaccination schedule reduced the incidence of chronic disease and, therefore, sought to patent an abstract mental process about a natural phenomenon.[159] Classen, on the other hand, argued that they did not claim a scientific truth but, instead, described a method for reducing the incidence of chronic immune-mediated disorders. The District Court stated that the correlation between vaccination schedules and the incidence of immune-mediated disorders was a natural phenomenon,[160] and that the issue was whether the claimed method simply described this correlation.[161] The District Court explained that the claimed method in the '283 patent was for 'a method of determining whether an immunization schedule affects the incidence or severity of a chronic immune-mediated disorder in a treatment group of mammals, relative to a control group of mammals'. In particular, this involved: (a) immunisation of a treatment group; and (b) a comparison of the incidence of chronic immune-mediated disorders in the treatment group relative to a control group.[162] It continued that, although articulated as a process, the '283 patent did not claim a specific technique or technical process

---

[154]   Ibid.

[155]   *Association for Molecular Pathology v Myriad Genetics, Inc* 132 S. Ct. 1794; 182 L. Ed. 2d 613 (2012).

[156]   304 Fed. Appx. 866 (Fed. Cir. 2008).

[157]   Ibid. at 867.

[158]   *Classen Immunotherapies Inc. v Biogen Idec*, 2006 U.S. Dist. LEXIS 98106 (D. Md., Aug. 16, 2006).

[159]   Ibid. at 11.

[160]   Ibid.

[161]   Ibid.

[162]   Ibid.

of testing vaccine safety. It further explained that, since the '283 patent described only a general inquiry of whether the proposed correlation between an immunisation schedule and the incidence of chronic disorders existed, it was indistinguishable from the idea itself and that the applicant sought to patent an unpatentable natural phenomenon.[163] The District Court, therefore, held that it was an attempt to patent an unpatentable natural phenomenon.[164]

In relation to the '139 and '739 patents, the District Court noted that they claimed 'a method of immunizing a mammalian subject' which required: (a) comparing the incidence of immune-mediated disorders in treatment groups with different vaccination schedules; and (b) immunising patients on a schedule identified as low risk.[165] It continued that, although described as a process for immunising 'mammalian subjects', the '139 and '739 patents did not describe a particular vaccine or vaccine schedule; rather, they described 'a process by which different immunization schedules are compared and the schedule which has the lowest correlation to chronic disorders is selected'.[166] The District Court explained that, like the '283 patent, the '139 and '739 patents described little more than an inquiry of the extent of the proposed correlation between vaccines and chronic disorders. It continued that, although the '139 and '739 patents included the active step of immunising patients in accordance with a schedule determined to be low risk, '[i]nsignificant post-solution activity will not transform an unpatentable principle into a patentable process'.[167] As a result, the District Court held that, since the '139 and '739 patents were an indirect attempt to patent the idea that there was a relationship between vaccine schedules and chronic immune-mediated disorders, they were an attempt to patent an unpatentable natural phenomenon.[168]

It might be said that the difficulty with the District Court's decision in *Classen* was that the trial judge made reference to both the natural phenomenon and the mental process as the basis on which he decided the claimed method was not patentable under section 101. At first blush, this argument seems attractive, but the point about the comparing/correlating claims is that the physician would have to go through the mental process of comparing the information and then determining that the correlation exists in the particular case under consideration. After examining the

---

[163] Ibid. at 12.
[164] Ibid.
[165] Ibid.
[166] Ibid.
[167] Ibid., quoting *Diehr*.
[168] Ibid.

information gathered, the physician would then determine whether in light of that information a particular illness exists or, as in the case in *Classen*, determine the optimal immunisation schedule for the patient. However, that determination is based on the physician observing and concluding (the mental process) that a particular correlation exists. In the classic diagnostic method claims, the physician would determine, given particular symptoms, that a particular disease exists – the correlation being the existence of these symptoms and the disease (natural phenomenon). Therefore, the trial judge in *Classen*, arguably, got it right in so far as he appreciated the distinction between the two even though he did not articulate it as such.

(b) The Federal Circuit: first judgment

On appeal, the Federal Circuit, in light of its decision in *In re Bilski*,[169] affirmed the District Court's decision, clarifying that the claims were neither 'tied to a particular machine or apparatus' nor did they 'transform[] a particular article into a different state or thing'.[170] This is not surprising since the Federal Circuit had only recently revisited the issue of the patent-eligible subject matter and the test for determining patentability under section 101 in its *en banc* decision in *In re Bilski*. It, therefore, did not want to have to look at the issue again. However, the Federal Circuit's rejection of the patent, on the basis of its decision *In re Bilski*, did not tell us anything about how it would have arrived at that conclusion in light of the two-pronged test it had only recently accepted therein. In *In re Bilski*, the Federal Circuit had provided a 'definitive test' for determining whether a process was patent-eligible under section 101, namely: a claimed process is directed to patentable subject matter if (a) 'it is tied to a particular machine or apparatus'; or (b) 'it transforms a particular article into a different state or thing'.[171] Under the *In re Bilski* 'machine or transformation test', 'the use of a specific machine or transformation of an article must impose meaningful limits on the claim's scope to impart patent-eligibility' and 'the involvement of the machine or transformation in the claimed process must not merely be insignificant extra-solution activity'.[172] The question of whether this test is the *sole* test for determining patentability has now been considered by the Court in *Bilski* and was examined in the previous chapter.

---

[169] 545 F.3d 943 (Fed. Cir. 2008) (*en banc*).
[170] *Classen* at 867.
[171] *In re Bilski* at 953.
[172] Ibid. at 961–2.

(c) The Federal Circuit: judgment on remand

This first decision of the Federal Circuit in *Classen* was vacated and remanded by the Court, in light of its decision in *Bilski*, back to the Federal Circuit for reconsideration. The Federal Circuit has now done so.[173] At the centre of the decision in *Classen*, as mentioned before, were two claims as summarised by Moore J in her dissent: (a) claim '283 required two steps: (1) *immunising* a group of mammals according to a schedule and then (2) *comparing* the incidence of a chronic immune-mediated disorder in the group to a control group;[174] and (b) whereas '139 and '739 claims required two steps: (1) *compare* the incidence of chronic immune-mediated disease in two groups of mammals who were immunised according to different schedules and then (2) *immunise* a mammal according to the lower-risk schedule.[175] The central question was whether these claims were patent-eligible under section 101. The first Federal Circuit decision, which held the claims unpatentable in 2008, was written by Moore J, with whom Newman and Farnan JJ agreed. In the second Federal Circuit decision (2011), the majority decision was written by Newman J, with whom Rader CJ agreed. However, Moore J dissented while Rader CJ provided some additional views of his own.

Newman J, writing for the majority, claimed that she reviewed the question of eligibility with the Court's guidance in *Bilski* that, rather than adopting categorical rules that might have wide-ranging and unforeseen impacts, exclusions from patent-eligibility should be considered in view of the particular case and applied narrowly.[176] She claimed that, as a result of the Court's decision in *Bilski*, the 'machine or transformation test' was not the sole standard of eligibility for patenting so the Federal Circuit could again review the District Court's decision, with the benefit of the Federal Circuit's analyses of eligibility in *Research Corp*,[177] *Prometheus*[178] and *AMP v USPTO*.[179] After examining some early cases on the interpretation of section 101, she reiterated that '[t]hese principles, based on the statute and elaborated in the common law of patents, continue to be

---

[173] *Classen Immunotherapies Inc. v Biogen Idec* 659 F.3d 1057 (Fed. Cir. 2011). The ideas in this section have been derived, in part, from E. Ventose, 'Patenting Methods of Medical Treatment in the United States' (2012) *Journal of Intellectual Property Law and Practice* 80.

[174] Ibid. at 1076.

[175] Ibid. at 1077–8.

[176] Ibid. at 1059.

[177] 627 F.3d 859 (Fed. Cir. 2010).

[178] 628 F.3d 1347 (Fed. Cir. 2010), cert. granted (June 20 2011).

[179] 653 F.3d 1329 (Fed. Cir. 2011).

reinforced'.[180] After examining the Court's decisions in *Chakrabarty, Diehr* and *Bilski,* she stated that she would follow the Court's lead in the recognition of the separation of the section 101 'categories' of eligible subject matter from the section 102 'conditions' of patentability.[181]

Newman J opined that the District Court held that none of the Classen claims met the threshold under section 101 of eligibility for patenting, reasoning that the method claimed in all three patents included the mental step of reviewing the relevant literature to determine the lower-risk immunisation schedule.[182] She continued that precedent had recognised that the presence of a mental step was not of itself fatal to section 101 eligibility and that the 'infinite variety' of mental and physical activity negates application of a rigid rule of ineligibility. Classen stated that: first, its claims included physical steps of immunisation, and were not entire sets of steps occurring only in the mind; second, the immunisation step was conducted after selection of a lower-risk schedule, as in the '139 and '739 claims, or that immunisation produced information about immunisation effects, as in the '283 claims; and, third, its claims were not directed to an abstract idea like the commodity hedging method in *Bilski.*[183] After noting that the Court in *Bilski* did not define the term 'abstract', and the difficulty of providing such an all-purpose definition, Newman J relied on the Federal Circuit's decision in *Research Corp* for the view that: 'this court also will not presume to define "abstract" beyond the recognition that this disqualifying characteristic should exhibit itself so manifestly as to override the broad statutory categories of eligible subject matter and the statutory context that directs primary attention on the patentability criteria of the rest of the Patent Act.'[184] Applying this, she held that the claims of the '139 and '739 patents were directed to a method of lowering the risk of chronic immune-mediated disorders, including the physical step of immunisation on the determined schedule. In her view, these claims were directed to a specific, tangible application, concluding that the subject matter of these two patents traversed the coarse eligibility filter of section 101.[185] The first question was how this was to be measured. However, Newman J was of the view that claim 1 of the '283 patent claimed the idea of comparing known immunisation results that were, according to the patent, found in the scientific literature but did not require using this information for immunisation

---

[180] *Classen* at 1064.
[181] Ibid. at 1065.
[182] Ibid.
[183] Ibid.
[184] Ibid.
[185] Ibid. at 1066.

purposes.[186] There was no information in the claimed method concerning how it was to be applied to solve a problem or to achieve a given result. This claim, she continued, stood in contrast to the '139 and '739 patents' claims, which included the subsequent step of immunisation on an optimum schedule.[187]

In her view, claim 1 of the '283 patent stated the idea of collecting and comparing known information. She then referred to the Federal Circuit's decision in *AMP v USPTO* for the view that methods that simply collect and compare data, without applying the data in a step of the overall method, might fail to traverse the section 101 filter.[188] The act of comparing and collecting data could be considered as pre-solution steps that are not patentable under section 101. Newman J stated that the '139 and '739 claims were not simply the '283 patent steps in reverse, as the dissent argued, continuing that the 'immunizing' in the '283 patent referred to the gathering of published data, while the immunising of the '139 and '739 patents' claims was the physical implementation of the mental step claimed in the '283 patent. Noting that the '283 patent merely invited the reader to determine the content of existing knowledge, she continued that the '283 claims did not include putting any knowledge gained to practical use, but were directed to the abstract principle that variation in immunisation schedules may have consequences for certain diseases.[189] The claims of the '139 and '739 patents, however, required the further act of immunisation in accordance with a lower-risk schedule, thus moving from abstract scientific principle to specific application. Newman J, therefore, concluded that the immunisation step moved the '139 and '739 claims through the coarse filter of section 101, while the abstraction of the '283 claim was unrelieved by any movement from principle to application.[190]

Newman J rejected Classen's reliance on the Federal Circuit's decision in *Prometheus*, stating that the analogy was inapt because the claims in *Prometheus* were for a method of controlling individualised dosages of a specific drug by measuring its metabolic products in the blood of individual patients, while the patents in *Classen* operated on published information to determine general immunisation schedules.[191] The principles applied in *Prometheus*, she continued, supported patent-eligibility in *Classen* that included such transformative steps, but were not relevant to

---

[186]   Ibid. at 1067.
[187]   Ibid.
[188]   Ibid.
[189]   Ibid.
[190]   Ibid. at 1068.
[191]   Ibid.

claims which required no more than referring to known information but did not include immunisation in light of that information. Viewing the representative claims of the patents in *Classen* in accordance with their purported scope, Newman J concluded that the claims of the '139 and '739 patents reasonably met the threshold of section 101 eligibility.[192]

Rader CJ claimed that the patent-eligibility doctrine always had significant unintended implications because patent-eligibility was a 'coarse filter' that excluded entire areas of human inventiveness from the patent system on the basis of judge-created standards.[193] He noted that eligibility restrictions usually engendered a healthy dose of claim-drafting ingenuity by patent claim drafters who devise new claim forms and language that evade the subject-matter exclusions. Rader CJ explained that these evasions added to the cost and complexity of the patent system and might cause technology research to shift to countries where protection was not so difficult or expensive.[194] In his view, careful claim-drafting or new claim forms could often avoid eligibility restrictions and, consequently, eligibility then became a game where lawyers learn ingenious ways to recast technology in terms that satisfy eligibility concerns. He cited two well-known examples of claim-drafting to circumvent eligibility restrictions: the Beauregard claim (United States) and the Swiss-type claim (Europe).[195] Rader CJ was of the view that '[w]hen careful claim drafting or new claim formats avoid eligibility restrictions, the doctrine becomes very hollow' and that '[e]xcluding categories of subject matter from the patent system achieves no substantive improvement in the patent landscape'.[196] In his view, these language games imposed high costs on patent prosecution and litigation and 'the new games can cheat naive inventors out of their inventions due to poor claim drafting'; and '[m]oreover, our national innovation policy takes on characteristics of rewarding gamesmanship'.[197]

Rader CJ argued that, in addition to gamesmanship, eligibility restrictions increased the expense and difficulty in obtaining a patent; accepting that, by creating obstacles to patent protection, the real-world impact was to frustrate innovation and drive research funding to more hospitable locations.[198] He explained that if one nation made patent protection difficult, it would drive research to another, more accommodating, nation;

---

192 Ibid.
193 Ibid. at 1074.
194 Ibid.
195 Ibid.
196 Ibid. at 1074–5.
197 Ibid. at 1075.
198 Ibid.

he was of the opinion that, with some considerable blame on its eligibility doctrines, Europe lost innovation investment in biotechnology to the United States. As a result, Rader CJ argued that the United States became the world leader in biotechnology innovation but cautioned that the tide could turn against the United States too.[199] In his view, the effect of eligibility restrictions could send innovation investment elsewhere, emphasising that perhaps an accommodating clinic in another country would be happy to take the additional funding and opportunity. In concluding, he reiterated that judges should tread carefully when imposing new limits on the protection for categories of human innovation.[200]

Moore J dissented principally on the ground that all the claims at issue were to a fundamental scientific principle so basic and abstract as to be unpatentable subject matter under section 101.[201] She accepted that Classen claimed a monopoly over the scientific method itself, adding that, in *Prometheus*, the Federal Circuit held the asserted claims, which recited a method comprising administering a specific drug to a subject and determining the level of the drug in that subject, were directed to patentable subject matter. Although agreeing with the majority that, notwithstanding both the *Prometheus* and *Classen* claims involved administering a drug (immunising in *Classen*), the analogy between the decisions in *Prometheus* and *Classen* was inapt, Moore J noted the Federal Circuit in *Prometheus* explained that administered drugs did not pass through the body untouched without affecting it, thus the human body necessarily underwent a transformation.[202] It was unfortunate that Moore J accepted the premise of the Federal Circuit's decision in *Prometheus*, namely, the existence of transformative steps in the claimed method, when, as argued above, that seemed non-existent. She explained that the Federal Circuit in *Prometheus* did not stop its analysis at the generality of the transformation concept but distinguished *In re Grams*, holding that the transformative steps in the claims were not merely data-gathering steps or insignificant post-solution activity. In addition, Moore J claimed the Federal Circuit in *Prometheus* concluded that the claims, which were drawn to the administration of specific drugs providing 6-thioguanine to a subject and then measuring specific metabolites, did not pre-empt broadly the use of any natural correlation but, rather, recited specific treatment steps with specific drugs.[203] She was of the view that none of this analysis existed in the

[199]   Ibid.
[200]   Ibid.
[201]   Ibid. at 1077.
[202]   Ibid.
[203]   Ibid.

majority decision in *Classen*, pointing out there was no consideration of the extent of pre-emption by the staggeringly broad and abstract claims. Moore J noted the claims in *Classen* were not directed to any specific treatment steps or drugs or even any specific chronic immune disorder.[204] She rejected the majority's reasoning, asserting that, with all due respect to them, she could see no distinction between the '283 claims and '139 and '739 claims which warranted different treatment.

After noting her summary of the claims (mentioned above), Moore J claimed, '[w]hile [she] confess[es] the precise line to be drawn between patentable subject matter and abstract idea is quite elusive, at least for me, this case is not even close'.[205] She continued that there was virtually no difference between these two claims for the purposes of our section 101 analysis: one involved immunising and then comparing ('283 patent); the other comparing then immunising ('739 patent). The '283 patent, in her view, only claimed the scientific method as applied to the field of immunisation and contained no limitations on the type of drug to immunise with, the schedules that should be used for the immunisation, the type of chronic immune disorder to look for or any limitation on the control group.[206] Moore J claimed that it was harder to imagine a more conceptually abstract claim in the immunisation area: the claims were directed to a thought apart from any concrete realities, specific objects or actual instances. Similarly, she explained that the '139 and '739 patents specified no specific immune disease, drug or schedule: first, these claims covered any kind of comparison between any two schedules, using any drugs and comparing the incidence of any chronic immune disease; and, second, after the user performed this completely abstract mental comparison, the user should then immunise the subject with the drug they choose on the schedule they deemed lowest risk.[207] In her view, these claims did nothing more than suggest that two immunised groups could be compared to determine which one was better.

Citing from *Flook*, *Diehr* and *Bilski*, Moore J stated that, although the line between a patentable 'process' and an unpatentable 'principle' was not always clear, the claims at issue clearly crossed that line, asserting that that Classen sought to pre-empt the field was readily apparent as his claims required only two steps: immunising and comparing.[208] She continued that having discovered a principle – that changing the timing of immunisation

---

204   Ibid.
205   Ibid. at 1078.
206   Ibid.
207   Ibid.
208   Ibid.

may change the incidence of chronic immune-mediated disorders – Classen sought to keep it for himself. The claim to the use of the scientific method to study the incidence of chronic immune-mediated disorders, in her view, would pre-empt the field of study, and would prevent any investigation into any immunogen, known or unknown, any disease, known or unknown, over any period of time.[209] Moore J was of the view that where a patent pre-empted an idea, a basic building block of science, within a field of study, the patent in practical effect was a patent on the idea itself, noting that the intent and effect of the Classen claims was clear: to keep others from exploring the same principle. In other words, nobody else could search for new immunogens, for use of new immunisations, to treat either existing or currently unknown chronic immune-mediated disorders without infringing.[210] Moore J added that, first, Classen's '283 patent was to use the scientific method by immunising groups and comparing results; second, the immunisation step in the '283 patent was nothing more than a data-gathering step necessary to explore the effects of different immunisation schedules; and, third, the '739 patent claim covered the comparison of any two schedules for any drug and chooses the one with lower incidence of any chronic immune disease and then immunises. She reasoned that, therefore, the immunisation step of the '739 patent, like updating the alarm limit in *Flook*, was nothing more than a post-solution activity: the post-solution immunisation did not transform the unpatentable principle – that a correlation existed between vaccination schedules and incidence of chronic immune disease – into a patentable process.[211]

She was of the view that: first, the fact that the claimed method was both useful and used tangible tools did not change the ultimate purpose of the claim to monopolise that natural phenomenon and pre-empt the field of study; and, second, nor did the fact that someone must carry out the immunisation to trigger the natural response which was subsequently compared with the control group.[212] Moore J claimed that inventors, like Classen, were not without incentives to innovate in this area, stating that he could claim: first, a method of treating a chronic immune-mediated disorder by using a new and specific immunisation schedule; second, new therapeutic immunogens which were identified as potential compounds of interest; or, third, a specific testing method to assay and explore his new discovery. In her view, Classen did none of these but, instead, claimed the

---

[209]   Ibid. at 1079.
[210]   Ibid.
[211]   Ibid.
[212]   Ibid. at 1080.

study of and merely compared whether the timing of immunisation affects chronic immune-mediated disorders.[213] Observing that Classen sought to monopolise the process of discovery itself, albeit limited to a single field, she stated that the American patent system does not award a monopoly that precludes others from using the basic procedures of scientific investigation to study the same phenomenon. Moore J pointed out that where 'the claims so clearly offend the constitutional imperative to promote the useful arts, where they preempt all application of a principle or idea, it is entirely appropriate to hold them unpatentable subject matter before reaching anticipation, obviousness, or any other statutory section that might also prove invalidity'.[214]

Moore J rejected the majority's reliance on the Federal Circuit's decision in *Research Corp* (that if the specified method is 'functional and palpable', the claims are drawn to statutory subject matter), questioning: first, how does one determine whether any given method or claim is 'functional' or 'palpable'?; and second: is this a return to the rejected notions of 'useful, concrete, and tangible'?[215] She further rejected the majority's reasoning, stating that: first, it 'points to nothing else in the claims and does not at all consider how these staggeringly broad claims will preempt the entire immunization field from considering any two schedules prior to immunizing any patient with any drug – clearly a sweepingly broad principle'; and second, that she could not 'agree that this single physical immunization step makes this principle patentable subject matter'.[216] Moore J explained that '[t]ying an abstract idea to a tangible result or a specific field of endeavor does not make the idea any less abstract', adding that: first, the scientific method is an abstract idea, fundamental to all scientific inquiry, and must be a tool reserved to all men, regardless of its specific application; second, no one is entitled to patent using the scientific method to discover a cure for a newly discovered disease – undeniably a tangible result – merely because they discovered the disease itself; and, third, Classen's claims readily illustrated that linking a natural phenomenon or abstract idea to a useful or practical result was no barrier for a competent patent drafter attempting to monopolise unpatentable subject matter.[217] As a result, she concluded that the Classen claims were directed to unpatentable subject matter.

---

[213]　Ibid.
[214]　Ibid.
[215]　Ibid. at 1081.
[216]　Ibid.
[217]　Ibid.

E   CONCLUSION

The failure of the Federal Circuit in *Prometheus* to fully grasp the nature of the claims at issue and accepting that they were methods of medical treatment means that patentees could claim patent protection for any claim as long as it is related to a method of medical treatment. Patent eligibility should not be determined on the basis of the usefulness of the invention, but, rather, whether it meets the statutory criteria. In any event, the claims at issue in *Prometheus* arguably were not really diagnostic methods at all. It was then left to the Federal Circuit's next decision in *Classen*, which involved similar claims, to either follow *Prometheus* or completely reject the application of the 'machine or transformation test' to medical diagnostic claims.

The decision by the majority of the Federal Circuit in *Classen* shows, yet again, that the Court should rein in to finally determine the scope of medical and diagnostic method patents in the United States. The majority accepts a tenuous basis for distinguishing the '139 and '739 patents' claims from the '283 patent claims, finding the former patentable while holding the latter unpatentable. This is laid bare by Moore J, dissenting, who found that the claims were indistinguishable and unpatentable under section 101. The decision of the Federal Circuit in *AMP v USPTO*, which related to a classic diagnostic method, determined the real test of the patentability of medical diagnostic claims. In that decision, the Federal Circuit made it clear that genetic diagnostic methods that simply contain abstract mental steps necessary to compare two different nucleotide sequences would not be patent-eligible; whereas those which contain transformative steps central to the purpose of the claimed process would be patentable under section 101. However, the real difficulty remains with the methods claims, in particular, determining whether such claims are transformational at all.

Since the issue of medical patents has produced inconsistent decisions in the Federal Circuit, the Court has clarified some of the teething issues in *Prometheus*, which was decided in March 2012. This decision of the Court will be considered in the next chapter. Fortunately, the Court had a myriad of Federal Circuit decisions, namely *Prometheus* (two decisions), *Classen* ('two' decisions) and *AMP v USPTO* to assist it in determining whether medical methods, medical diagnostic methods, genetic diagnostic methods and treatment or dosage regimes are patentable under section 101 of the Patent Act. It will be no surprise if *Classen* and *AMP* are also decided by the Court by June 2013.

6. Consideration by the Supreme Court

A   INTRODUCTION

As was seen in Chapter 5, in the 1980s the Federal Circuit had initially considered the issue of patent protection for diagnostic and medical treatment methods without much success. In the main, they ruled that such methods were not patentable under section 101. The Court's decisions in *Benson*, *Flook* and *Diehr* provided some guidance on the issue of patent-eligibility which were used by the CCPA and the Federal Circuit, especially in recent years, to determine the question of whether patent protection should be provided for medical methods, in particular, diagnostic methods. None of these decisions reached the Court. However, one unremarkable decision which raised the question of patent protection for diagnostic methods only tangentially reached the Court. That decision was *Laboratory Corporation*,[1] where the Court, although granting *certiorari* to determine the issue of whether a diagnostic method essentially fell afoul of section 101, rejected the claim without deciding the issue. However, a dissent by Breyer J provided an initial view of three members of the Court on the issue of patent protection for medical and diagnostic methods.

Although the dissenting opinion in *Laboratory Corporation* has no precedential value, it was, nonetheless, used by some District Courts to justify rejecting similar claims as unpatentable subject matter, but the Federal Circuit made clear that that opinion has little value. The reliance on *Laboratory Corporation* was, however, short-lived since the Court has handed down its decision in *Prometheus*.[2] This decision is now the leading authority on patenting medical and diagnostic methods in the United States. However, of the three dissenters in *Laboratory Corporation*,

---

[1]   548 U.S. 124, 126 S. Ct. 2921, 165 L. Ed. 2d 399 (2006) (dismissing the writ of *certiorari* as improvidently granted). Twenty-one amicus briefs were filed, including the Intellectual Property Owners Association, IBM, the Public Patent Foundation, AARP and the American Heart Association.

[2]   *Mayo Collaborative Services v Prometheus Labs* 132 S. Ct. 1289; 182 L. Ed. 2d 321 (2012).

namely, Breyer, Souter and Stevens JJ, only Breyer J is still on the Court. After deciding *Prometheus*, the Court remanded *Classen* and *AMT v USPTO* back to the Federal Circuit for reconsideration in light of its decision in *Prometheus*. However, *AMT v USPTO* raises the issue of not only genetic diagnostic method patents but also gene (product) patents, so it is likely that the Court will soon also hear that decision.

B   A DISSENTING VIEW

The question of whether a diagnostic method was patentable arose directly for consideration by the Court in *Laboratory Corporation*. In that decision, the jury found that the claimant (LabCorp) had indirectly infringed the defendant's patent (the '658 patent). The '658 patent claimed a method for detecting cobalamin and folate deficiency. Both are B vitamins and their deficiency can cause various illnesses in the human body, namely, vascular disease, cognitive dysfunction, birth defects and cancer. However, if this deficiency is detected at an early stage, vitamin B supplements can treat this deficiency. University Patents Inc. developed a test which was able to identify the deficient vitamin and it formed the basis of the '658 patent, whose claims read as follows:

> 13. A method for detecting a deficiency of cobalamin or folate in warm-blooded animals comprising the steps of: assaying a body fluid for an elevated level of total homocysteine; and correlating an elevated level of total homocysteine in said body fluid with a deficiency of cobalamin or folate.

The '658 patent was eventually licensed to LabCorp, which originally performed total homocysteine assays, but then switched to a total homocysteine assay developed by another company. Metabolite sued LabCorp for infringement and succeeded in the District Court, which held that LabCorp infringed the '658 patent and that the claims at issue were not invalid.

On appeal, the Federal Circuit, accepting a broad construction of the patent, agreed with the District Court's conclusion that 'correlate' meant 'to establish a mutual or reciprocal relationship between'.[3] It noted that the mutual relationship was established when an elevated homocysteine level was present, whereas a reciprocal relationship was established when

---

[3]   *Metabolite Labs Inc. v Laboratory Corporation of America Holdings* 370 F.3d 1354, 1364 (Fed. Cir. 2004).

an elevated homocysteine level was absent.[4] LabCorp argued that the claim should only cover a mutual relationship because 20 per cent of the assays correlated elevated levels of homocysteine to diagnose a B vitamin deficiency.[5] The Federal Circuit accepted that claim 13 was only infringed when the assays performed by LabCorp revealed elevated levels of homocysteine and that approximately 80 per cent of the assays LabCorp processed revealed unelevated levels of homocysteine.[6] However, the majority of the Federal Circuit vacated the jury's verdict that the assays resulting in unelevated levels of homocysteine infringed claim 13, and further vacated and remanded the jury's verdict on damages for recalculation based only on those infringing assays that demonstrated elevated levels of homocysteine.[7]

LabCorp petitioned the Court to review the decision of the Federal Circuit. The Court invited the government to brief on the following question:

> Respondent's patent claims a method for detecting a form of vitamin B deficiency, which focuses upon a correlation in the human body between elevated levels of certain amino acids and deficient levels of vitamin B. The method consists of the following: First, measure the level of the relevant amino acids using any device, whether the device is, or is not, patented; second, notice whether the amino acid level is elevated and, if so, conclude that a vitamin B deficiency exists. Is the patent invalid because one cannot patent 'laws of nature, natural phenomena, and abstract ideas'? *Diamond v. Diehr*, 450 U.S. 175, 185 (1981)

The Solicitor-General, in his reply, accepted that claim 13 described more than a natural phenomenon, since it did not merely recite a natural relationship between elevated total homocysteine and deficiencies in the B vitamins, but also claimed a diagnostic method based on that relationship – assaying for total homocysteine in order to determine cobalamin or folate deficiency.[8] He claimed that whether the application of the natural relationship was patentable might depend on facts that were not well developed in the record, particularly because the lower courts did not discuss the validity of claim 13 under the natural phenomenon doctrine.[9] The Solicitor-General stated that the natural relationship between elevated homocysteine and deficiencies in the B vitamins was an unpatentable

---

[4] Ibid.

[5] Ibid.

[6] Ibid.

[7] Ibid.

[8] Brief for the United States as Amicus Curiae at 8, *Laboratory Corporation v Metabolite Labs*, 126 S. Ct. 2921 (No. 04-607), 2005 WL 3533248.

[9] Ibid. at 9.

'principle in natural philosophy or physical science'.[10] Consequently, he urged the Court to deny the petition.[11] The Court rejected his advice and granted review only in respect of question 3 in the petition, namely:[12]

> Whether a method patent setting forth an indefinite, undescribed, and non-enabling step directing a party simply to 'correlat[e]' results can validly claim a monopoly over a basic scientific relationship used in medical treatment such that any doctor necessarily infringes the patent merely by thinking about the relationship after looking at a test result.

Notwithstanding the Court had granted *certiorari* to decide the question of whether a method patent directing a party simply to 'correlate' test results could validly claim a monopoly over a basic scientific relationship such that any doctor necessarily infringes the patent merely by thinking about the relationship after looking at a test result, it decided not to rule on the question, but dismissed the writ as improvidently granted.[13]

Breyer J, along with Souter and Stevens JJ, dissented, arguing that the Court should have ruled on the question because those who engaged in medical research, who practised medicine and who, as patients, depended upon proper health care, might well benefit from the Court's authoritative answer.[14] He then proceeded to examine the principles emerging from the leading Court decisions of *Benson*, *Flook* and *Diehr*, namely, excluded from patent protection are 'laws of nature, natural phenomena, and abstract ideas'.[15] In his view, this principle was grounded not 'in any claim that "laws of nature" are obvious, or that their discovery is easy, or that they are not useful', but, '[r]ather, the reason for the exclusion is that sometimes too much patent protection can impede rather than "promote the Progress of

---

[10]   Ibid. at 10.

[11]   Ibid. at 5.

[12]   The questions were: 1. Whether liability can be imposed for wilfully inducing patent infringement under 35 U.S.C. section 271(b) based solely on evidence that a party has disseminated a basic scientific fact to others. 2. Whether an express limitation in a patent claim can be ignored so as to allow the patent to cover the exact opposite of what was claimed. 3. Whether a method patent setting forth an indefinite, undescribed and non-enabling step directing a party simply to 'correlat[e]' test results can validly claim a monopoly over a basic scientific relationship used in medical treatment such that any doctor necessarily infringes the patent merely by thinking about the relationship after looking at a test result (Petition for Writ of Certiorari, Metabolite, 126 S. Ct. 2921 (No. 04-607), 2004 WL 2505526.).

[13]   *Laboratory Corporation* at 125.

[14]   Ibid. at 126.

[15]   Ibid.

Science and useful Arts," the constitutional objective of patent and copyright protection'.[16] Breyer J claimed that, contrary to the first assertion, 'research into such matters may be costly and time-consuming; monetary incentives may matter; and the fruits of those incentives and that research may prove of great benefit to the human race'.[17] He explained that '[t]he problem arises from the fact that patents do not only encourage research by providing monetary incentives for invention',[18] but that, '[s]ometimes their presence can discourage research by impeding the free exchange of information, for example by forcing researchers to avoid the use of potentially patented ideas, by leading them to conduct costly and time-consuming searches of existing or pending patents, by requiring complex licensing arrangements, and by raising the costs of using the patented information, sometimes prohibitively so'.[19] He emphasised that '[p]atent law seeks to avoid the dangers of overprotection just as surely as it seeks to avoid the diminished incentive to invent that underprotection can threaten' and that '[o]ne way in which patent law seeks to sail between these opposing and risky shoals is through rules that bring certain types of invention and discovery within the scope of patentability while excluding others'.[20] He concluded by claiming that: first, phenomena of nature, though just discovered, mental processes and abstract intellectual concepts are the basic tools of scientific and technological work (*Benson*);[21] and, second, treating 'fundamental scientific principles as "part of the storehouse of knowledge" and manifestations of laws of nature as "free to all men and reserved exclusively to none"' (*Funk Bros.*),[22] the Court was reflecting 'a basic judgment that protection in such cases, despite its potentially positive incentive effects, would too often severely interfere with, or discourage, development and the further spread of useful knowledge itself'.[23]

As was mentioned above, one of the first questions to be answered before one could determine whether claims are excluded from patent protection under the criteria accepted in *Benson*, *Flook* and *Diehr*, is: what exactly do the claims cover? In other words, one must determine the inventive concept embodied in the claims. It is only then that could one determine whether the *invention* is patent-eligible. In the instant case, the question would be:

---

[16] Ibid. at 126–7.
[17] Ibid. at 126.
[18] Ibid. at 127.
[19] Ibid.
[20] Ibid.
[21] Ibid.
[22] Ibid. at 127–8.
[23] Ibid. at 128.

what, then, did the respondents invent? As noted above, the claims were for a method for detecting a deficiency of cobalamin or folate in warm-blooded animals comprising two steps, namely: first, assaying a body fluid for an elevated level of total homocysteine; and, secondly, correlating an elevated level of total homocysteine in said body fluid with a deficiency of cobalamin or folate.[24] In respect of the claimed method at issue, Breyer J claimed, '[t]he question before us is whether claim 13 . . . is invalid in light of the "law of nature" principle'.[25] He noted that the Federal Circuit agreed with the District Court that claim 13's 'correlating' step simply meant 'relating total homocysteine levels to cobalamin or folate deficiency, a deficiency in both, or a deficiency in neither'. [26] Breyer J further noted that the Federal Circuit 'did not address LabCorp's argument that, *if so construed*, claim 13 must be struck down as an improper effort to obtain patent protection for a law of nature'.[27]

He rejected the 'technical procedural reason for not [answering the question posed], namely, that LabCorp did not refer in the lower courts to [section] 101 of the Patent Act, which sets forth subject matter that is patentable, and within the bounds of which the "law of nature" principle most comfortably fits'.[28] Additionally, Breyer J argued that '[t]here is also a practical reason for not [answering the question posed], namely, that [the Court] might benefit from the views of the Federal Circuit, which did not directly consider the question'.[29] He claimed that, '[n]onetheless, stronger considerations argue for our reaching a decision', namely: first, 'the technical procedural objection is tenuous' as 'LabCorp argued the essence of its present claim below' when it, *inter alia*, 'explicitly stated in its petition for *certiorari* that, "if the Court allows the Federal Circuit opinion to stand . . . [respondents] would improperly gain monopolies over basic scientific facts rather than any novel inventions of their own"'.[30] In addition, Breyer J found that he could 'find no good practical reason for refusing to decide the case' because: first '[t]he relevant issue has been fully briefed and argued by the parties, the Government, and 20 *amici*'; second, '[t]he record is comprehensive, allowing us to learn the precise nature of the patent claim, to consider the commercial and medical context (which the parties and *amici* have described in detail), and to become familiar

---

[24]   Ibid. at 129.
[25]   Ibid. at 132.
[26]   Ibid. at 131.
[27]   Ibid. (emphasis in original).
[28]   Ibid. at 132.
[29]   Ibid.
[30]   Ibid. at 133.

with the arguments made in all courts'; third, '[n]either the factual record nor the briefing suffers from any significant gap'; fourth, '[n]o party has identified any prejudice due to our answering the question'; and, fifth, 'there is no indication that LabCorp's failure to cite [section] 101 reflected unfair gamesmanship'.[31] He concluded by noting that '[o]f course, further consideration by the Federal Circuit might help us reach a better decision' because '[l]ower court consideration almost always helps'.[32] However, Breyer J was convinced that 'the thoroughness of the briefing leads me to conclude that the extra time, cost, and uncertainty that further proceedings would engender are not worth the potential benefit'.[33] In addition, he reiterated that he 'believe[d] that important considerations of the public interest – including that of clarifying the law in this area sooner rather than later – argue strongly for our deciding the question presented now'.[34]

On the facts, Breyer J then sought to define the invention claimed by the respondent, as alluded to before. He noted that, '[a]s construed by the Federal Circuit, claim 13 provided those researchers with control over doctors' efforts to use that correlation to diagnose vitamin deficiencies in a patient'.[35] Claim 13 of the patent was based on the discovery that 'an elevated level of homocysteine in a warm blooded animal is correlated with folate and cobalamin deficiencies'.[36] The question for him was: '[d]oes the law permit such protection or does claim 13, in the circumstances, amount to an invalid effort to patent a "phenomenon of nature"?'[37] He conceded that 'the category of non patentable "[p]henomena of nature," like the categories of "mental processes" and "abstract intellectual concepts," is not easy to define'.[38] However, Breyer J was of the opinion that '[a]fter all, many a patentable invention rests upon its inventor's knowledge of natural phenomena; many "process" patents seek to make abstract intellectual concepts workably concrete; and all conscious human action involves a mental process'.[39] This much is true – and the question becomes the method by which the patent claims the *application* of the phenomena of nature. It is the application that constitutes patentable subject matter – not the underlying natural phenomena on which it is based. He continued,

---

[31] Ibid.
[32] Ibid.
[33] Ibid.
[34] Ibid. at 134.
[35] Ibid.
[36] Ibid.
[37] Ibid.
[38] Ibid.
[39] Ibid.

'[n]or can one easily use such abstract categories directly to distinguish instances of likely beneficial, from likely harmful, forms of protection'.[40] He concluded, however, that the instant case was 'not at the boundary' and that: first, '[i]t does not require us to consider the precise scope of the "natural phenomenon" doctrine or any other difficult issue'; and, second, in his view, 'claim 13 is invalid no matter how narrowly one reasonably interprets that doctrine'.[41] In other words, the decision was a clear one in that the Court would not have to determine the precise contours of the 'natural phenomenon' doctrine in order to decide this case.

Breyer J asserted, '[t]here can be little doubt that the correlation between homocysteine and vitamin deficiency set forth in claim 13 is a "natural phenomenon"'.[42] This, he noted, was what the petitioner argued. If the claimed method embraced a 'natural phenomenon', the question of whether it was patentable would turn on whether it applied it or whether the claims simply recited the correlation without more. In addition, he continued that this was also accepted by the Solicitor-General in the following terms: '[t]he natural relationship between elevated total homocysteine and deficiencies in the B vitamins is an unpatentable "principle in natural philosophy or physical science".'[43] Moreover, he claimed that even the respondents conceded the argument as follows: '[t]he correlation between total homocysteine and deficiencies in cobalamin and folate that the Inventors discovered could be considered, standing alone, a "natural phenomenon" in the literal sense: It is an observable aspect of biochemistry in at least some human populations.'[44]

The respondents argued 'that the correlation is nonetheless patentable because claim 13 packages it in the form of a "process" for detecting vitamin deficiency, with discrete testing and correlating steps'.[45] In addition, they claimed that claim 13 was a patentable '*application* of a law of nature' because, considered as a whole, it: first, entailed a physical transformation of matter, namely, the alteration of a blood sample during whatever test was used (citing *Cochrane* and *Benson*);[46] and, second, produced a 'useful, concrete, and tangible result', namely, detection of a vitamin deficiency (citing *State Street Bank*).[47] It is immediately clear that

---

[40] Ibid.
[41] Ibid. at 135.
[42] Ibid.
[43] Ibid.
[44] Ibid.
[45] Ibid.
[46] Ibid. at 135–6 (emphasis added).
[47] Ibid. at 136.

the respondents were trying to ground their claim in the application of the correlation by noting that it comprised a process for determining vitamin deficiency. However, if the correlation alone could produce that result then the claimed method added nothing to the 'natural phenomenon'. It is this recognition that made the applicant further argue that the claimed method entailed a physical transformation, namely, the alteration of the blood sample. This so-called 'transformation' did not form part of the actual claimed method in that it was not part of the actual *treatment* of the patient. It was simply part of the data-gathering step in the multi-step method that characterises diagnostic methods.

Breyer J responded that, in his view, 'the cases to which the respondents refer do not support their claim' *since* '[n]either *Cochrane* nor [*Benson*] can help them because the process described in claim 13 is *not* a process for transforming blood or any other matter'.[48] The actual transformation, in other words, was not the central part of the claimed method.

These arguments by the respondent were rejected by Breyer J, who argued that '[c]laim 13's process instructs the user to (1) obtain test results and (2) think about them', questioning: '[w]hy should it matter if the test results themselves were obtained through an unpatented procedure that involved the transformation of blood?'[49] In his view, '[c]laim 13 is indifferent to that fact, for it tells the user to use *any* test at all' and that, '[i]ndeed, to use virtually any natural phenomenon for virtually any useful purpose could well involve the use of empirical information obtained through an unpatented means that might have involved transforming matter'.[50] Additionally, he claimed that '[n]either *Cochrane* nor [*Benson*] suggests that that fact renders the phenomenon patentable'.[51] Breyer J also argued that '[n]either does the Federal Circuit's decision in *State Street Bank* help the respondents' because '[t]hat case does say that a process is patentable if it produces a "useful, concrete and tangible result" . . . But this Court has never made such a statement and, if taken literally, the statement would cover instances where this Court has held the contrary.'[52] He also claimed the Court has invalidated a patent for: first, 'a system for triggering alarm limits in connection with catalytic conversion despite a similar utility, concreteness, and tangibility' (*Flook*); and, second 'a process that transforms, for computer programming purposes, decimal figures into binary figures – even though the result would seem useful, concrete,

---

48   Ibid. (emphasis in original).
49   Ibid.
50   Ibid.
51   Ibid.
52   Ibid.

and at least arguably (within the computer's wiring system) tangible' (*Benson*).[53]

Breyer J explained that, '[a]t most, respondents have simply described the natural law at issue in the abstract patent language of a "process"', '[b] ut they cannot avoid the fact that the process is no more than an instruction to read some numbers in light of medical knowledge'.[54] The respondents, in his opinion, have merely explained how the natural law worked – they provided information about the correlation and how it worked. He noted that '[o]ne might, of course, reduce the "process" to a series of steps, e.g., Step 1: gather data; Step 2: read a number; Step 3: compare the number with the norm; Step 4: act accordingly. But one can reduce any process to a series of steps.'[55] Although, to be fair to the respondents, the fact that they had reduced the diagnostic method to a series of steps was not, of itself, determinative of the issue of patent-eligibility because, as Breyer J continued, '[t]he question is what those steps embody' and that, in the instant case, 'aside from the unpatented test, they embody only the correlation between homocysteine and vitamin deficiency that the researchers uncovered'.[56] As a result, he concluded that the correlation was an unpatentable 'natural phenomenon' and there was nothing in claim 13 that added anything more of significance.[57]

Breyer J also argued that if he was correct in his conclusion that the patent was invalid, 'then special public interest considerations reinforce[d] [his] view that [the Court] should decide this case': first, '[t]o fail to do so threatens to leave the medical profession subject to the restrictions imposed by this individual patent and others of its kind. Those restrictions may inhibit doctors from using their best medical judgment'; second, 'they may force doctors to spend unnecessary time and energy to enter into license agreements'; third, 'they may divert resources from the medical task of health care to the legal task of searching patent files for similar simple correlations'; and, fourth, 'they may raise the cost of health care while inhibiting its effective delivery'.[58] Breyer J continued that, even if he was wrong in relation to the patent-eligibility of the claims at issue, 'it still would be valuable to decide this case' because: first, 'doing so would help diminish legal uncertainty in the area, affecting a "substantial number of patent claims"'; second, '[i]t would permit those in the medical profession

---

53   Ibid. at 137.
54   Ibid.
55   Ibid.
56   Ibid. at 137–8.
57   Ibid. at 138.
58   Ibid.

better to understand the nature of their legal obligations'; and, third, '[i]t would help Congress determine whether legislation is needed. Cf. 35 U.S.C. [section] 287(c) (limiting liability of medical practitioners for performance of certain medical and surgical procedures).'[59] He then concluded that '[i] n either event, a decision from this generalist Court could contribute to the important ongoing debate, among both specialists and generalists, as to whether the patent system, as currently administered and enforced, adequately reflects the "careful balance" that "the federal patent laws . . . embod[y]".'[60]

C A UNANIMOUS OPINION

1 Introduction

It might be recalled that the claim under consideration by the Court in *Prometheus* was for a method of optimising therapeutic efficacy for treatment of an immune-mediated gastrointestinal disorder. The main claim of the invention was that the blood levels of certain metabolites of some thiopurine drugs used for treatment of immune-mediated gastrointestinal disorders correlate with toxic side effects of the thiopurine drugs. One typical claim was as follows:

> A method of optimizing therapeutic efficacy for treatment of an immune-mediated gastrointestinal disorder, comprising: (a) administering a drug providing 6-thioguanine to a subject having said immune-mediated gastrointestinal disorder; and (b) determining the level of 6-thioguanine in said subject having said immune-mediated gastrointestinal disorder, wherein the level of 6-thioguanine less than about 230 pmol per 8x108 red blood cells indicates a need to increase the amount of said drug subsequently administered to said subject and wherein the level of 6-thioguanine greater than about 400 pmol per 8x108 red blood cells indicates a need to decrease the amount of said drug subsequently administered to said subject.

As mentioned in the previous chapter, the District Court in *Prometheus* held that the patents claimed the correlations between certain thiopurine drug metabolite levels and therapeutic efficacy and toxicity. As a result, it found that these correlations were natural phenomena and not patentable inventions because the correlations resulted from a natural body process.[61]

---

[59] Ibid.
[60] Ibid.
[61] Invalidity Opinion, 2008 WL 878910 at 9.

On appeal, the Federal Circuit in *Prometheus* held that the claims at issue satisfied the 'machine or transformation test' and were, therefore, patent-eligible.[62] The Federal Circuit, in its second decision, on reconsideration, affirmed its 2009 decision, holding that the 'machine or transformation test', as applied to the Prometheus claims, led to a clear and compelling conclusion that they passed muster under section 101, adding that they did not encompass laws of nature or pre-empt natural correlations.[63] Judge Moore, dissenting, argued that the claims did nothing more than suggest that two immunised groups be compared to determine which one was better and, after citing from *Chakrabarty*, *Diehr* and *Bilski*, held that, consequently, they were unpatentable under section 101.

2   The Opinion of the Court in *Prometheus*

(a)   Rationale for the exceptions

Breyer J, speaking for a unanimous Court, noted that section 101 of the Patent Act contained an important implicit exception for the laws of nature, natural phenomena and abstract ideas, citing, *inter alia*, *Diehr*, *Bilski* and *Chakrabarty*.[64] Breyer J had delivered the opinion of the three dissenting justices in *Laboratory Corporation*. The Court claimed that the monopolisation of the basic tools of scientific and technological work, namely, phenomena of nature, mental processes and abstract intellectual concepts (all of which are not patentable), through the grant of a patent, might tend to impede innovation more than it would tend to promote it. In other words, this was the rationale for this implicit exception.[65] Noting that too broad an interpretation of this exclusionary principle could evis-cerate patent law (because all inventions at some level embody, use, reflect, rest upon or apply laws of nature, natural phenomena or abstract ideas), the Court claimed that it was the *application* of the implicit exceptions that was key. In its opinion, to transform effectively an unpatentable law of nature into a patenteligible application of such a law, one must do more than simply state the law of nature while adding the words 'apply it'.[66] The Court was of the view that upholding these patents would risk dispropor-tionately tying up the use of the underlying natural laws, and inhibit their use in the making of further discoveries. Two clear points were being made by the Court: first, patent protection for these basic tools of scientific and

---

[62]   581 F.3d 1336 (Fed. Cir. 2009).
[63]   628 F.3d 1347 (Fed. Cir. 2010).
[64]   132 S. Ct. 1289; 182 L. Ed. 2d 321 (2012) at 1.
[65]   Ibid. at 2.
[66]   Ibid. at 3.

technological work would impede innovation because future inventors would not be able to use these freely without first seeking a licence from the patentee; and, second, these exclusions should be interpreted in a sensible way since all inventions, at some level, involve such laws of nature, natural phenomena or abstract ideas. To distinguish between the patentable and the unpatentable invention, the court must focus on and isolate the application of the laws of nature, natural phenomena or abstract ideas. Only the applications of these are patentable, because they would tie up the use of those underlying laws and, thereby, impede innovation.

The Court explained that its jurisprudence has repeatedly emphasised a concern that patent law should not inhibit further discovery by improperly tying up the future use of laws of nature. This was the key to the jurisprudence of the Court in this area. Citing statements from *Bilski*, *Benson* and *Flook*, it noted that these statements reflected the fact that, even though rewarding with patents those who discovered new laws of nature and the like might well encourage their discovery, those laws and principles, considered generally, were 'the basic tools of scientific and technological work'. The Court, although accepting that it was the function of patent law to reward discoveries, still felt that those basic tools of scientific and technological work should not form the basis of a patent. As a result, the Court cautioned that there was a danger that the grant of patents that tied up their use would inhibit future innovation premised upon them, and that this danger became acute when a patented process amounted to no more than an instruction to 'apply the natural law', or otherwise foreclosed more future invention than the underlying discovery could reasonably justify. The rationale for this was that such basic tools were building blocks of most inventions, depending on the level of abstractness at which they were viewed. If this is correct then an invention which simply claims one or more of those basic tools would preclude other inventors from either also patenting that same basic tool or using it, however tangential, in a future invention. The patentee of this basic tool would, therefore, get a patent monopoly over all inventions, however created, which applied that basic tool.

(b) Guiding principles
The Court said that the patent claims at issue covered processes that helped doctors who used thiopurine drugs to treat patients with auto-immune diseases that determined whether a given dosage level was too low or too high.[67] In its view, the claims purported to apply natural laws

---

[67] Ibid. at 3.

describing the relationships between the concentration in the blood of certain thiopurine metabolites and the likelihood that the drug dosage would be ineffective or induce harmful sideeffects. The claimed method was therefore aimed at producing information that enabled the physician to decide on the optimum treatment for a particular patient. The question for the Court was whether the claimed processes transformed these unpatentable natural laws into patenteligible *applications* of those laws.[68] The Court was of the opinion that the following principles may be gleaned from the Court's jurisprudence under section 101: first, they warn against interpreting patent statutes in ways that make patent-eligibility depend simply on the draftsman's art without reference to the principles underlying the prohibition against patents for natural laws (citing *Flook*); second, they warn against upholding patents which claim processes that too broadly pre-empt the use of a natural law (citing *Benson*);[69] third, they insist that a process that focuses upon the use of a natural law should also contain other elements or a combination of elements (sometimes referred to as an 'inventive concept') sufficient to ensure that the patent, in practice, amounts to significantly more than a patent upon the natural law itself (citing *Flook* and *Bilski*). Applying these principles, the Court held that the process claims at issue did not satisfy these conditions (and were, therefore, unpatentable), in particular, the steps in the claimed processes (apart from the natural laws themselves) that involved well-understood, routine, conventional activity previously engaged in by researchers in the field.[70] It also held that upholding the patents would risk disproportionately tying up the use of the underlying natural laws, inhibiting their use in the making of further discoveries. Two points are worthy of note: the first is the Court was making it plain that the routine activities engaged in by physicians should not be patent-eligible. But, arguably, this should relate not to patentability under section 101 of the Patent Act, but, rather, to section 102, which deals with novelty; second, the Court emphasised that such patents risk preventing further innovation that made use of such underlying natural laws.

(c) The claims at issue

The Court claimed that the case before it lay at the intersection of these basic principles; namely, it concerned patent claims covering processes that help doctors who use thiopurine drugs to treat patients with autoimmune

---

68 Ibid.
69 Ibid.
70 Ibid. at 4.

diseases determine whether a given dosage level was too low or too high.[71] The claimed method, as mentioned in the previous chapter, was not a method of medical treatment since it was not directed at the treatment of the patient per se. It was simply a method of determining the correct dosage for the patient; it did not even purport to claim an actual dosage to be administered to patients generally or a specific patient. What it sought to do was to provide information to the physician, who would then make the decision as to whether to reduce or increase the amount of the drugs administered to the patient to achieve the optimum result. Arguably, like patent protection on dosages regimes, it provides information but, unlike these, it is the physician who has ultimate responsibility in determining the actual dosge for the patient that would result in some positive therapeutic benefit.

It opined that the patents at issue concerned the use of thiopurine drugs in the treatment of autoimmune diseases, such as Crohn's disease and ulcerative colitis, explaining further that when a patient ingests a thiopurine compound, his body metabolises the drug, causing metabolites to form in his bloodstream.[72] The Court noted that, because the way in which people metabolise thiopurine compounds varies, the same dose of a thiopurine drug affected different people differently, and it had been difficult for doctors to determine whether for a particular patient a given dose was too high, risking harmful side effects, or too low, and so likely ineffective. It continued that, at the time the discoveries embodied in the patents were made, scientists already understood that the levels in a patient's blood of certain metabolites, including, in particular, 6-thioguanine and its nucleotides (6–TG) and 6-methyl-mercaptopurine (6–MMP), were correlated with the likelihood that a particular dosage of a thiopurine drug could cause harm or prove ineffective.[73] Therefore, there was nothing novel about the discovery of the correlation between the existence in the patient's blood of certain metabolites with the success or otherwise of a particular dosage of a thiopurine drug. The Court pointed out that those in the field did not know the precise correlations between metabolite levels and likely harm or ineffectiveness; however, the patent claims at issue set forth processes embodying researchers' findings that identified these correlations with some precision.[74] The patent, therefore, was not for the actual precise correlations but the process for determining them. A patent

---

[71] Ibid.
[72] Ibid.
[73] Ibid.
[74] Ibid. at 5.

for the precise ones were, presumably, not sought because the nature of the patent was for personalised medicine and the precise correlation would be patient specific and, therefore, a patent on this would not be possible. The patent merely provided the physician with more information about how the correlation worked. It was then for the physician to use that information the best way he saw fit to treat his patient. Therefore, it is highly unlikely that the provision of information alone, without any application of that information to treat the patient (as in the instant case), would be worthy of patent protection under section 101.

The Court explained that Prometheus's patents set forth laws of nature – namely, relationships between concentrations of certain metabolites in the blood and the likelihood that a dosage of a thiopurine drug will prove ineffective or cause harm.[75] It explained that: first, while it took a human action (the administration of a thiopurine drug) to trigger a manifestation of this relation in a particular person, the relation itself existed in principle apart from any human action; and, second, the relation was a consequence of the ways in which thiopurine compounds were metabolised by the body – entirely natural processes. Therefore, it held that a patent that simply described that relation set forth a natural law.[76] The question for the Court was whether the claims did significantly more than simply describe these natural relations. In other words: did the patent claims add *enough* to their statements of the correlations to allow the processes they described to qualify as patenteligible processes that *applied* natural laws?[77] In its view, the answer to that question was no. This much was clear since the patent was a method for determining whether the correlation existed in a particular patient's case. It achieved nothing else. However, the information gathered was important because it enabled the physician to make the decision on whether an increase or decrease in the dose was required for that particular patient.

The Court reiterated that if a law of nature is not patentable, then neither is a process reciting a law of nature, unless that process has additional features which provide practical assurance that the process is more than a drafting effort designed to monopolise the law of nature itself.[78] It explained that a patent, for example, could not simply recite a law of nature and then add the instruction 'apply the law'. Therefore:[79]

---

[75]   Ibid. at 8.
[76]   Ibid.
[77]   Ibid. at 8–9.
[78]   Ibid. at 9.
[79]   Ibid.

Einstein, we assume, could not have patented his famous law by claiming a process consisting of simply telling linear accelerator operators to refer to the law to determine how much energy an amount of mass has produced (or vice versa). Nor could Archimedes have secured a patent for his famous principle of flotation by claiming a process consisting of simply telling boat builders to refer to that principle in order to determine whether an object will float.

In its view, the claimed process told doctors interested in the subject about the correlations that the researchers discovered, recited: an 'administering' step, a 'determining' step, and a 'wherein' step; however, these additional steps were not themselves natural laws but neither were they sufficient to transform the nature of the claim.[80] The claimed method did nothing more than explain, through a series of steps, how the correlation worked. The Court opined that: first, the 'administering' step simply referred to the relevant audience, namely, the doctors who treat patients with certain diseases with thiopurine drugs; second, the 'wherein' clauses simply told a doctor about the relevant natural laws, at most adding a suggestion that he should take those laws into account when treating his patient (in other words, these clauses tell the relevant audience about the laws while trusting them to use those laws appropriately where they are relevant to their decision-making);[81] and, third, the 'determining' step told the doctor to determine the level of the relevant metabolites in the blood, through whatever process the doctor or the laboratory wished to use.[82] It noted that: first, as the patents stated, methods for determining metabolite levels were well known in the art; and, second, scientists routinely measure metabolites as part of their investigations into the relationships between metabolite levels and efficacy and toxicity of thiopurine compounds. The Court continued that this last step told doctors to engage in well-understood, routine, conventional activity previously engaged in by scientists who work in the field.[83] It cautioned that purely 'conventional or obvious' 'presolution activity' was normally not sufficient to transform an unpatentable law of nature into a patent-eligible application of such a law.

Therefore, the Court held that to consider the three steps as an ordered combination added nothing to the laws of nature that were not already present when the steps were considered separately, continuing that anyone who wanted to make use of these laws must first administer a thiopurine drug and measure the resulting metabolite concentrations, and so the combination amounts to nothing significantly more than an instruction

---

80   Ibid.
81   Ibid.
82   Ibid. at 10.
83   Ibid.

to doctors to apply the applicable laws when treating their patients.[84] It emphasised that, in summary, the three steps simply told doctors to gather data from which they might draw an inference in light of the correlations.[85] The Court also held that: first, the claims informed a relevant audience about certain laws of nature; second, any additional steps consisted of well-understood, routine, conventional activity already engaged in by the scientific community; and, third, those steps, when viewed as a whole, added nothing significant beyond the sum of their parts taken separately.[86] Consequently, it concluded that the steps were not sufficient to transform the unpatentable natural correlations into patentable applications of those regularities to satisfy section 101 of the Patents Act.

(d)   Confirmation by controlling precedents

The Court asserted that a more detailed consideration of its controlling precedents reinforced its conclusion that the claimed method at issue was unpatentable.[87] It stated that the cases most directly on point were *Diehr* and *Flook*, two cases in which the Court reached opposite conclusions about the patent-eligibility of processes that embodied the equivalent of natural laws. The *Diehr* process (held patent-eligible) related to a method for moulding raw, uncured rubber into various cured, moulded products; the process used a known mathematical equation, the Arrhenius equation, to determine when (depending upon the temperature inside the mould, the time the rubber had been in the mould, and the thickness of the rubber) to open the press.[88] The Court explained that, although in *Diehr* the Court pointed out that the basic mathematical equation, like a law of nature, was not patentable, it found the overall process patent-eligible because of the way the additional steps of the process integrated the equation into the process as a whole.[89] Importantly, it pointed out that in *Diehr* it nowhere suggested that all these steps, or at least the combination of those steps, were in context obvious, already in use or purely conventional.[90] In the Court's opinion, these other steps apparently added to the formula something that, in terms of patent law's objectives, had significance – they transformed the process into an *inventive application* of the formula. It noted that the process in *Flook* (held not patentable) provided a method

---

84   Ibid.
85   Ibid. at 10–11.
86   Ibid. at 11.
87   Ibid.
88   Ibid.
89   Ibid. at 11–12.
90   Ibid. at 12.

for adjusting 'alarm limits' in the catalytic conversion of hydrocarbons.[91] The Court explained that in *Flook* it characterised the claimed process as doing nothing other than providing an unpatentable formula for computing an updated alarm limit, adding that the steps in the claimed process were all 'well known' to the point where, putting the formula aside, there was no 'inventive concept' in the claimed application of the formula.[92]

The Court held that the claims at issue presented a case for patentability that was *weaker* than the (patent-eligible) claim in *Diehr* and *no stronger* than the (unpatentable) claim in *Flook*.[93] In its view, beyond picking out the relevant audience, namely, those who administered doses of thiopurine drugs, the claim simply told doctors to: (1) measure (somehow) the current level of the relevant metabolite; (2) use particular (unpatentable) laws of nature (which the claim set forth) to calculate the current toxicity/inefficacy limits; and (3) reconsider the drug dosage in light of the law. The Court continued that these instructions added nothing specific to the laws of nature other than what was well-understood, routine, conventional activity, previously engaged in by those in the field.[94] Additionally, it pointed out that since they were steps that must be taken in order to apply the laws in question, the effect was simply to tell doctors to apply the law somehow when treating their patients. The Court reasoned that the process in *Diehr* was not so characterised and those in *Flook* were characterised in roughly this way which, in its view, explained the different outcomes on patentability between the two cases.[95]

(e) The laws of nature

The Court pointed out that its decisions have repeatedly emphasised the concern that patent law not inhibit further discovery by improperly tying up the future use of laws of nature.[96] After citing passages from *Benson*, *Flook* and *Bilski*, it claimed that statements in these cases reflected the fact that, even though rewarding with patents those who discover new laws of nature and the like might well encourage their discovery, those laws and principles, considered generally, were the basic tools of scientific and technological work.[97] Consequently, they should not be available as patents, as such. This, in the Court's opinion, means that there was a danger that

---

[91] Ibid.
[92] Ibid. at 13.
[93] Ibid.
[94] Ibid.
[95] Ibid.
[96] Ibid. at 16.
[97] Ibid. at 17.

the grant of patents that tie up their use would inhibit future innovation premised upon them, a danger that would become acute when a patented process amounted to no more than an instruction to 'apply the natural law', or otherwise foreclosed more future invention than the underlying discovery could reasonably justify.[98]

The Court argued that the laws of nature at issue in this case were *narrow* laws that might have limited applications, but accepted that the patent claims that embodied them nonetheless implicated the concern that patent law should not inhibit further discovery by improperly tying up the future use of laws of nature. In its view, the claims simply told a treating doctor to measure metabolite levels and to consider the resulting measurements in light of the statistical relationships they described.[99] They did nothing more than provide the doctor with more information about his patient so as to enable him to better treat that patient. As such, the Court held that, in doing so, they: first, tied up the doctor's subsequent treatment decision whether or not that treatment changed in light of the inference he had drawn using the correlations; and, second, threatened to inhibit the development of more refined treatment recommendations (like that embodied in Mayo's test), that combine Prometheus's correlations with later discovered features of metabolites, human physiology or individual patient characteristics. Importantly too for the Court was that the 'determining' step was set in highly general language that covered all processes that made use of the correlations after measuring metabolites, including later discovered processes that measured metabolite levels in new ways.[100]

However, the Court cautioned that it need not, and did not, decide whether, if the steps at issue were less conventional, these features of the claims would prove sufficient to invalidate them because, in its opinion, the steps added nothing of significance to the natural laws themselves.[101] It explained further that unlike, for example, a typical patent on a new drug or a new way of using an existing drug, the patent claims at issue did not confine their reach to particular applications of those laws. The Court argued that the presence of the basic underlying concern that these patents tied up too much future use of laws of nature simply reinforced its conclusion that the processes described in the patents were not patent-eligible, while eliminating any temptation for the Court to depart from its established case law precedent.[102]

---

98   Ibid.
99   Ibid. at 18.
100   Ibid.
101   Ibid.
102   Ibid. at 18–19.

(f) Other arguments

Other arguments in favour or against protection for the claims at issue were also considered by the Court. The first was that of the Federal Circuit, which, on two occasions, held that the claimed processes were patent-eligible, since they involved transforming the human body by administering a thiopurine drug and transforming the blood by analysing it to determine metabolite levels.[103] The Court responded that: first, the first of these transformations, however, was irrelevant; second, the 'administering' step simply helped to pick out the group of individuals who were likely interested in applying the law of nature; and third, the second step could be satisfied without transforming the blood, should science develop a totally different system for determining metabolite levels that did not involve such a transformation.[104] It then concluded that, regardless, in stating that the 'machine or transformation test' was an 'important and useful clue' to patentability, the Court had neither said nor implied that the test trumped the 'law of nature' exclusion adding that this being so, the test failed in the instant case.[105]

The second, argued by Prometheus, was that because the particular laws of nature that its patent claims embodied were narrow and specific, the patents should be upheld.[106] The Court explained that it was encouraged to draw distinctions among laws of nature based on whether or not they would interfere significantly with innovation in other fields now or in the future.[107] However, it cautioned that the underlying functional concern at issue in the instant case was a relative one: how much future innovation was foreclosed relative to the contribution of the inventor.[108] The Court was of the opinion that: (1) a patent upon a narrow law of nature might not inhibit future research as seriously as would a patent upon Einstein's law of relativity, but the creative value of the discovery was also considerably smaller; (2) even a narrow law of nature (such as the one before the Court) could inhibit future research; and (3) the Court's cases have not distinguished among different laws of nature according to whether or not the principles they embody are sufficiently narrow. In its view, this was understandable because the courts and judges were not institutionally well suited to making the kinds of judgements needed to distinguish among different

---

[103] Ibid. at 19.
[104] Ibid.
[105] Ibid.
[106] Ibid.
[107] Ibid. at 19–20.
[108] Ibid. at 20.

laws of nature.[109] This, it continued, explained why the Court's cases have endorsed a bright-line prohibition against patenting laws of nature, mathematical formulas and the like, which served as a somewhat more easily administered proxy for the underlying 'building-block' concern.

The third was that of the Government, which urged the Court to accept that other statutory provisions, namely, section 102 (novelty), section 103 (obviousness) and section 112 (enabling disclosure) could perform the 'screening function' rather than section 101.[110] If this approach were to be accepted, the Court claimed that it would make the 'law of nature' exception to section 101 patentability a dead letter, adding that this approach was not consistent with prior Court case law. Whilst recognising that, in evaluating the significance of additional steps, the section 101 patent-eligibility inquiry and, perhaps, the section 102 novelty inquiry might sometimes overlap, the Court noted that they need not always overlap.[111] Therefore, it held that to shift the patent-eligibility inquiry entirely to these later sections risked creating significantly greater legal uncertainty, while assuming that those sections could do work that they were not equipped to do. As a result, the Court declined the Government's invitation to substitute sections 102, 103 and 112 inquiries for the better-established inquiry under section 101.[112] The debate that had plagued the Federal Circuit is now over – courts must, where appropriate, decide the issue of patent-eligibility under section 101 before addressing the other issues under sections 102, 103 and 112. It will be remembered that the decision of the Federal Circuit in *MySpace* produced a sharp split in the opinion of the court as to the proper approach when considering challenges to patent-eligibility under section 101 of the Patent Act. The majority, Plager and Newman JJ, were of the view that the matter should be disposed of under sections 102 and 103 of the Patent Act, rather than under section 101. Mayer J dissented. The approach of the majority has now been rejected by the Court in *Prometheus*.

The fourth related to the arguments of principle and policy for and against patent protection for medical treatment and diagnostic methods. Those who, like Prometheus, argued for patent protecton claimed that a principle of law denying patent coverage would interfere significantly with the ability of medical researchers to make valuable discoveries, particularly in the area of diagnostic research.[113] They argued that research was expen-

---

109   Ibid.
110   Ibid. at 21.
111   Ibid.
112   Ibid. at 22.
113   Ibid.

sive, including that leading to the discovery of laws of nature; it made the United States the world leader in this field; and it required protection. Others, namely, the medical experts, argued strongly against a legal rule that would make the present claims patent-eligible, invoking policy considerations that point in the opposite direction.[114] The Court claimed that it did not find this kind of difference of opinion surprising because patent protection was, after all, a two-edged sword. It claimed that, on the one hand, the promise of exclusive rights provides monetary incentives that lead to creation, invention and discovery and, on the other hand, the very exclusivity could impede the flow of information that might permit, indeed spur, invention by, for example, raising the price of using the patented ideas once created, requiring potential users to conduct costly and time-consuming searches of existing patents and pending patent applications, and requiring the negotiation of complex licensing arrangements.[115]

The Court continued that, at the same time, a patent law's general rules must govern inventive activity in many different fields of human endeavour, with the result that the practical effects of rules that reflect a general effort to balance these considerations may differ from one field to another.[116] In rejecting these and other arguments made, the Court concluded that it must: first, hesitate before departing from established general legal rules lest a new protective rule that seems to suit the needs of one field produce unforeseen results in another; and, second, recognise the role of Congress in crafting more finely tailored rules where necessary.[117] However, it cautioned that it need not determine in the instant case whether, from a policy perspective, increased protection for discoveries of diagnostic laws of nature was desirable.

D APPLYING *PROMETHEUS*

1 Medical Methods

Within ten days of the Court handing its decision in *Prometheus*, the District Court had occasion to apply it to a similar medical treatment method in *SmartGene Inc v Advanced Biological Laboratories SA*.[118] In that decision, the plaintiff filed a motion for partial summary judgment,

---

[114] Ibid. at 23.
[115] Ibid.
[116] Ibid.
[117] Ibid. at 24.
[118] 212 U.S. Dist. LEXIS 44138 (March 30 2012).

contending that the 'patents in dispute' were facially invalid under section 101 of the Patent Act because the subject matter was ineligible for patent protection.[119] The patents at issue, '988 and '786, were entitled 'Systems, Methods and Computer Program Products for Guiding the Selection of Therapeutic Treatment Regimens' and related to a system, method and computer program for guiding the selection of therapeutic treatment regimens for complex disorders by ranking available treatment regimens and providing advisory information. Claim 1 of the '786 patent was as follows: a method for guiding the selection of a therapeutic treatment regimen for a patient with a known disease or medical condition by: (a) having the user input information into a 'computing device' comprising three databases, including: (i) a medical conditions database; (ii) a database containing expert rules for selecting a treatment regimen; and (iii) an advisory information database; (b) having the computing device generate a ranked listing of therapeutic treatment regimens for the patient; and (c) generating advisory information based on patient information and expert rules.[120]

Howell J delivered the judgment of the District Court, commenting that he would focus the analysis on claim 1 of the '786 patent, because the language for claim 1 in both the '786 and '988 patent was nearly identical.[121] The District Court concluded that the differences between the various method and system claims within the patents in dispute were immaterial with respect to whether the patents constituted eligible subject matter under section 101 and that, accordingly, the pending motion turned on whether claim 1 of the '786 patent constituted eligible subject matter under section 101 of the Patent Act.[122] After referring to the Court's decisions, namely, *Chakrabarty*, *Benson*, *Bilski* and *Prometheus*, concerning the scope of section 101, it claimed that the issue before it was whether the patents in dispute were abstract such that they did not constitute patentable subject matter.[123] The District Court explained that a court might conduct a section 101 analysis before it conducted a formal construction of claims.[124] It continued, in respect of the level of deference that should be paid to the United States Patent Office (PTO), that the fact that the PTO conducted re-examinations of the patents in dispute did not trigger higher deference on the issue of subject-matter patentability because the PTO could not

---

[119]   Ibid. at 2.
[120]   Ibid. at 20.
[121]   Ibid. at 5.
[122]   Ibid. at 5–6.
[123]   Ibid. at 16.
[124]   Ibid. at 17.

review subject-matter eligibility during a re-examination proceeding.[125] As a result, the District Court concluded that the matter at issue was not dealing with matters previously covered during the re-examination proceedings.

The plaintiff argued that the patents in dispute constituted ineligible patent subject matter because: (1) they were directed to abstract ideas and mental processes; and (2) they failed the 'machine or transformation test' articulated in *Bilski*, and were thus invalid.[126] In support of this, it asserted that the patents in dispute were 'directed to nothing more than a mental process in which a person, for example, a physician, engages when determining a treatment for a patient suffering from a disease or a medical condition'.[127] The defendants countered that: (1) the claims at issue were not directed to an abstract idea; and (2) although the 'machine or transformation test' was not the sole test for patentability, the patents in dispute satisfied that test. They further argued that the patents in dispute described an interactive system, method and computer program to assist the physician in keeping track of potential treatment regimens and optionally ranking those regimens based on the patient's personal information, adding that, rather than supplanting the role of the physician, as the plaintiff suggested, the invention sought to improve patient treatment by giving the physician reference to a program which could exceed his or her own capabilities.[128]

The District Court stated that, guided by Court and Federal Circuit precedent in this area, it would proceed with the analysis by (a) examining section 101 as a 'threshold' inquiry into patent validity; (b) reviewing the Court's case law 'guideposts' on the subject of patent subject-matter eligibility; and then (c) examining whether the patents in dispute (i) satisfied the 'machine or transformation test', and (ii) constituted eligible subject matter irrespective of the 'machine or transformation test'.[129] It continued that although it did not formally construct the claims on which there was disagreement between the parties, it would then (d) examine the claim construction proposals to inform its section 101 analysis. The District Court proceeded to examine each of the following Court precedents: *Benson*, *Flook*, *Diehr*, *Bilski* and *Prometheus*, concluding that the relevant precedents and tests demonstrated that the patents in dispute constituted

---

[125] Ibid. at 17–18.
[126] Ibid. at 19.
[127] Ibid. at 19–20.
[128] Ibid. at 20–21.
[129] Ibid. at 21.

ineligible subject matter and were thus invalid.[130] In respect of the most recent Court precedent, *Prometheus*, it claimed that that decision concerned patent claims covering a process aimed to aid doctors administering thiopurine drugs to treat patients with autoimmune disease.[131]

Applying *Benson*, *Flook*, *Bilski* and *Prometheus*, the District Court held that the patents in dispute did no more than describe an abstract mental process engaged in routinely, either entirely within a physician's mind or potentially aided by other resources in the treatment of patients.[132] Like the process in *Prometheus*, the claims at issue simply provided the doctor with more information that enabled him to better treat the patient. It accepted the view in *Prometheus* that mental processes and abstract intellectual concepts were simply not patentable for the sound reason that 'monopolization of those tools through the grant of a patent might tend to impede innovation more than it would tend to promote it'.[133] The District Court opined that the claim at issue was more like the claim in *Flook* and *Prometheus* because it was merely a recitation of abstract steps, rather than an innovation that adds something 'specific to the laws of nature [or abstract ideas] other than what is well-understood, routine, conventional activity, previously engaged in by those in the field',[134] citing *Prometheus*. It continued that the claims were also analogous to the claim in *In re Meyer*, which, as was seen in Chapter 3, was a process for gathering neurological testing data, inputting it into a computer and using a formula to infer whether certain neurological elements are functioning. In disallowing the claims, the CCPA rejected the argument that the invention was 'concerned with replacing, in part, the thinking processes of a neurologist with a computer', concluding instead that 'the process recited is an attempt to patent a mathematical algorithm rather than a process for producing a product as in [*Diehr*]'.[135] In the instant case, the District Court noted that the defendants claimed that 'the purpose of [their] invention was to provide the practitioner with help, to give the practitioner more than he could have just in his mind', but rejected this argument because the patents in dispute were even more abstract than those in *In re Meyer*, which at least involved a mathematical algorithm.

It first examined the '786 patent step by step in the context of the Court's precedent, as happened in *Prometheus*, before proceeding to the

---

[130]   Ibid.
[131]   Ibid. at 32.
[132]   Ibid. at 34.
[133]   Ibid.
[134]   Ibid. at 35.
[135]   Ibid. at 36.

'machine or transformation test' that the Court highlighted as an 'important tool' in the section 101 analysis.[136] In respect of the first step of the claimed method (a method for guiding the selection of a therapeutic treatment regimen for a patient with a known disease or medical condition), the District Court explained that this process was one that was performed in doctors' offices every day, adding that: first, a doctor speaks with a patient, who describes his or her ailments; and, second, the doctor recalls or looks up possible treatment regimens, and then advises the patient about the treatment regimen options, and the recommendation for treatment.[137] This step merely described the process by which information is taken from a patent who is examined and a view formed as to the ailment from which he is suffering and the treatment regimen suggested to cure that illness. It stated that there was nothing in the second step (providing patient information to a computing device comprising three knowledge databases) that was any different from the process a doctor went through in real time when he evaluated a patient by taking a medical history and obtaining information pertinent to the patient's condition and documenting the same in a medical chart. The District Court continued that: first, the patents' reference to three databases also mimicked the evaluative process involved in the treatment of patients; and, second, the claim did not add anything to the process that doctors regularly engaged in mentally when evaluating and treating patients.[138] This step related to the mental process that can also take place in the doctor's mind after examining the patient to first determine the ailment and then suggest the appropriate treatment regimen. It was of the opinion that the other step (having the computing device generate a ranked listing of therapeutic treatment regimens for the patient) merely described what went on in the mind of a doctor in evaluating and ranking possible treatment options for a patient based upon the benefits and counter-indicators of each option. This step could also be performed in the mind of the doctor before determining the actual treatment regimen. In relation to the final step (generating advisory information based on patient information and expert rules), the District Court stated that it understood this step as corresponding to a doctor generating a treatment plan for a patient.[139] As a result, it concluded that these steps described abstract ideas that were commonly performed by medical professionals in evaluating, considering and constructing treatment options

---

136   Ibid.
137   Ibid. at 38.
138   Ibid. at 39.
139   Ibid. at 40.

for a patient presenting a specific medical condition. The District Court then concluded, following *Prometheus*, that the claims tracked the abstract mental processes of a doctor treating a patient, which meant that they were abstract ideas and unpatentable under section 101 of the Patent Act.[140] The claims at issue in *SmartGene* were, therefore, remarkably similar to those at issue in *Prometheus*, so the decision of the District Court that they were unpatentable was not surprising at all.

The District Court then proceeded to determine whether the claims were nonetheless valid under the 'machine or transformation test' utilised in some of the Court and Federal Circuit precedents.[141] It noted that although the Court in *Bilski* rejected the Federal Circuit's statement that that test was the exclusive test for determining patent-eligibility under section 101, the Court in *Bilski* did not foreclose the use of the 'machine or transformation test' as a useful and important clue and an investigative tool for determining whether some claimed inventions were processes under section 101. The District Court claimed that, recently, in *Prometheus*, the Court rejected not the 'machine or transformation test' but the Federal Circuit's *application* of that test to the claims at issue therein.[142] As noted in the previous chapter, the Federal Circuit in *Prometheus* had twice concluded that the transformation prong of the 'machine or transformation test' was satisfied because the claimed process involved 'transforming the human body by administering a thiopurine drug and transforming the blood by analyzing it to determine the metabolite levels'. However, the Court in *Prometheus* described as 'irrelevant' the transformation on which the Federal Circuit upheld the patent at issue since no part of the so-called 'transformation' required the claimed process.[143] As such, the District Court decided to employ the 'machine or transformation test' as a useful investigative tool. Under the 'machine or transformation test', a process claim is patentable if: (a) it is tied to a particular machine or apparatus; or (b) it transforms a particular article into a different state or thing. Added to these were two limitations, namely, (i) the use of a specific machine or transformation of an article must impose meaningful limits on the claim's scope to impart patent-eligibility and, (ii) involvement of the machine or transformation in the claimed process must not be merely insignificant extra-solution activity.[144]

In relation to the machine prong of the test, namely, that a claimed

---

[140] Ibid.
[141] Ibid. at 41.
[142] Ibid. at 42.
[143] Ibid. at 43.
[144] Ibid. at 43–4.

process must be tied to a particular machine or apparatus, the District Court found that the patents in dispute did not satisfy the machine prong for two reasons.[145] The first was that the claims of the patents in dispute did not refer to any 'particular' machine; so that, although the claims mention a 'computing device', those references were insufficient to satisfy the machine test. In rejecting the defendants' arguments that the figures and specification specify how the computer was to be specially programmed to implement the claimed method, the District Court explained that the patents in dispute included no special programming code, nor provided any specific algorithms that the computers would use to perform the database-matching or synthesis of expert rules, advisory information, treatment regimens and patient information.[146] Therefore, it concluded that, to the extent the claims referenced a machine at all, they referenced a 'general purpose computer' which did not satisfy the machine prong.[147] In rejecting numerous citations by the defendants, the District Court ruled the case law was clear that allowing a process to become patentable simply because it was computer-aided and constituted a practical application would render the subject-matter eligibility criteria contained in section 101 meaningless.[148] In addition, it noted, the fact that the '786 claim relied in part on four other patents for its inference database did not save the defendants' claim under section 101 because, in its view, general references to other patents as 'examples' of components of a structure without any detail as to implementation or combination was simply insufficient to identify a structure in the claims.[149] The District Court held that this was fatal for the defendants' claims, finding that nothing in their proposed claim construction helped them satisfy the 'machine' prong of the 'machine or transformation test'.

The second reason was that the computing device referenced in the claims was incidental to the claimed invention, and was not used for more than 'insignificant post-solution activity', and thus did not satisfy the 'machine' prong.[150] The District Court was of the view that: first, as in *Flook*, the computing device was merely a means of improving an existing process, which did not make the claims of the patents-in-dispute patentable; and, second, when the computer was functioning simply to speed up a process, this did not make the process patentable. Therefore, it concluded

---

[145]   Ibid. at 45.
[146]   Ibid. at 46.
[147]   Ibid. at 47.
[148]   Ibid. at 49–50.
[149]   Ibid. at 51–2.
[150]   Ibid. at 52.

that, in respect of the patents-in-dispute, the computing device referenced in the claims appeared to be doing nothing more than speeding up the research and mental processes that a doctor normally went through when evaluating the best treatment options or regimen for a given patient.[151] Consequently, the District Court held that Claim 1 of the '786 patent did not satisfy the 'machine' prong of the 'machine or transformation test'.

In respect of the 'transformation prong' of the 'machine or transformation test', a claimed process must 'transform a particular article into a different state or thing'. The plaintiffs argued that the claims merely took one form of information (i.e., patient information, therapeutic treatment regimens and advisory information) and represented it in a different form (i.e., lists of therapeutic treatment regimens and advisory information), concluding that such manipulations of information were insufficient to meet the 'transformation' prong of the test.[152] The defendants countered that the system created the ability for a physician to interact with a program and view and develop a treatment regimen for a patient. The District Court noted that the Court and Federal Circuit had offered some guidance in deciphering whether a process satisfied the transformation prong: first, the transformation must be central to the purpose of the claimed process (*Bilski*); second, mere manipulation or reorganisation of data did not satisfy the transformation prong (*CyberSource*); and, third, purported transformations or manipulations simply of public or private legal obligations or relationships, business risks, or other such abstractions simply could not meet the test because they were not physical objects or substances, nor were they representative of physical objects or substances (*In re Bilski*).[153] It continued that although the Court in *Prometheus* rejected the Federal Circuit's application of 'transformation' (that claimed processes were patent-eligible where they involved 'transforming the human body'), the Court did not retreat from a transformation analysis as part of a subject-matter patentability test under section 101.[154]

The District Court then examined recent Federal Circuit authorities on the issue of patent-eligibility under section 101 of the Patent Act. It then cited *CyberSource* for the view that even if computers simplified data-gathering and computation functions, a claimed invention was unpatentable if it might be entirely performed through mental processes.[155] It then concluded that the '786 patent did not involve any transformation and

---

[151] Ibid. at 53.
[152] Ibid.
[153] Ibid. at 54.
[154] Ibid. at 54–5.
[155] Ibid. at 56.

that, like *Bilski* and *CyberSource*, the alleged transformation performed in the defendants' patents was more akin to a manual reorganisation of treatment options. As such, the District Court held that the claimed method did not satisfy the transformation prong of the 'machine or transformation test'.[156]

Nonetheless, the District Court held that a claimed method might still constitute eligible subject matter despite failing to satisfy the 'machine or transformation test',[157] adding that an examination of Federal Circuit precedent, however, only reaffirmed that the defendants' patents in dispute were abstract and did not constitute patent-eligible subject matter.[158] It observed that, while the claims in *Ultramercial* could not be performed as 'purely mental steps' and involved a number of steps with complex computer programming, the claimed inventions could be performed – and, in fact, were routinely performed – in the minds of physicians who were evaluating patients and selecting therapeutic treatment options for them.[159] The District Court reasoned, therefore, that the patents in dispute were more like the claimed invention in *CyberSource* – a process for detecting credit card fraud in Internet transactions – which the Federal Circuit concluded could be performed exclusively in the human mind. In its opinion, the claims at issue, like those in *CyberSource*, involved the 'organization of data' and did 'not require the method to be performed by a particular machine', which meant that they suffered from the same defects as the claims in *CyberSource* and were, consequently, not patentable.[160] The District Court continued that the Federal Circuit's decision in *Dealertrack* only reinforced its view that the patents in dispute were not patentable, reiterating that, in light of this precedent, it found that the claims mirrored the mental processes that a physician performed – and this embodied the 'basic tools of scientific and technological work' that were free to all men and reserved exclusively to none.[161] In addition, it explained that the computing device references in the patents might be 'programmed to perform very different tasks in very different ways', and, therefore, could not serve as a significant limitation or constraint on the claimed invention.

Although stating that it was not necessary for it to formally construct the claims, the District Court noted that the defendants' proposed construction of the disputed claims only reinforced its view that these claims

---

156   Ibid.
157   Ibid. at 58–9.
158   Ibid. at 59.
159   Ibid. at 60.
160   Ibid. at 60–61.
161   Ibid. at 62.

were unpatentable.[162] In its view, it was the claimed steps of the invention, and not the specification, that must impose meaningful limits on the claims' scope in order to cabin the claimed invention's potential reach. As a result, the District Court held that the claim language in claim 1 of the '786 patent failed to enforce any meaningful limits on the scope and breadth of the claimed invention.[163] It explained that the contours of the patents, with no definition as to which information was pertinent, combined with the broadest possible construction of the terms, could encompass far more than the common understanding of therapeutic treatment regimens and could, for example, include financial information about the patient and the most economic treatment options available. The District Court therefore held that this was reminiscent of the situation in *Benson* where the Court expressed concern that a claim was 'so abstract and sweeping as to cover both known and unknown uses', which could 'vary from the operation of a train to verification of drivers' licenses to researching the law books for precedents' and 'be performed through any existing machinery or future-devised machinery or without any apparatus'.[164] It held that the breadth of the proposed constructions only underlined the abstractness of claim 1 of the '786 patent and, citing *Dealertrack*, concluded that the claims were invalid as being directed to an abstract idea pre-emptive of a fundamental concept or idea that would foreclose innovation in this area.[165] Therefore, it held that the claims constituted ineligible subject matter under section 101 and were, therefore, invalid.[166]

2   Computer-implemented Methods

The Federal Circuit has yet again forayed into the issue of patentability under section 101 of the Patent Act. This time, it does so with the guidance of the Court's recent decision in *Prometheus*. Although this decision, *CLS Bank International v Alice Corporation Pty Ltd*,[167] is not specifically concerned with the patentability of medical treatment or diagnostic method claims, its importance lies in the approach adopted by the majority and dissenting judges concerning the proper test to be adopted by the Federal Circuit in respect of patent-eligibility under section 101. Linn J wrote the majority opinion and O'Malley J agreed. In their view, the patents covered

---

[162]   Ibid. at 65.
[163]   Ibid.
[164]   Ibid. at 66–7.
[165]   Ibid. at 67.
[166]   Ibid. at 68.
[167]   2012 U.S. App. LEXIS 13973 (Fed. Cir. 2012).

a computerised trading platform for exchanging obligations in which a trusted third party settles obligations between a first and second party so as to eliminate 'settlement risk'. Settlement risk was defined as the risk that only one party's obligation will be paid, leaving the other party without its principal.[168] They continued that a trusted third party eliminated this risk by either: (a) exchanging both parties' obligations; or (b) exchanging neither obligation. The District Court granted CLS Bank's motion for summary judgment, accepting all four patents as invalid for failure to claim patent-eligible subject matter.[169]

After examining some of its own precedent, and those of the Court, the Federal Circuit noted that the District Court's decision ultimately turned on, and the appeal was primarily directed to, the issue of whether the claimed inventions fell within the 'abstract ideas' exception to patent-eligibility.[170] It explained that, while the Court's recent decision in *Prometheus* reiterated the trilogy of 'implicit' exceptions to patent-eligibility, including the exception for abstract ideas, it did not directly address how to determine whether a claim was drawn to an abstract idea in the first instance. The Federal Circuit continued that the abstractness of the 'abstract ideas' test to patent-eligibility had become a serious problem, leading to great uncertainty and to the devaluing of inventions of practical utility and economic potential.[171] Citing from the Court's decision in *Bilski* and its own decisions in *In re Alappat* and *Research Corp*, it claimed that, notwithstanding these well-intentioned efforts and the great volume of pages in the Federal Reporters treating the abstract ideas exception, the dividing line between inventions that were directed to patent-ineligible abstract ideas and those that were not remained elusive.[172] After examining further decisions that have looked to the notion of 'pre-emption' to further elucidate the 'abstract idea' exception, the Federal Circuit explained, while every inventor was granted the right to exclude, or 'pre-empt', others from practising his or her claimed invention, no one was entitled to claim an exclusive right to a fundamental truth or disembodied concept that would foreclose every future innovation in that art.[173] In its opinion, the essential concern was not pre-emption, per se, but the extent to which pre-emption resulted in the foreclosure of innovation.[174] The Federal Circuit noted claims that

---

[168]   Ibid. at 2.
[169]   Ibid. at 9.
[170]   Ibid. at 19.
[171]   Ibid. at 19–20.
[172]   Ibid. at 20.
[173]   Ibid. at 23–4.
[174]   Ibid. at 24.

were directed to no more than a fundamental truth and foreclosed, rather than fostered, future innovation were not directed to patent-eligible subject matter under section 101. As a result, it concluded no one could claim the exclusive right to all future inventions.[175]

The Federal Circuit claimed that the mere implementation on a computer of an otherwise ineligible abstract idea would not render the asserted 'invention' patent-eligible,[176] citing *Fort Properties*, *Dealertrack* and *CyberSource*. It was of the opinion that it could appreciate that a claim drawn to a specific way of doing something with a computer was likely to be patent-eligible, whereas a claim to nothing more than the idea of doing that thing on a computer might not.[177] However, the Federal Circuit noted, even with that appreciation, that great uncertainty remained, and the core of that uncertainty was the meaning of the 'abstract ideas' exception. It explained that any claim could be stripped down, or simplified, removing all of its concrete limitations, until at its core, something that could be characterised as an abstract idea was revealed.[178] The Federal Circuit argued that nothing in the Court's precedent, nor in the Federal Circuit's precedent, allowed a court to go hunting for abstractions by ignoring the concrete, palpable, tangible and otherwise not abstract invention the patentee actually claimed. It continued it was fundamentally improper to paraphrase a claim in overly simplistic generalities in assessing whether the claim fell under the limited 'abstract ideas' exception to patent-eligibility under section 101.[179] The Federal Circuit explained: first, patent-eligibility must be evaluated based on what the claims recited, not merely on the ideas upon which they were premised; and, second, in assessing patent-eligibility, a court must consider the asserted claim as a whole. As a result of this, the Federal Circuit held that when – after taking all of the claim recitations into consideration – it was not manifestly evident that a claim was directed to a patent-ineligible abstract idea, that claim must not be deemed for that reason to be inadequate under section 101.[180]

In respect of the instant claims, the Federal Circuit stated they were directed generally to the exchange of obligations between parties using a computer.[181] It noted that, while the method, system and media claims fell within different statutory categories, the form of the claim at issue

---

175   Ibid. at 25.
176   Ibid. at 27.
177   Ibid. at 28–9.
178   Ibid. at 29.
179   Ibid. at 30.
180   Ibid. at 31.
181   Ibid. at 32.

did not change the patent-eligibility analysis under section 101. The Federal Circuit argued that because mere computer implementation could not render an otherwise abstract idea patent-eligible, the analysis must consider whether the asserted claims (method, system and media) were substantively directed to nothing more than a fundamental truth or disembodied concept without any limitation in the claims tying that idea to a specific application.[182] For it, the determination of whether Alice's claims were directed to nothing more than a fundamental truth or disembodied concept required the Federal Circuit to consider the scope and content of the claims. As such, the Federal Circuit noted that the patent specifications were consistent with the understanding that each asserted claim required computer implementation.[183] In its view, although computer implementation indicated that the claims would likely satisfy the 'machine' prong of the 'machine or transformation test', the mere fact of computer implementation alone did not resolve the patent-eligibility question.[184]

The Federal Circuit was of the opinion that, unlike *Bilski*, *CyberSource*, *Dealertrack* and *Fort Properties*, it was 'difficult to conclude that the computer limitations here do not play a significant part in the performance of the invention or that the claims are not limited to a very specific application of the concept of using an intermediary to help consummate exchanges between parties'.[185] It asserted that the 'limitations of the claims *as a whole*, not just the computer implementation standing alone, are what place meaningful boundaries on the meaning of the claims in this case'.[186] In respect of the claims at issue, it held that they covered the practical application of a business concept in a specific way, which required computer-implemented steps of exchanging obligations maintained at an exchange institution by creating electronically maintained shadow credit and shadow debit records. Additionally, the Federal Circuit explained that the limitations requiring specific 'shadow' records left broad room for other methods of using intermediaries to help consummate exchanges, whether with the aid of a computer or otherwise and, thus, did not appear to pre-empt much in the way of innovation.[187] It further explained that while the use of a machine in these limitations was less substantial or limiting than the industrial uses examined in *Diehr* (curing rubber) or *Alappat* (a rasteriser), the presence of these limitations prevented it from finding it

---

[182] Ibid. at 34.
[183] Ibid. at 35–6.
[184] Ibid. at 39.
[185] Ibid. at 39–40.
[186] Ibid. at 41 (emphasis in original).
[187] Ibid.

manifestly evident that the claims were patent-ineligible under section 101. As a result, it held that that Alice's method, system and product claims were directed to statutory subject matter under section 101.[188]

Prost J penned a vigorous dissent, commenting that: first, the majority resisted the Court's unanimous directive in *Prometheus* to apply the patentable subject-matter test with more vigour; and, second, worse yet, it created an entirely new framework that in effect allowed courts to avoid evaluating patent-eligibility under section 101 whenever they so desired.[189] Noting she also found it difficult to answer the questions presented in the case with absolute certainty, Prost J nonetheless believed that precedent and common sense counselled that the asserted patent claims were abstract ideas repackaged as methods and systems. She was of the view that when it came to subject-matter patentability, the Federal Circuit did not write on a blank slate, because only a few months ago, the Court in *Prometheus* reversed the Federal Circuit in a section 101 case for a second time in its last three terms, hinting (not so tacitly) that its subject-matter patentability test was not sufficiently exacting.[190]

Prost J claimed that the majority had failed to follow the Court's instructions in *Prometheus* – not just in its holding, but more importantly in its approach.[191] In her view, the majority did not inquire, as the Court in *Prometheus* mandated, whether the asserted claims include an inventive concept but, rather, devised a new approach to subject-matter patentability, namely, the Federal Circuit must now avoid deciding a section 101 case unless unpatentability was 'manifestly evident'. In so doing, the majority questioned whether the Court's abstract idea test in *Prometheus* was workable at all.[192] She would have been more empathetic if the majority's approach was based on a case-specific determination, made upon the application of the Court's abstract idea test to the asserted claims. Prost J observed that the bulk of the majority's analysis focuses on the fact that the claims required 'computer implementation', which the majority itself deemed insufficient to pass muster under section 101.[193] She claimed: first, there was no explanation why the specific computer implementation in the instant case brought the claims within patentable subject matter; and, second, the majority merely posited that the additional limitations in the claims 'can be characterized as being integral to the [invention]', but it

---

[188]   Ibid. at 42.
[189]   Ibid.
[190]   Ibid. at 43.
[191]   Ibid. at 44.
[192]   Ibid. at 45.
[193]   Ibid.

did not explain whether they should be characterised as such, and what 'integral' meant in the context of section 101 in the first place.[194]

Prost J explained the basic idea behind the claimed invention was the use of an intermediary in a financial transaction: in a transaction between parties 'A' and 'B', a middle-man collected funds from 'A' but would not pass them to 'B' until 'B' had also performed.[195] In her view, not only was this basic idea of 'credit intermediation' not just abstract; it was also literally ancient. Prost J referred to the majority's view that the invention was not the computer implementation but, rather, 'the claims as a whole' that made the invention patentable.[196] She claimed that, without any need for computer implementation, there was nothing in the method steps themselves that brought the invention within patentable subject matter. Prost J continued that, stripped of jargon, representative method claim 33 simply broke down the idea of a financial intermediary into four steps: (a) creating a debit and credit account for each party; (b) checking the account balances in the morning; (c) adjusting the account balances through the day; and (d) paying the parties at the end of the day if both parties have performed.[197] Applying *Prometheus*, she concluded that the claim in effect presented an abstract idea and then said 'apply it' and this was not enough.

Prost J criticised the majority's objection that it was impermissible for the court to rewrite claims as it saw them, asserting 'that is precisely what courts do in claim construction everyday'.[198] She continued, in respect of the majority's view that the 'shadow records' somehow limited the claim, that 'the claims use "shadow" to simply define an account that is used to track a party's payments (the account is a shadow of the party's performance)'.[199] Prost J explained this was not a limiting feature at all and any financial intermediation would in one way or another use a 'shadow' account, concluding: first, the representative method claim did not limit the method steps in a way that the Court considered meaningful; and, second, it merely recited the steps of performing as an intermediary in a financial transaction, which was an abstract idea, nothing more and nothing less. She stated that *Benson*, *Dealertrack* and *Fort Properties* should have compelled the Federal Circuit to hold that the asserted method claims in the instant case were abstract.[200] Prost J continued: first,

---

194 Ibid. at 46.
195 Ibid.
196 Ibid. at 47.
197 Ibid.
198 Ibid. at 49.
199 Ibid.
200 Ibid. at 51.

the connection between the basic idea behind the claimed invention and the use of computers was not any stronger in the instant case than the relationship between the binary conversion system and the shift register in *Benson*, or the credit application system and computers in *Dealertrack*; and, second, unlike in *Benson* and *Dealertrack*, the representative method claim did not even recite the use of a computer. She then asserted that, while some of the dependent claims recited computers, the specification showed that the use of computers was simply incidental.[201]

In respect of the system claims, Prost J stated that they presented a closer question, in part, because the Court has not decided a section 101 case that involved system claims.[202] In her opinion, there 'is a perfectly reasonable argument that system claims are never abstract as a matter of law'; and that she did not believe the Federal Circuit was free to decide that system claims might never be abstract.[203] Noting that '[a] brightline rule that brings all systems within patentable subject matter is also easy to comprehend and administer', Prost J explained that doing so would: first, conflict with the Court's admonition against putting form before substance in this area of patent law; and, second, eviscerate the abstract idea test altogether. Such an approach should be avoided because any method claim that used a general-purpose computer might also be drafted as a system (containing computers) that carried out the method.[204] As a result, she agreed with the majority that the mere fact that a claim recited a system did not put it beyond the abstract idea test.[205] Prost J clarified that once it was accepted that system claims might be abstract, however, there was little room to suggest that the system claims at issue fell within patentable subject matter, adding that the Court had directed the Federal Circuit to inquire whether the claim limitations added to the abstract idea were inventive. This, in her opinion, did not permit the Federal Circuit to collapse the obviousness and novelty inquiries into section 101; the claims and the specification might be consulted in some cases in order to conclude that the additions were mere pre- or post-solution activity.[206] However, Prost J argued there might be cases in which the Federal Circuit could easily tell that the invention was not about systems or computers, i.e., it was merely an abstract idea clothed as something more tangible – in such cases, the Federal Court should not defer the threshold question of patentability to other provisions of the

[201]   Ibid. at 52.
[202]   Ibid.
[203]   Ibid. at 53.
[204]   Ibid.
[205]   Ibid. at 54.
[206]   Ibid.

Act; rather, where the case squarely presented the issue, it must invalidate the patent under section 101.[207]

Stating that the case at issue was one such case, Prost J reiterated that, apart from the abstract idea of avoiding transaction risk by using financial intermediaries, representative system claim 1 of the '720 patent recited: (1) a computer memory that contains account balance information; and (2) a computer that could track the account balance.[208] After examining the various claims, she held that even a quick glance at the '720 patent revealed that the claimed invention was not about physical systems; it was the abstract idea of risk management in financial transactions carried out on an already known infrastructure. Prost J then concluded that that invention, even if new, was an unpatentable abstract idea.[209] She claimed that the Federal Circuit, as mandated by the Court in *Prometheus*, must look beyond the non-inventive aspect of the claims and ask whether the remaining portion was an abstract idea. Applying that approach to the instant case, she held it unavoidably led to the conclusion that, similar to the method claims, the asserted system claims were not patentable.

E   CONCLUSION

The Court's decision in *Prometheus* made it clear that careful claim-drafting alone would not make a claim patent-eligible if the claimed method sought to tie up the laws of nature. To be patent-eligible (i.e., to transform an unpatentable law of nature into a patent-eligible *application* of such a law), a patent must do more than simply state the law of nature while adding the words 'apply it'. In other words, the patent must limit its reach to a particular *inventive application* of the law. The Court emphasised that claimed processes are not patentable unless they have *additional features* that provide practical assurance that the processes are *genuine application* of those laws rather than drafting efforts designed to monopolise the correlations. Patentees should ensure that the claims show how the laws of nature are applied in the claimed method to be patent-eligible under section 101. Additionally, the Court, following *Flook* and *Bilski*, reiterated that prohibition against patenting abstract ideas could not be circumvented by attempting to limit the use of the formula to a particular technological environment (in *Prometheus*, it was doctors who

---

[207]   Ibid.
[208]   Ibid. at 55.
[209]   Ibid. at 57.

treat patients with thiopurine drugs). It also noted, distinguishing *Diehr*, that the claims should include unconventional steps to satisfy the subject-matter requirement; however, where, as in *Prometheus*, the claims comprised well-understood, routine, conventional activity previously engaged in by scientists who work in the field, it would not suffice for patentability under section 101. Also, importantly, was that the Court affirmed its decision in *Bilski* that, although the 'machine or transformation test' is an 'important and useful clue' to patentability, it was not determinative; and it has neither said nor implied that the test trumps the 'laws of nature' exclusion.

7. Conclusions

A INTRODUCTION

Although the issue seems of recent vintage, especially in light of the number of cases currently before the Federal Circuit (and those recently decided by it), the courts in the United States and the USPTO have confronted this issue of whether patent protection should be provided for medical procedures and diagnostic methods for over a century. The question was always whether the legal requirements of patentability were met; and, initially, when medical procedure patents were rejected, it was usually on the basis that they were not new. They were not rejected on the ground that they were *incapable* of being patentable subject matter. *Ex parte Brinkerhoff* was the only case that held they were not patentable because of the uncertainty of the results of such treatments. The fallacy of that argument was made clear in *ex parte Scherer*, which overruled *ex parte Brinkerhoff* to the extent that it had held medical procedures were not patentable subject matter under section 101 of the Patent Act.

The courts did not question the availability of medical procedure patents on the basis that they may be contrary to public policy or unethical. The only case where this was hinted was *Martin*, where Chesnut J pointed out that '[t]*he professional ethics of doctors and surgeons are more consistent with the widespread use of their medical and surgical discoveries for the benefit of mankind than in obtaining a monopoly to control their discoveries for personal commercial advantage*. In this respect it would seem also that public interest is here involved.'[1] Although he rightly pointed out that a method of medical treatment raised some public health considerations, he did not proceed to provide any discussion of the issue.

For over 50 years the legal position in the United States was settled and physicians and others alike patented medical treatments and diagnostic methods. The *Pallin v Singer* case served as the catalyst for various bills that were introduced in Congress to exclude medical procedures from patent protection. This was achieved with the enactment of the MPAA, which did not exclude medical procedures from patent protection. It

---

[1]   96 F Supp 689 (DC DM 1951).

maintained the status quo but provided immunity to physicians and related health care entities from patent infringement suits to ensure that they were not hindered in the treatment of patients. It also sought to address the concerns of the opponents to medical procedure patents by excluding new uses of pharmaceutical products, machines and bio-technological process patents from the scope of the MPAA. The MPAA attempted a compromise between patenting methods of medical treatment and the incentives of the patent system. Methods of medical treatment, and diagnostic methods, remained patentable while the remedies available to the patentee, *vis-à-vis* a medical practitioner or a related health care entity, were removed. A different route from that taken in Europe was adopted, but the end result was the same, namely, providing physicians with no patent restrictions on the methods of treatment that they use to treat their patients.

B   THE CONTEXT

While there has been a resurgence of the issue of patenting methods of medical treatments, in particular, diagnostic methods, the Court has only recently finally pronounced on the issue in its decision in *Prometheus*. It missed an opportunity in the 2006 *Laboratory Corporation* case where the minority argued that the insufficiency in the record of decisions of lower courts dealing with the issue should not have been a reason not to decide the matter. Before the Court's 2012 decision in *Prometheus*, a plethora of Federal Circuit decisions dealt with the same issue, namely, *Prometheus* and *Classen*, but in June 2010 the Court vacated these decisions and remanded them to the Federal Circuit for reconsideration in light of its decision in *Bilski*. On reconsideration, the Federal Circuit in *Prometheus* reaffirmed its previous decision and decided two other cases dealing with medical and diagnostic methods, namely, *Classen* and *AMP v USPTO*. For the time being, the decision of the Court in *Bilski* made no difference to the analysis of the Federal Circuit in these decisions. The Court's decision in *Prometheus* has settled the issue of medical and diagnostic methods in the United States. *Classen* and *AMP v USPTO*, on reconsideration by the Federal Circuit in light of the Court's decision in *Prometheus*, might also be decided by the Court.

This chapter provides concluding remarks on the issue of patenting medical methods in the United States. It also considers, *inter alia*, whether methods of medical treatments and diagnostic methods: first, can be excluded based on the 'machine or transformation test'; second, are abstract ideas; and, third, can be considered as unpatentable subject matter per se. An examination of whether these issues apply equally to patenting genetic diagnostic methods is also explored.

C DEFINING DIAGNOSTIC METHODS

Typically, diagnostic methods, using the analysis of the Enlarged Board of Appeal of the European Patent Office (EBA) in *CYGNUS/Diagnostic method*,[2] include: (i) the examination phase involving the collection of data; (ii) the comparison of these data with standard values; (iii) the finding of any significant deviation, i.e., a symptom, during the comparison; and (iv) the attribution of the deviation to a particular clinical picture, i.e., the deductive medical or veterinary decision phase. This is very similar to what Breyer J formulated in *Laboratory Corporation*, namely: (i) gather data; (ii) read a number; (iii) compare the number with the norm; and (iv) act accordingly. The differences between the two are: first, the EBA's step (i) is Breyer J's steps (i) and (ii); second, Breyer J's formulation does not have step (iii) of *CYGNUS/Diagnostic method*; and, third, Breyer J's formulation does not have step (iv) of *CYGNUS/Diagnostic method*. It would seem that Breyer J's formulation is wider than that of *CYGNUS/ Diagnostic method*, since the latter does not say exactly what one is doing the comparison for and, consequently, what further steps must be done with the information found. In a sense, then, most of the decisions considered in this book are not strictly diagnostic methods, based on the definition accepted in *CYGNUS/Diagnostic method*. Such claims usually involve gathering and analysing data and comparing it to determine whether a particular correlation is satisfied. That correlation, in the strict diagnostic method claim, is the determination that a particular medical condition exists or whether a patient has a predisposition to that medical condition.

In *Prometheus*, the Court explained that that the claim simply told doctors to: (1) measure (somehow) the current level of the relevant metabolite; (2) use particular (unpatentable) laws of nature (which the claim set forth) to calculate the current toxicity/inefficacy limits; and (3) reconsider the drug dosage in light of the law. Step (1) in *Prometheus* is similar to step (i) in *Laboratory Corporation* and steps (i) and (ii) of *CYGNUS/Diagnostic method*. The comparison step, arguably, is found in step (2) of *Prometheus* and step (ii) of *CYGNUS/Diagnostic method* and step (iii) of *Laboratory Corporation*. It must be noted that, although the three steps in *Prometheus*

---

[2] (G 01/04) [2006] EPOR 15. See E.D. Ventose, *Medical Patent Law: The Challenges of Medical Patents* (Edward Elgar, Cheltenham, UK 2011) 184–228.

do not contain an explicit reference to a comparison step, this must be implied in step (2), which uses the law of nature to calculate the current toxicity/inefficacy limits. Step (iii) of *CYGNUS/Diagnostic method* (the finding of any significant deviation, i.e., a symptom, during the comparison) must be implicit in step (2) of *Prometheus*. It is expressly found in step (iii) of *Laboratory Corporation*.

In *In re Grams*, the claimed method was to determine whether a particular abnormal condition existed in a patient. Similarly, in *In re Meyer*, the claimed method was for determining whether a malfunction existed in a patient and in *In re Griffin*, the claimed method was for diagnosing an increased risk for thrombosis or a genetic defect causing thrombosis. All of these methods would be considered as diagnostic methods since they all contained the steps necessary for making a diagnosis. The difference between the claims in *In re Grams* and *In re Griffin* was that, in *In re Grams*, the claims sought to find whether the patient had a particular medical condition, whereas the claim in *In re Griffin* sought to determine whether the patient had a genetic defect causing thrombosis, or whether there existed in that patient an increased risk for thrombosis. *In re Griffin* type claims are wider since they are able not only to tell whether the patient has a particular genetic disorder, but whether that patient is predisposed to having one. As such, they both essentially perform related but different functions of determining whether a patient has a particular illness or whether there is a strong possibility that he might develop it later. Therefore, it makes little difference, in terms of patentability, whether the patent claims a particular medical condition or a predisposition to that medical condition. Where a claim suggests a particular treatment for the patient, that further treatment would be an independent therapeutic method and not a diagnostic one.

The claimed method in *Laboratory Corporation* was to determine whether the patient had cobalamin or folate deficiency, both or neither. This was a quintessential diagnostic method since all four steps were extant in the claimed method. In *Classen*, the claimed method was for determining the efficiency of an immunisation schedule on a group of patients. This would not be considered as a diagnostic method since the information gathered does not determine whether the patient is suffering from a particular disease but, rather, whether the dosages need to be adjusted to better treat that patient for the disease already being treated. In *Prometheus*, the claimed method was similar to the ones in *Classen* in that it claimed a method for optimising the therapeutic efficiency of treatment of an immune-mediated gastrointestinal disorder. In both *Classen* and *Prometheus*, there were no steps (ii)–(iv) based on the decision of the EBA in *CYGNUS/Diagnostic method*. This was not surprising since the purpose of the information gathered was not to determine whether the patient was suffering from an illness, as was the case in *In re Meyer*, *In re Grams*, *In re Griffin* (and at least predisposed to such an illness) and *Laboratory Corporation* but, rather, to determine the optimum dosage regime for that patient in respect of treatment already administered for an illness already ascertained. This necessitates an answer to the separate question of whether dosage or treatment regimes are patentable under section 101.

In *Prometheus*, the claimed method was not directed at the dosage regime at all but at how to determine whether a particular patient needed an adjustment in the dosage administered. In other words, it did not determine the actual dosage for the patient, but allowed the physician, based on the information provided, to determine a patient-specific dosage regime. This involved: first, administering the drug to the patient; and, second, determining the levels of metabolite of the drug subsequent to administration. That level then would determine whether an increase or decrease in the amount of drug administered was necessary. The claimed method was not a diagnostic method since it did not involve determining whether the patient had any ailment based on examination then comparing the information gathered to normal values and then a diagnosis made by the doctor. In fact, the claimed method used an existing treatment regime for the patient and sought simply to determine how effective it was by measuring the metabolites product subsequent to administering the drug to the patient. The Court in *Prometheus* claimed that the instructions in the claimed method added nothing specific to the laws of nature other than what was well-understood, routine, conventional activity, previously engaged in by those in the field. In other words, since they were steps that must be taken in order to apply the laws in question, the effect was simply to tell doctors to apply the natural law somehow when treating their patients.

The Court was of the view that this was simply an attempt to monopolise the laws of nature – namely, relationships between concentrations of certain metabolites in the blood and the likelihood that a dosage of a thiopurine drug will prove ineffective or cause harm. It continued that if a law of nature is not patentable, then neither is a process reciting a law of nature unless that process has additional features which provide practical assurance that the process is more than a drafting effort designed to monopolise the law of nature itself.

D   MACHINE OR TRANSFORMATION TEST

It will be remembered that the Federal Circuit in *In re Bilski* had asserted that the 'machine or transformation test' was the sole test for determining whether a process is patentable under section 101. In *Bilski*, the Court rejected that view, asserting that that test was a useful one, or a clue to patentability of a process under section 101, and that it was not at all the sole test. Now that the 'machine or transformation test' has been discredited, it means that the Federal Circuit's tortuous reasoning, using the transformation part of the test in *Prometheus* to find that methods of optimising therapeutic efficiency of treatment of an immune-mediated gastrointestinal disorder, needs to be revisited. The Court vacated the Federal Circuit's decision in *Prometheus* and remanded it back to the Federal Circuit for reconsideration in light of the Court's decision in *Bilski*. In *Prometheus*, the Federal Circuit had held that the method in question transformed an article into a different state or thing on the basis of the change which occurred in the human body following the administration of the drug. It must be pointed out that the claimed method itself must effect that transformation. However, the method in question was simply the process for determining an optimised treatment of the human body. In other words, it was directed at the process for making that determination whereby the physician was to make some observations concerning how effective certain dosages were. It was, therefore, not directed to the actual treatment of the patient for, if it were, it would be a method of treating the human body. Arguably, there was no transformation of the human body based on the claimed method that Prometheus sought to patent. It is even more inconceivable that the second part of the test could ever be satisfied in light of the requirement that the invention be tied to a particular machine or apparatus. As was seen in Chapter 4, the Federal Circuit, on reconsideration, applied the 'machine or transformation test', in the same way it did in *Prometheus*, in its second decision in *Prometheus* to find the claims at issue patentable.

This error was laid bare by the Court's decision in *Prometheus*. The Court, it will be remembered, responded that: first, the first of these transformations, however, was irrelevant; second, the 'administering' step simply helped to pick out the group of individuals who were likely interested in applying the laws of nature; and, third, the second step could be satisfied without transforming the blood, should science develop a totally different system for determining metabolite levels that did not involve such a transformation. It then concluded that, regardless, in stating that the 'machine or transformation' test was an 'important and useful clue' to patentability, the Court had neither said nor implied that the test trumped the 'law of nature' exclusion, adding that, this being so, the test failed in the instant case.

Similarly, the Court earlier had vacated the Federal Circuit's decision in *Classen* and remanded it to the Federal Circuit for reconsideration in light of the Court's decision in *Bilski*. The Federal Circuit in *Classen* had found that the claimed method for determining appropriate dosages to be given to a treatment group, by comparing associated disorders to that of a controlled group, did not meet the 'machine or transformation test' set forth in *In re Bilski*. The Federal Circuit gave no reasons why the claimed method did not meet that test, although the point is now moot in light of the Court's rejection, in *Bilski*, of the 'machine or transformation test' as the sole test for patentability under section 101 and its reaffirmation of this point in *Prometheus*.

E NATURAL PHENOMENA

In rejecting the 'machine or transformation test' as the sole test for patentability, the Court in *Bilski* did not articulate any specific test that should be used by the Federal Circuit to determine patentability under section 101, observing that guideposts are to be found in its precedents, namely, *Benson*, *Flook* and *Diehr*. The Court observed that the Patents Act was intended to encompass new and unforeseen inventions, and that new technologies may call for new inquiries, even pointing out advanced diagnostic medicine techniques as one such technology. However, it specifically made clear that it was not commenting on the patentability of such techniques. This means that to be patentable the methods of medical treatment, including diagnostic methods, must not fall under the exclusions from patent protection for abstract ideas, for example: mathematical algorithms; natural phenomena; and laws of nature, according to an unbroken line of authorities from the Court. Similarly, the Court in *Prometheus* stressed that its decisions have repeatedly emphasised the concern that patent law not inhibit further discovery by improperly tying up the future use of laws of nature.

The question now is whether methods of medical treatment, in particular, diagnostic methods, are abstract ideas, natural phenomena or part of the laws of nature. It is clear they are not abstract ideas and do not cover the laws of nature. The more specific question that will be addressed now is whether diagnostic methods are natural phenomena. It will be remembered that Breyer J accepted this in *Laboratory Corporation* and the District Court judges in both *Prometheus* and *Classen* held the claimed methods were natural phenomena. In *Benson*,[3] the Court noted '*[p]henomena of nature*, though just discovered, *mental processes*, and abstract intellectual

---

[3] 409 U.S. 63 (1972).

concepts are not patentable, as they are the basic tools of scientific and technological work'.[4] It then quoted its statement in *Funk Bros. Seed Co. v Kalo Inoculant Co.*,[5] which reads: '[h]e who discovers a hitherto unknown phenomenon of nature has no claim to a monopoly of it which the law recognizes. If there is to be invention from such a discovery, *it must come from the application of the law of nature to a new and useful end.*'[6] The Court noted that statement applied to process claims as well, although in *Funk Bros* it was there considering a product claim.[7] The Court in *Benson* noted that '[t]ransformation and reduction of an article "to a different state or thing" is the clue to the patentability of a process claim that does not include particular machines'.[8] This is apt where the process leads to the production of a particular thing, but it does not apply where the process leads to information as with the case of diagnostic methods – the method simply tells us from what disease the patient is suffering. Clearly, this does not involve the transformation or reduction of an article, contrary to the holding of the Federal Circuit in both of its decisions in *Prometheus*.

In respect of the claimed method at issue in *Benson* for converting binary-coded decimal numerals into pure binary numerals, the Court held that the 'mathematical formula involved here has no substantial practical application except in connection with a digital computer, which [meant that, if granted,] the patent would wholly preempt the mathematical formula and in practical effect would be a patent on the algorithm itself'.[9] What, therefore, does this say about patentability under section 101? If the claimed method embraces an unpatentable natural phenomenon, for example, it must have some substantial practical application outside the claimed method. If it does not, it would mean that the patent would wholly pre-empt the natural phenomenon and would effectively be a patent on the natural phenomenon itself. This prompts the necessary question of whether a diagnostic method contains or recites natural phenomenon. As mentioned above, two District Court judges thought as much, and so did the dissenting justices in *Laboratory Corporation*.

In *Flook*,[10] the Court had to consider whether the identification of a limited category of useful, though conventional, post-solution applications of such a formula made a method for updating alarm limits, where

---

4   Ibid. at 67 (emphasis added).
5   333 U.S. 127 (1948).
6   Ibid. at 130 (emphasis added).
7   *Benson* at 68.
8   Ibid. at 70.
9   Ibid. at 71–2.
10 437 U.S. 584 (1978).

the only novel feature was a mathematical formula, eligible for patent protection.[11] It noted that '[t]he line between a patentable "process" and an unpatentable "principle" is not always clear'.[12] The Court noted the 'notion that post-solution activity, no matter how conventional or obvious in itself, can transform an unpatentable principle into a patentable process exalts form over substance', observing that a 'competent draftsman could attach some form of post-solution activity to almost any mathematical formula'.[13] Therefore, it ruled that it was absolutely clear the respondent's application contained no patentable invention.[14] Although the Court in both *Benson* and *Flook* found that the claimed method was unpatentable, because it attempted to monopolise an algorithm, it was left to *Diehr*[15] to articulate the circumstances in which a claimed method that includes an excluded subject matter will, nonetheless, still be patentable.

It will be remembered that in *Diehr* the question for the Court was whether a process for curing synthetic rubber, which included in several of its steps the use of a mathematical formula and a programmed digital computer, was patentable subject matter under section 101.[16] The Court, relying on its previous precedents, including *Benson* and *Flook*, noted the claimed method for a physical and chemical process for moulding precision synthetic rubber products fell within the section 101 categories of possibly patentable subject matter.[17] It continued that that conclusion was 'not altered by the fact that in several steps of the process a mathematical equation and a programmed digital computer are used'.[18] The Court then distinguished *Benson* on the basis that the claims were held unpatentable because the 'sole practical application of the algorithm was in connection with the programming of a general purpose digital computer'.[19] It also distinguished *Flook* on the basis that 'the application sought to protect a formula for computing this number'.[20] The Court then concluded that, in contrast, the patentee in *Diehr* did not seek to patent a mathematical formula but only sought patent protection for a process of curing synthetic rubber. It continued that although the process admittedly employed

---

[11] Ibid. at 585.
[12] Ibid. at 589.
[13] Ibid. at 590.
[14] Ibid. at 594.
[15] 450 U.S. 175 (1981).
[16] Ibid. at 177.
[17] Ibid. at 184.
[18] Ibid. at 185.
[19] Ibid. at 185–6.
[20] Ibid. at 186.

a well-known mathematical equation, they did not seek to pre-empt the use of that equation, but, rather, sought only to foreclose from others the use of that equation in conjunction with all of the other steps in their claimed process.[21] The Court reasoned that it was obvious one did 'not need a computer to cure natural or synthetic rubber, but if the computer use incorporated in the process patent significantly lessens the possibility of "overcuring" or "undercuring" the process as a whole does not thereby become unpatentable subject matter'. [22]

Citing *Benson* and *Flook*, the Court asserted that these decisions lent support to its conclusion that a claim drawn to subject matter, otherwise statutory, does not become non-statutory simply because it uses a mathematical formula, computer program or digital computer.[23] It reiterated that it was 'now commonplace that an *application* of a law of nature or mathematical formula to a known structure or process may well be deserving of patent protection'.[24] The Court held that the claims were 'nothing more than a process for molding rubber products and not as an attempt to patent a mathematical formula'.[25] It was of the opinion that when 'a claim recites a mathematical formula (or scientific principle or phenomenon of nature), an inquiry must be made into whether the claim is seeking patent protection for that formula in the abstract'.[26] Relying on its previous decisions of *Benson* and *Flook*, the Court reasoned that 'a mathematical formula as such is not accorded the protection of our patent laws, and this principle cannot be circumvented by attempting to limit the use of the formula to a particular technological environment'.[27] In addition, it explained that insignificant post-solution activity will not transform an unpatentable principle into a patentable process.[28] If this were not the case, the Court said that it 'would allow a competent draftsman to evade the recognized limitations on the type of subject matter eligible for patent protection'.[29] It claimed that 'when a claim containing a mathematical formula implements or applies that formula in a structure or process which, when considered as a whole, is performing a function which the patent laws were designed to protect (*e.g.*, transforming or reducing

---

[21] Ibid.
[22] Ibid. at 187.
[23] Ibid.
[24] Ibid. (emphasis in original).
[25] Ibid. at 191.
[26] Ibid.
[27] Ibid.
[28] Ibid. at 191–2.
[29] Ibid. at 192.

an article to a different state or thing), then the claim satisfies the requirements of [section] 101'.[30] Consequently, the Court held the claim was not an attempt to patent a mathematical formula but, rather, to be drawn to an industrial process for the moulding of rubber products.[31]

The EBA in *CYGNUS/Diagnostic method* held that 'as the deductive or veterinary decision phase, diagnosis for curative purposes in itself is an intellectual exercise, unless, as a result of developments in the field of technology, a device capable of reaching diagnostic conclusions can be used'.[32] It was, therefore, not surprising the EBA held that the deductive medical or veterinary decision phase, as an intellectual exercise, was not a patentable invention within the meaning of Article 52(1) of the European Patent Convention (EPC).[33] The EBA in *CYGNUS/Diagnostic method* has observed that 'diagnosis' included 'activities which are not normally practised on the body but predominantly involve *mental acts*, i.e. activities of a non-technical nature performed by a medical professional, such as the steps of comparing the data with normal values and recording any significant deviation and attributing the deviation to a particular clinical picture'.[34] Article 52(1)(c) EPC excludes from patent protection, *inter alia*, schemes, rules and *methods for performing mental acts*. The extent to which the final part of diagnostic methods require the physician to think about whether a diagnosis can be made based on the information presented, it would be unpatentable in light of the requirement in *Benson* that, *inter alia*, *phenomena of nature*, though just discovered, and *mental processes* are not patentable as they are the basic tools of scientific and technological work. In addition, the mental step the physician is required to make is a determination of whether the patient is suffering from a particular disease based on the symptoms, which have been identified. Where it has been discovered that elevated levels of certain amino acids meant that there was deficient levels of vitamin B, there is no doubt, as Breyer J held in *Laboratory Corporation*, this correlation would be a natural phenomenon.

The question is whether this reasoning applies as a matter of principle to all diagnostic methods, or whether the patentability of each claimed method should be decided on a case-by-case basis to determine whether the natural phenomenon has some substantial practical application outside the claimed method itself. This, arguably, cannot be determined without considering each claimed method in the context of the applicable

---

[30] Ibid.
[31] Ibid. at 192–3.
[32] *CYGNUS/Diagnostic method* (G 01/04) at para. 5.2.
[33] Ibid. at para. 5.5.
[34] Ibid. at para. 3.5.

technology. It is reasonable to assume that, if such a correlation were found, unless there are other correlations that determine whether that particular illness or deficiency is present in the human body, it would not have any substantial use outside the context of making that diagnosis. It is possible to argue that the natural phenomenon is only used in the diagnostic method; but that matters little if its only or substantial application would be in that diagnostic method, meaning that the inventor would effectively have a monopoly on the natural phenomenon itself. In such cases, there is hardly any way around this argument, unless other uses of that natural phenomenon are available. Would it matter in such circumstances that the patentee's diagnostic method might be the only one such use of the natural phenomenon, and that he would have a monopoly of that natural phenomenon when used as a method of diagnosis?

In *Prometheus*, the Court claimed that statements in its decisions of *Benson*, *Flook* and *Bilski*, concerning the implicit exceptions to patentability under section 101, reflected the fact that even though rewarding with patents those who discover new laws of nature and the like might well encourage their discovery, those laws and principles, considered generally, were the basic tools of scientific and technological work. Therefore the laws of nature should not be patentable per se, but should be available to everyone to ensure that innovation in every field of endeavour continued uninhibited by patents. The Court argued that the laws of nature at issue in this case were narrow laws that might have limited applications, but accepted the patent claims that embodied them nonetheless implicated the concern that patent law should not inhibit further discovery by improperly tying up the future use of laws of nature. Although the laws of nature were limited, the Court reasoned that the central concern was no less relevant since there was still potential that patents on these could prevent others from using the applicable law of nature. Further, if the Court were to draw a line for narrow laws of nature, policing the boundaries would be difficult and made it clear that it had not yet devised a method of doing so. At the forefront of the Court's consideration was the fact that the patent did not seek to apply the laws of nature but only to monopolise it in a treatment regimen for patients.

In its view, the claims simply told a treating doctor to measure metabolite levels and to consider the resulting measurements in light of the statistical relationships they described. They did nothing more than provide the doctor with more information about his patient so as to enable him to better treat that patient. As such, the Court held that, in doing so, they: first, tied up the doctor's subsequent treatment decision as to whether or not that treatment changed in light of the inference he had drawn using the correlations; and, second, threatened to inhibit the development of more refined treatment recommendations (like that embodied in Mayo's test), that combine Prometheus's correlations with later discovered features of metabolites, human physiology or individual patient characteristics. Also important for the Court was that the 'determining' step was set in highly general language that covered all processes that made use of the correlations after measuring metabolites, including later discovered processes that measured metabolite levels in new ways.

However, the Court in *Prometheus* cautioned that it need not, and did not, decide whether, if the steps at issue were less conventional, these features of the claims would prove sufficient to invalidate them, because, in its opinion, the steps added nothing of significance to the natural laws themselves. Further, it explained that unlike, for example, a typical patent on a new drug or a new way of using an existing drug, the patent claims at issue did not confine their reach to particular applications of those laws. The Court argued that the presence of the basic underlying concern that these patents tied up too much future use of laws of nature simply reinforced its conclusion that the processes described in the patents were not patent-eligible, while eliminating any temptation for the Court to depart from its established case-law precedent.

F   GENETIC DIAGNOSTIC METHODS

The decision of the Federal Circuit in *AMP v USPTO* provides a much needed insight into the question of whether a diagnostic method using genes is patentable under section 101 of the Patent Act. In respect of the 'genetic diagnostic method' claims, it held that the claims to 'comparing' or 'analyzing' two gene sequences fell outside the scope of section 101 because they claimed only abstract mental processes. Since the claims did not apply the step of comparing two nucleotide sequences in a process but, rather, comprised the entire process claimed, the Federal Circuit held that they were unpatentable under section 101. Just like the claims at issue in *Prometheus*, the claimed methods of comparing or analysing nucleotide sequences failed to satisfy the 'machine or transformation test', and were instead directed to the abstract mental process of comparing two nucleotide sequences. As a result the Federal Circuit concluded that the claims failed to be patent-eligible under section 101.

It will be remembered that the Federal Circuit explained the claimed 'screening method claim' comprised the steps of: (1) 'growing' host cells transformed with an altered BRCA1 gene in the presence or absence of a potential cancer therapeutic; (2) 'determining' the growth rate of the host cells with or without the potential therapeutic; and (3) 'comparing' the growth rate of the host cells. These steps, in its opinion, included more than the abstract mental step of looking at two numbers and 'comparing' two host cells' growth rates. However, in light of the decision of the Court in *Prometheus*, it is unlikely that this claim would survive a section 101 inquiry. The Federal Circuit's view that: first, the steps of 'growing' transformed cells in the presence or absence of a potential cancer therapeutic, was an inherently transformative step involving the manipulation of the cells and their growth medium; and, second, the step of 'determining' the cells' growth rates, a step that also necessarily involved physical manipulation of the cells, was open to question since the Court in *Prometheus* held that similar steps in that decision were irrelevant to the application of the transformation part of the 'machine or transformation test'.

Similarly, it is hoped that if the Court were to decide this case on appeal, it would clarify the new 'test' emerging post-*Bilski* in the Federal Circuit, which was applied to this 'screening method claim' to find it patent-eligible. In *AMP v USPTO* the Federal Circuit also held that the claim was not so 'manifestly abstract' as to claim only a scientific principle, and not a patent-eligible process. The Court in *Prometheus* did not use such a test or approve it to find the claims at issue unpatentable under section 101.

While the reasoning of the Federal Circuit on the 'genetic diagnostic method' claims is unassailable, its conclusion on the 'screening method' claim is open to question since the alleged transformation, like those found by the Federal Circuit in *Prometheus*, seems irrelevant and, further, its use of this new test of 'manifestly abstract' has not been endorsed by the Court. The reasoning of the Court in *Prometheus* would support the reasoning and conclusion of the Federal Circuit in *AMP v USPTO* in relation to the 'genetic diagnostic method' claims and its conclusion is unlikely to change on appeal to the Court. The Court in *Prometheus* asked whether the patent claims added *enough* to their statements of the correlations to allow the processes they described to qualify as patent-eligible processes that *applied* natural laws. If one were to ask a similar question in relation to the claim at issue, the conclusion would be no. Such a conclusion would be consistent with the Court's view that if a law of nature is not patentable, then neither is a process reciting a law of nature, unless that process has additional features which provide practical assurance that the process is more than a drafting effort designed to monopolise the law of nature itself. As the Federal Circuit concluded, the claimed methods merely described the abstract mental process of comparing two nucleotide sequences. Nothing in the 'screening method' claim would differentiate it, in principle, from the 'genetic diagnostic method' claim and, consequently, the reasoning in respect of the latter should apply equally to find the screening method also unpatentable under section 101.

This means that the use of genes in a diagnostic method does not per se make a difference to the applicable principles – the question always is whether the claimed method added anything specific to the laws of nature other than what is well-understood, routine, conventional activity previously engaged in by those in the field. In determining this, one must keep in mind the Court's caution in *Prometheus* that there was a danger that the grant of patents that tie up their use would inhibit future innovation premised upon them.

G CONCLUSION

The Court in *Prometheus* has decided the question of whether medical treatment or diagnostic methods are patentable in the United States. This decision makes it plain that such methods are not per se excluded from patent-eligibility under section 101 of the Patent Act. A specific claim relating to a diagnostic method or a method of medical treatment by surgery or therapy might be unpatentable because it did nothing but recite one of the laws of nature without any application of that law of nature in respect of a treatment regime for the patient. Such patents, the Court emphasised, implicated a serious concern that patent law should not inhibit further discovery by improperly tying up the future use of laws of nature. The Court has now articulated its view on granting such patents, emphasising that the ethical or public health concerns are beyond the limit of section 101 and, correctly, are not factors that it should take into account in making subject-matter eligibility determinations. As mentioned above, two other decisions will be making their way to the Court again, namely, *Classen* and *AMP v USPTO*. These will provide the Court with ample opportunity to further elucidate on the issue of patenting medical and genetic diagnostic methods.

What is also of interest is that the public policy and other ethical considerations, which were brandished to justify the passage of the MPAA in 1996, did not feature at all in the decision of the Court in *Prometheus*. In fact, the Court did reference these considerations, both for and against patent protection for medical treatment and diagnostic methods, only to say that it must: first, hesitate before departing from established general legal rules lest a new protective rule that seems to suit the needs of one field produce unforeseen results in another; and, second, recognise the role of Congress in crafting more finely tailored rules where necessary. It then concluded, stating that it need not determine in the instant case whether, from a policy perspective, increased protection for discoveries of diagnostic laws of nature was desirable.

Bibliography

B.G. Alten, 'Left to One's Own Devices: Congress Limits Patents on Medical Procedures' (1998) 8 *Fordham Intell. Prop. Media & Ent. LJ* 837.

S.D. Anderson, 'A Right without a Remedy: The Unenforceable Medical Procedure Patent' (1999) 3 *Marq Intell Prop L Rev* 117.

S.J.R. Bostyn, 'The Critical Analysis of the (Non)-Patentability of Diagnostic Methods and the Consequences for BRCA1 Gene Type Patents in Europe' (2003) *Bio-Science L R* 111.

C.C. Brinckerhoff, 'Medical Methods Patents and the Fifth Amendment: Do the New Limits on Enforceability Effect a Taking?' (1996) 4 *U Balt Intell Prop LJ* 147.

T.F. Cotter, 'Do Federal Uses of Intellectual Property Implicate the Fifth Amendment?' (1998) 50 *Fla L Rev* 529.

I.J. Fellner, 'Patentability of Therapeutic Methods' (1946) 28 *JPOS* 90.

W.E. Havins, 'Immunising the Medical Practitioner "Process" Infringer: Greasing the Squeaky Wheel, Good Public Policy or What?' (1999) 77 *Uni Det Mercy L Rev* 51.

C.J. Katopis, 'Patients v. Patents?: Policy Implications of Recent Patent Legislation' (1997) 71 *St. John's L Rev* 329.

W.B. Lafferty, 'Statutory and Ethical Barriers in the Patenting of Medical and Surgical Procedures' (1996) 29 *J Marshall L Rev* 891.

B.J. Meier, 'The New Patent Infringement Liability Exception for Medical Procedures' (1997) 23 *J Leg* 265.

S.L. Nichols, 'Hippocrates, the Patent-Holder: The Unenforceability of Medical Procedure Patents' (1997) 7 *Geo. Mason L Rev* 227.

R.M. Portman, 'Legislative Restriction on Medical and Surgical Procedure Patents Removes Impediments to Medical Progress' (1996) 4 *U Balt Intell Prop LJ* 91

E. Ventose, *Medical Patent Law: The Challenges of Medical Patents* (Edward Elgar, Cheltenham, UK 2011).

E. Ventose, 'Patenting Methods of Medical Treatment in the United States' (2012) *Journal of Intellectual Property Law and Practice* 80.

E. Ventose, 'Patent Protection for the BRCA1 Gene and Genetic Diagnostic Methods in the United States' (2012) *Journal of Intellectual Property Law and Practice* 7.

W.W. Yang, 'Patent Policy and Medical Procedure Patents' (1995) 1 *B U J Sci & Tech L* 5.

Index